THE Myth
OF Excellence

THE Myth
OF Excellence

Why **Great** Companies
Never Try to Be the Best at Everything

Fred Crawford and
Ryan Mathews

CROWN
BUSINESS
NEW YORK

Published by Crown Business, New York, New York.
Member of the Crown Publishing Group.

Random House, Inc. New York, Toronto, London, Sydney, Auckland
www.randomhouse.com

CROWN BUSINESS and colophon are trademarks of Random House, Inc.

Printed in the United States of America

DESIGN BY LYNNE AMFT

Library of Congress Cataloging-in-Publication Data
Crawford, Fred.
    The myth of excellence : why great companies never try to be the best at everything/
Fred Crawford and Ryan Mathews.—1st ed.
    Includes bibliographical references and index.
    1. Marketing research—Case studies.   2. Consumer behavior—Case studies.
3. Shopping—Case studies.   I. Mathews, Ryan.   II. Title.
HF5415.2 .C76 2001
658.8'34—dc21
                                                                    2001017344

ISBN 0-609-60820-7

10 9 8 7 6 5 4 3 2

First Edition

For Chris and Luke (I love you guys—sorry I've missed so many evenings) and our families—Fred, Margaret, Ron, Debbie, Ray, Ryan, John, Jeanette, Johnnie, and Michael.

—Fred Crawford

For Sierra and Gabriel, who grew into the two most amazing people it's been my pleasure to meet, mostly when I wasn't smart enough to be watching.

—Ryan Mathews

Acknowledgments

WE WOULD BOTH LIKE to thank our publishing team: agent extraordinaire Raphael Sagalyn of The Sagalyn Agency, who gave us our first, sometimes hard, lessons in publishing; John Mahaney, the spiritual leader of the Crown Publishing Group, whose editorial guidance helped shape both our thinking and final product; Jonathan Slonim, editorial assistant, for his liaison work on our behalf; and Will Weisser, Debbie Koenig, and the rest of the Crown promotional and advertising team.

Special recognition needs to be given to three individuals, each of whom placed an indelible stamp on this project. Without their efforts this book literally would not have been possible. Marcella Mosier brought a remarkable and tireless faith to this effort—even when our direction was unclear—and contributed content, provided insight, delivered against project goals, and in the process helped shape what became Consumer Relevancy. Priscilla Donegan contributed her insights, thoughts, and discipline; forced this manuscript into readability through tireless editing; made us act like adults; broke the ties; and donated hours to this project nobody should have given or been asked for. Finally, to Rebecca Sue River, thanks for everything—and we do mean everything.

A special mention also goes to Susan Buddenbaum, whose insights and early contributions provided the momentum for what today has become Consumer Relevancy. And thanks also to Bob Stanojev, who put us together in the first place. Other important early contributors included Bernie Thiel and Syed Hoda.

The Myth of Excellence simply wouldn't have been written without the cooperation and support of several individuals and companies. Feargal Quinn charmed himself to the top of this list by providing great access into his own company, providing invitations into other companies, and once again proving himself to be one of the best hosts and friends to be found anywhere in this world. We recommend that any reader finding herself or himself in Ireland stop by to visit Superquinn, and please buy something while you're there.

Thanks also go to our other Irish friends: Patrick Campbell, Donal O'Brien, and Paul O'Toole of Campbell-Bewley Group, and Derek McDonagh and Edward Stephenson of Jurys Doyle Hotel Group. Staying on the international note, special thanks to Bill Keon and the entire Pueblo family in San Juan.

Returning stateside we want to thank: Catherine Baum of Stanley Martin; Janet Kraus at Circles; Claudia Kotchka at Tremor; Craig Schnuck, his family, and the staff at Schnuck Markets; Ross Roeder and the staff at Smart & Final; Ron Pearson and his staff at Hy-Vee; John Gottfried, Ned Visser, and Andrew Arons at Gourmet Garage; Mike Himes and the other good vibrations at Record Time; Bob Carpenter and the team at Dollar General.

Five other companies assisted us in our early work, helping Consumer Relevancy take on its initial shape: Domino's Pizza, Ames, Eddie Bauer, Southwest Airlines, and Midwest Express.

Special thanks also go out to Wesley Wright, Jimmy Wright, Roger Kidd, and the rest of the team at Diversified Retail Solutions. Thanks also to Don Dufek for his efforts in initially helping shape Consumer Relevancy. The following companies and associations were kind enough to give us support, encouragement, resources, and, most important, platforms: Georgia-Pacific, Procter & Gamble, the Grocery Manufacturers of America, Kellogg, Unilever Bestfoods, C&A, British American Tobacco, and Royal Dutch Ahold.

Fred extends thanks to the Cap Gemini Ernst & Young family for putting up with all of the trials and tribulations of this project. To Terry Ozan, Dale Wartluft, Bob McIlhattan, Berend Brix, and Geoff Unwin, thanks very much for your support. Also, a special thanks to Stephanie Shern at Ernst & Young LLP, who got me focused on this in the first place. To Doug Dickson and Stella Goulet, thanks for all your hard work and support. To Charlie Gottdiener, who took the concept of Consumer Relevancy and helped shape it into something tangible, thanks a lot. To all of the CPRD team around the globe, thanks for all your hard work and dedication to our practice and to the concept of Consumer Relevancy. And while we said it together, to Rebecca and Marcie, an encore thanks!

To Bake, Burke, Bow, MTV, Spiro, Heath, and the crew, rock on.

And again to the home team, Chris and Luke, who make it all worthwhile.

Ryan would also like to thank the FirstMatter team: Watts Wacker, futuring's cosmic cowboy and my comrade-in-arms, for the sage publishing advice, creative counsel, patience, and friendship; Mary DeVito, whose great organizational skills, logistical expertise, and attention to large and small details both professional and personal were invaluable in the completion of this manuscript; Darrell Stewart, the special librarian with the big heart and a constant friend through several vocational incarnations; and last but not least Michael Strother, who managed to keep the hardware, software, and wetware running in sync, no small task given my admitted technological limitations.

I would also like to thank Tara, Mark, Rochelle, Liz, and the other Motor City friends and neighbors whose qualitative responses helped confirm our original quantitative findings; the Wacker family—Betsy, Cal, and Lee—who provided food, shelter, and a true home away from home; Syed Hoda, for the exciting car rides in Puerto Rico and the interest in this project as it developed; friends, especially Mark Baum, Mike Maurer, Russ Hockin, Joe Finegan, Craig MacDonald, and John Gray, each of whom made a unique contribution to both this book and all the activities surrounding its creation. Encore thanks to Priscilla, Rebecca Sue, and Marcie. And a special thanks goes out to Rick Jackson, whose intuitive understanding of the principles in this book allows him to operate the finest shoe shine stand in Detroit's Metro Airport, for the friendship and good conversation that brightened many a morning and confirmed that what we are saying here is right.

Again for Gabe and Sierra, who have helped me in ways they may not fully understand or appreciate for decades to come. And finally, a wink and a nod to WTB and PTH, because without at least a little magic, life wouldn't be half as much fun.

Contents

Preface

"It's not what you don't know that hurts you, it's what you know that ain't so."
—MARK TWAIN

MARK TWAIN COULDN'T HAVE been more right, especially when it comes to modern business strategy and execution. Over the past three years, we've conducted research that jolted us out of our personal smug assumptions about the nature of business. What we "knew" about business was keeping us from seeing the changing realities of commerce. Perhaps like you, we had ample reason to believe that we had a handle on the nature of business, a deep understanding of what customers wanted from the companies that served them, and a better than average insight into what makes commerce tick. We believed that when customers talked about price, they naturally meant they wanted the lowest price available. We were wrong. We also believed that—given a choice—customers would naturally always prefer the highest product quality. Again, we were wrong. And, perhaps most significant of all, we believed that all businesses should strive to be the best they can be at everything they do. Frankly, we discovered we couldn't have been more wrong about this, and we hope our experience sets off some alarm bells in your head.

What we discovered was that, across the globe and across all industries, businesses are spending billions of dollars sending poorly aimed—and in some cases offensive—messages to their customers and leaving literally billions more on the table each day. Instead of talking to customers in a language they can understand and find meaningful, most businesses are actually demonstrating—through advertising, marketing, merchandising, product assortment and selection, transactional terms, and service levels—that they don't respect or even know whom they are doing business with. To paraphrase the G. B. Shaw aphorism about the British and the Americans, businesses and customers are increasingly separated by a common language. The words used by both are the same, but the meanings are entirely different.

Companies large and small are offering customers everything except what those customers really want. Every business day, thousands of businesses spend millions of dollars on focus groups, surveys, and processing call-center reports, all to limited avail. In almost every trade sector, all businesses—including market leaders—live in the shadow of unforeseen competitive threats. Just consider how many local businesses, from supermarkets and sporting-goods stores to jewelry and hardware stores, spent years confident that they knew their customers and what those customers valued. Imagine how comfortable they felt and how secure they thought their businesses were, until Wal-Mart opened up in their towns and—armed with a superior understanding of customers and what they wanted—summarily put them out of business. Or imagine how confident IBM and, yes, even Xerox were that they understood the needs of the computer user, until their market dominance was usurped by "upstarts" such as Microsoft, Dell, Gateway, and Apple. Think about how Apple itself fell prey to the same trap. The bottom line: Global business—and perhaps more important to you, your business—is inexorably, and unknowingly, marching toward a crisis point.

The bad news: Today's market leaders across all commercial sectors are in jeopardy. We are poised on the brink of a customer revolution, a revolution whose demands could not be more clearly articulated: Recognize and respect me as an individual and start doing business my way. The good news: Not only can the worst-case scenario be prevented, but also companies that pay attention to the lessons we've learned can avoid disaster and take advantage of an unprecedented growth opportunity.

It's true that the demand for new business practices is edging many businesses close to crisis, but it's also true that in a world of increasingly ubiquitous product quality, increasingly similar market offerings, standardized service levels, and relatively normalized if not standardized pricing, companies that crack the customer code and break from traditional business practices stand to gain disproportionate advantage over their competition. Our mission in *The Myth of Excellence* is both to describe the parameters of the threat to *your* business as well as map out a plan for *your* future success.

No matter how robust or poor the economy appears, and no matter how much sales and profits increase or decrease, commercial prosperity bears a frightening resemblance to a house of cards, because customers are deeply resentful and personally dissatisfied with their commercial experiences. For the first time in history, businesses are being asked to do something other than engage in commerce. Customers increasingly frustrated with the experience of their lives want reinforcement of personal—not just commercial—values. The terms of commercial engagement have changed, and changed forever; businesses that don't find ways to engage on the new terms will fail.

As a result of misunderstanding what customers really want and how best to serve those wants, even the world's most successful businesses have bought into what we have termed the myth of excellence—the false belief that a company ought to try to be good at everything it does. Misdiagnose the problem and you almost inevitably misdiagnose the solution. Because businesses focus on increasing transactional value rather than nurturing sustaining relationships, and increasing the value of a transaction rather than worrying about the values surrounding the transaction, they almost intuitively adopt strategies aimed at becoming the best at every aspect of a transaction, an approach that leads to a lack of enterprise focus, which in turns confuses and alienates customers.

We interviewed dozens of world-class business leaders, and time after time we heard how their companies offered customers the highest-quality products at the lowest prices, providing the easiest access to sales environments that were fun and characterized by the best service available. They had spent literal fortunes customizing their products and services based on what they "heard" their customers saying, but they consistently failed to "listen" to what those same customers were really saying. When we talked to their customers, we were told a much different story.

We heard CEOs boast of how well they customized their products and services against target markets only to watch their sales slide over the next few months. We interviewed companies in the course of researching this book that went bankrupt before the final draft was completed. And over and over again, we found companies overspending against any plausible hope of a return. Their experiences form the foundation of this book. Business isn't a Greek tragedy: Learning from the mistakes of others can help you change your fate.

For the purposes of our analysis, we have divided all commercial transactions into five elements or attributes: price, product, access, service, and experience. We identified these five attributes because they are present in every commercial transaction—business-to-consumer or business-to-business. We assigned a numerical value to each of these attributes, with 5 indicating market domination on an attribute, 4 indicating differentiation around an attribute, and 3 indicating that you've effectively met—but not exceeded—market competition on an attribute. We've termed the ability to see business through the customer's eyes and conduct business on terms that customers find meaningful on a personal level Consumer Relevancy. And we've found that you can profitably conduct business on these terms. Looking at the world through the lens of Consumer Relevancy, we found that the best companies have a strategy for *dominating* (i.e., being world-class) on *one* of the five attributes of product, price, access, experience, and service, *differentiating* on a second, and being at *industry par* (i.e., average) on the remaining three. On a 1-to-5 scale, where 5 is world-class, 3 is industry par, and 1 is unacceptable, a perfect score is 5, 4, 3, 3, 3. Two additional "rules" apply: There is a "no-man's-land" or "consumer underworld" into which no company should travel. As a result, you can't be below industry par on any one attribute. At the same time, you shouldn't attempt to be a 5 on more than one attribute and a 4 on more than one. If a business is below par on any attribute, it cannot be viable for very long, as consumers will reject its value proposition over time. If a business is a 5 on more than one attribute and a 4 on more than one, it has created needless differentiation and is leaving money on the table.

There is a growing gap between the content of a business transaction (the value of a product or service) and the context (the values surrounding doing business). We found business after business simply missing the point and believing that value was an effective commercial substitute for values and that transactions were an acceptable alternative to the relationships customers want. In companies trying to be great at everything, this misunderstanding created substantial value leakage. In companies that weren't so great, it was the first step toward disaster. Customers are looking for deeper levels of personal recognition and a clear statement of values, but their pleas are going largely unheeded by the businesses that serve them. The *context* in which your business engages consumers (in Wal-Mart's case, the absolute trust of an honest low price) has grown in importance, eclipsing the *content* of your product or service. Most businesses have been improving their product offering since opening their doors, yet the context surrounding the transaction has been an afterthought, a necessary evil in the mindless dash for differentiation. *Human values*, not commercial value, have become the contemporary currency of commerce.

Let's briefly go back to Wal-Mart and try and put some flesh on the bones. Wal-Mart is known as the price leader, but its prices are not always lowest. It dominates (earns a 5 rating) on price because consumers trust that its "everyday low prices" philosophy will provide them with an honest price in the low-price range, a price with no hidden gimmicks, and in all product categories. Wal-Mart's honesty and true understanding of what consumers value is reflected in Wal-Mart's values and how the company treats customers. Wal-Mart differentiates itself on product (earns a 4 rating). Product quality is high but not as high as key competitor Target. And on service, access, and experience, Wal-Mart is industry par, i.e., average (earns a 3 rating) in each of these attributes.

We don't believe all businesses are the same; in fact, we don't really believe any two businesses are identical. But we do believe we've found a process and methodology that can be customized and applied to any business from the corner barbershop to Microsoft with proportionately equal benefit. It begins by mapping out how all the stakeholders of a business really see that business; moves to an analysis of competitive factors; and, finally, allows you to create a future blueprint for your business. We'll also describe the great "white space" opportunity that lies just beyond your current grasp—the opportunity to both reduce operating costs and, more important, increase top-line sales and profits.

And, of course, there's another reason to read. Business is a two-way street, and everyone from Bill Gates to the Queen of England is somebody's customer. *The Myth of Excellence* helps bring understanding to both sides of the transaction, allowing businesses to see through the eyes of their customers—and vice versa.

THE Myth

OF Excellence

CHAPTER 1

Field Notes from the
Commercial Wilderness

THIS BOOK IS REALLY the diary of a journey—field notes from an expedition into the commercial wilderness, if you will. Our trek began with a survey, fairly modest in conception although broad in scope. After all, we thought we knew how consumers felt. Understanding consumer dynamics, analyzing marketplaces and market spaces, anticipating the impact of technological change on businesses and consumers, and looking into the future are all significant elements of our day-to-day business and personal lives. In retrospect, it is incredible how naive we really were—naive, but not unlike a lot of other businesspeople. Since we knew what we were looking for, we wanted the data to provide verification of our brilliant insights. Like a company polling its customers and rationalizing any negative comments, we expected the survey results to support our entrenched assumptions.

We assumed, for example, that consumers wanted the absolute lowest prices, the very best products, and lots of value-added services. We also expected them to tell us that they wanted shopping to be fun and entertaining. We were in for a shock.

Our real journey started when the data came back. We were sitting in the conference room of a restored Victorian home in Westport,

Connecticut, marveling at how it was possible for 5,000 Americans to be so wrong. Our initial research included more than 4,000 consumer telephone surveys and 1,000 additional Internet polls, covering a wide range of questions about various facets of the consumer/business relationship and the "average" shopping experience, followed up by hundreds of additional one-on-one conversations with consumers.

We had asked consumers some basic questions about relatively simple business transactions, or so we thought, and they'd blown it. They didn't get it. What had gotten into them? Slowly, the grim truth began to dawn on us: They weren't wrong. *We* were.

The survey results told us that consumers are looking for values, not just value. They wanted recognition as individual human beings, not just a 30 percent discount. While we had started asking questions about retail, we quickly began to see retail as a metaphor for something much broader. Life apparently wasn't too satisfying, and our initial respondents expected somebody or something—apparently business—to set things right.

We began to totally reevaluate our work. The survey tool we had developed was an excellent diagnostic, applicable to any business. But what did the results mean? We had thought about the notion of business simply in terms of the successful transfer of goods and services—basic buying and selling. Yet suddenly we felt more like social workers, wrestling with intangible issues like respect and trust. Like teenagers out for a joyride in a Ferrari Testarossa, we found ourselves behind the wheel of a vehicle whose power was much greater than we had initially anticipated. So we eased the clutch down, gingerly downshifted, and gently applied the brakes. We concentrated on understanding the tool, fine-tuned it and ran limited tests in real companies until we were sure the new insights that kept pouring in were correct. Then we spent a year focusing on in-depth analysis, conferring with our colleagues, conducting thousands of one-on-one consumer interviews and dozens of interviews with business leaders.

Gradually things became clearer. Over and over again, the responses of our pilot 5,000 respondents kept echoing back to us. The critical elements of a transaction, business-to-consumer or business-to-business, weren't capital, goods, and services—they were the human qualities of the people or companies exchanging those elements. It didn't seem to matter what business we were talking about. The lessons we first learned in the retail sector applied to any and all of the businesses we looked at, whether it was airlines, banks, auto companies, high-tech, insurance, or entertainment. Consumers' expectations had changed and changed radically. Unfortunately, not enough people in business had noticed. Some had, of course—the successful always do.

But even the most successful companies are often overspending and only partially achieving their aims. What led us to that conclusion? Our research caused us to see that every business transaction—from the simplest sale of goods to the most complex service offering—can be broken down to five attributes: price, service, access, experience, and product. We found that many companies tried to be "excellent" in all of these areas. This misguided strategy, which we've come to term the myth of excellence, had several failings: First, it's impossible for one company to be great at everything. Even Wal-Mart, arguably the most successful retailer in history, doesn't dominate its competitors on every attribute.

Second, even assuming a company could excel in all five areas, it would have difficulty communicating a clear value proposition to consumers. Imagine the confusion if Tiffany suddenly began advertising deep discount prices on emeralds, or McDonald's began offering free-range chicken and tofu. In selecting the attribute that defines their primary field of competition (the one on which a company seeks to dominate), the most successful consumer businesses hone the one that their target consumers value the most.

This seems simple enough, but it's surprising how often companies try to be the best at something their consumers don't want. Several years ago, for example, Kmart embarked on a campaign to make its line of clothing more upscale. As part of that campaign, the retailer began offering higher-priced Gitano designer jeans. The move, not surprisingly, was a resounding flop—the retailer's customers didn't believe designer clothes could be sold at Kmart prices. At the same time, Gitano hurt itself on the other end of its business, because upscale shoppers didn't believe that any brand sold by Kmart could still carry sufficient high-fashion cachet. On the other hand, the Martha Stewart line has been a great success, apparently because Kmart consumers believe that somebody who can make a candelabra out of wild gourds shares a sense of values with them. High fashion put the shoppers off. High craft seemed a bit more accessible. It wasn't that the Gitano jeans weren't a good value, it's that Kmart shoppers said to themselves that *low cost, high fashion* must somehow also mean *low quality.*

Finally, we found that even the most successful companies tended to be right for the wrong reasons—they weren't paying enough attention to what we came to recognize as a desperate cry for basic human values. It became increasingly clear to us that this was at the heart of the myth of excellence.

But if universal commercial excellence was a myth, what was the reality? We found the answer inside our original consumer data. There was, in fact, a way for businesses to answer consumers' demand for values on terms that the consumers could recognize, a way of speaking to customers in their own language. We call this Consumer Relevancy, a way of appropriately framing an offering that enhances its value to a customer. Again, we stopped. If we were right, how could we explain the longest uninterrupted period of prosperity in human history? What could be wrong? The answer, we found, is, Plenty.

The Eye of the Storm: The Forces Driving Change in Consumer Values

Something is wrong in industrialized societies across the globe—really, really wrong. Measured in historical terms, these are truly still the best of times. Yet despite all the material prosperity that surrounds us, we are living in some of the worst of personal times. There is a huge difference between economic and psychic well-being, between being able to afford physical comforts and feeling whole, between living in affluent surroundings and having a sense of connectedness. We're living our lives and running our businesses in the shadows of satisfaction. We look around at everything we have accomplished, everything we have built, and everything we own, but they somehow don't mean exactly what we thought they would.

Self-styled culture jammer and "adbuster" Kalle Lasn looks at our problem this way: "Take stock of your life. Look around at what you drive, wear, eat, smoke, read. Are these things *you*? Would an anthropologist, given a pile of all your material possessions, be able to assemble an accurate portrait of your personality? Would that portrait reflect a true original or a 'type'?"[1] There's something—some fundamental element—missing in our lives. We feel it every day, and so do you. Most of the time we blame the food, the schedule, or the stress, but intuitively we feel something is wrong that can't be fixed by a better diet, a few days off, or some hours in the gym. The hows and whys of what we're feeling take some explaining, but start by asking yourself a few simple questions:

- How frequently do you miss key life events (birthdays, anniversaries, even soccer games), and what toll is it taking on your family?
- How did it feel to watch the peace of the suburban American Dream shattered by the gunfire of Columbine, guns in the hands of affluent sixteen-year-olds from good homes?
- Do you ever wonder how we moved so quickly from a time when Gary Hart couldn't run for office to a time when Bill Clinton couldn't be removed?
- How often do you spend a day completely unplugged—no e-mail, voice mail, or pager?
- How do you verify that anything you read, see, or hear is true? Are margarine, red wine, aspirin, and eggs good or bad for you?

It's clear that on a macro level, things are changing, and not for the better. But what about on a micro level? What's going on every day in your life?

- Do you look forward to flying on any commercial airplane, and when was the last time you really enjoyed a flight?
- Is holiday shopping fun or just another duty eating away at your free time?

- Are you tired of standing in line at the supermarket or bank only to deal with someone who can't make eye contact or say hello?
- Do you fully understand how your health insurance works?

So, you're more affluent than your parents ever dreamed of being, but is your life *really* as good as theirs? The answer to this question is increasingly "no." But why?

Historically, we have looked to our social institutions to reinforce our personal values. Yet, as we have already hinted at and will document more fully in a moment, these institutions are chronically and repeatedly failing us. The search for values, like nature, abhors a vacuum. The fact that our social institutions no longer can be counted on as consistent sources of personal value or fulfillment doesn't mean our individual search for those qualities gets set aside. This creates a unique opportunity for businesses to fill this values gap, assuming they recognize it and move quickly. It's an opportunity that we as consumers do not explicitly request but will both appreciate and pay a premium for. It's an opportunity that provides businesses with a chance to simultaneously build their brand and increase market share and margin, a troika that does not present itself often.

Before we go any further, we'd like you to answer a few basic questions about your customers and your business:

- Do you really know why your customers behave as they do? What makes them buy from you, and what could you do that would lose their business?
- Do you know how a new—or existing—competitor could steal your business?
- What is the one thing you're not providing your customers today that they are secretly begging for?
- What are two things about your business that you cannot—under any circumstances—afford to change?

If you think you've got good answers to all these questions, we suggest you close this book, mix yourself a large martini, and enjoy the fruits of your labor. If, on the other hand, you have at least some niggling little doubts about your answers, we encourage you to keep reading. We suspect you're an expert in your business, but that doesn't offer much protection against becoming a victim of your own assumptions and past experience. In many respects, we are all experts on the nature and impact of commerce—not just as businesspeople, but because we all buy something every day. Things are changing, however, and if you're honest with yourself, you have to admit it's getting harder and harder just to stay even. We live in a world that is more stressful, less accommodating, moving faster, and, frankly speaking, tough to deal with. At the same time, much of the support infrastructure that has fortified and sustained us is breaking down. So what do we want?

The Perpetual Scavenger Hunt for Values

Human values—trust, respect, honesty, dignity, courtesy, ease—are the building blocks of any free, advanced society. Yet those very things are gradually but systematically being stripped away from our daily lives. We cannot enjoy product or service provision in an environment devoid of human values—values that are harder and harder to find in society. To understand exactly how this values gap impacts us, we first need to analyze our personal and social circumstances: What is changing around us that gives rise to a shift in our desires as consumers? Three key changes—societal devolution, personal time compression, and the proliferation of information and communication technologies—all occurring at once, are driving us to crave something different. Actually, it's less something different than it is a change in the relative weighting we assign to the context of a transaction. Let's examine these three factors:

1. **Societal devolution.** All human beings look to put themselves in situations where they recognize and relate to the values being portrayed around them. This obvious and fundamental truth explains why there are biker bars and martini bars, churches and synagogues, Republican and Democratic political parties, chat rooms on virtu-

ally every subject, and, while we may never understand why, Britney Spears fan clubs. But all of these different splinters are anchored by a core set of fundamental values. Everyone wants to be respected, to be treated well, not to be taken advantage of, to be recognized and valued: in short, to be validated as an individual. Historically, that responsibility hasn't fallen very heavily on goods and services providers. People were able to find such reinforcement in many places: family, government, their marriages, school, social-club membership, church. Each made a contribution, some more than others, to validating and reinforcing the value of the individual, the worth of their society, and the sanctity of their place in it.

But today much of this is changing. We're not suggesting that the world is coming to an end, but in dozens of small ways the edges of the social fabric are slowly unraveling. Some of these ways make us mildly, but unidentifiably, uncomfortable. Some cause us stress, and some make us question ideas and institutions that we were trained since birth to accept. One by one, the institutions that have historically safeguarded our values have begun to fail us. Our trust in government leaders is slowly eroding. In April 1966, with the Vietnam War raging, 66 percent of Americans *rejected* the view that "people running the country don't really care what happens to you." In December 1997, in the midst of the longest period of peace and prosperity in more than two generations, 57 percent of Americans *endorsed* that same view.[2] This is manifesting itself in voter turnout. Since 1960, the turnout for the U.S. presidential election has steadily declined, dropping below the 50 percent mark in 1988.

Families, too, have changed dramatically over the past four decades. According to a 2000 YMCA survey, more than 60 percent of the respondents believed communication with their children had deteriorated dramatically in the 1990s. American fathers spoke with their children 45 minutes a day on average in the 1960s. Today that "quality time" has shrunk to about six minutes. And as Swedish academics Kjell Nordström and Jonas Ridderstråle note in their book *Funky Business: Talent Makes Capital Dance,* "When the Norwegian furniture company Stokke launched its Tripp Trapp children's chair in France there was a disappointing response. Then it discovered why. Families did not sit down for meals together anymore. Even in France, home of gastronomy and convivial meals, families eat at different times. There simply wasn't a need for a chair that allowed children to sit comfortably at the same height as adults. So, a Norwegian company had to set about reeducating the French to eat meals with their kids."

Organized religion, once both the font and final preserve of aggregate human values, has lost its historic monopoly on the moral high ground. By 1996, only 38 percent of people in the United States worshiped each week,[3] while in the United Kingdom the number of people attending the Church of England each week dipped below the 1 million mark in 2000 for the first time since Henry VIII set up the Church.[4] Ambivalence has riddled the American Roman Catholic Church since the days of Vatican II. Protestants have seen their fundamentalist wing evolve into a decidedly more secular faction increasingly concerned with impacting elections rather than individual lives. In Israel, Orthodox and Reform Jews wrestle not only for control of the government but also of society, while Jews of Arab descent complain of being second-class citizens. Japan, which is both the world's most literate nation and Asia's most industrialized state, has birthed more than 500 new religions since the end of World War II.[5] Church attendance is down, while New Age religions from born-again Buddhism to Gaia flourish, as, in a search for values and meaning, more and more people try to create their own spiritual templates outside the context of traditional organized religion.

The same pattern holds true in education. At graduation, American high school students are behind students in 96 percent of the countries in the developed world in terms of math, reading, and science proficiency.[6] Not only have American schools consistently failed to educate—and therefore to communicate values—but also, from Columbine to Cleveland, they have come to embody *la vida loca* more than *in loco parentis.*

The upshot of all this is that traditional institutions have become less able to adequately reflect fundamental human values. As individuals, we unconsciously seek out reinforcement and ratification of our personal values and consciously reward those commercial institutions smart enough to build values into their offerings. This simple fact came across loud and clear in our research. While there are countless examples of this in our interviews, the following excerpt from our interview with Sandra, a working mother, sums it up well:

> There's one store that treats me, and most other moms, with respect and dignity. While most stores have a children's area, this store goes those others one better. It has a VCR, with a variety of movies, games, and a picnic table. The mothers now routinely come in and have a cup of coffee. They put their kids in the play area and bring their friends. They've developed relationships and discuss decorating their houses together. It's not unusual for them to be there an hour on average, but it's also not unusual for someone to be there two or three hours.

2. **Increased inability to keep pace with daily life.** Everywhere we turned during our research for this book, we heard it: "I simply can't keep up." From white-collar professionals we heard complaints of e-mail, voice mail, pager, cell phone, fax machine, and computer overload. The great experiment of the Information Age is claiming its early victims. From blue-collar professionals we heard complaints about technology-driven productivity expectations concurrent with staffing reductions, of the need to work two or even three jobs per family to maintain a standard of living or just get by, of the difficulty in getting adequate health insurance. U.S. Census Bureau data indicated that 16 percent of all Americans, or about 44 million people, do not have health insurance.[7] The situation is particularly pronounced in lower-income families. Nearly a third of Americans with

income levels below the poverty line, or about 11 million people, have no health insurance. And the gap between the haves and the have-nots is growing. According to Congressional Budget Office data, the after-tax income of the top one-fifth of America's population rose 43 percent between 1977 and 1999, compared with a decline of 9 percent for the bottom one-fifth. And from everybody we heard complaints of not enough time . . . to be a good father or mother, son or daughter, brother or sister, employee, coach, volunteer.

It is clear that expectations are rising and we are falling further behind. There are plenty of facts to support this claim. Here are a few:

- **Time pressure starts with too much work.** U.S. citizens work almost 2,000 hours a year on average, more than the Japanese, and nine workweeks more than the average European. "The Economic Policy Institute . . . has found that, together, parents in middle-class families work 3,335 hours per year on average, up from 3,200 (in the 1980s) and just over 3,000 (in the 1970s)."[8]

- **Stress is getting to us all—everywhere in the world.** A recent survey by the United Kingdom's Institute of Management found all of the survey respondents agreeing that stress had increased dramatically since 1993.[9]

- **Depression will soon hit almost as many of us as heart disease.** By the year 2020, the World Health Organization (WHO) estimates that depression will be the second leading cause of "lost years of healthy life" worldwide—behind only ischemic heart disease.[10] A recent University of Wisconsin study showed a 50 percent increase in the number of students going to campus counselors for depression, with nearly one-third taking mood-altering medication.[11] Sales of the antidepressants Prozac, Zoloft, and Paxil exceed $4 billion annually.

- **Suicide rates have risen globally.** "Since the mid-1950s, global suicide rates have jumped by 60 percent. This year, the WHO estimates 1 million people will die by their own hand. . . . In the United States, the suicide rate tops the homicide rate by 50 percent. Every day four Finns will commit suicide. And China, which makes up about 22 percent of the world's population, accounts for 44 percent of the world's suicides."[12]

3. **Proliferation of increasingly intrusive information and communication technologies.** Concurrent with the first two factors, there has been an explosion in the amount and availability of information in our lives. It may not be good or accurate information, but that is largely left for each of us to decipher. It is coming from everywhere: the Internet, cable television, billboards, radio, the backs of buses, and your broker. We live in an era where things are moving so fast, and breakthroughs (technical, medical, and otherwise) are coming so quickly that we don't know whom or what to believe.

   This proliferation comes at us from all directions:

   - The adoption rate of the Internet, PCs, and cell phones is phenomenal in historic terms. While it took television fifty-five years to reach 50 percent of the U.S. population, it's taken the Internet only thirty-two years; PCs, twenty-five years; and cell phones, twenty-four years. By July 2000, the number of households in the United Kingdom with Internet access increased from one in ten to one in four.

   - Cable television penetration continues to grow. More than 70 percent of U.S. households have access to cable. The number of available cable channels ranges from fifty at the low end to more than five hundred at the high end.

   - Advertising spending continues to soar. Spending on advertising overall is growing at a 6 percent to 8 percent rate annually—to a total of $353 billion worldwide.[13] Internet advertising has grown at a more rapid pace, reaching $7 billion worldwide in 1999.[14]

The impact of this media explosion is compounded by a growing granularity of media coverage. The Columbine tapes have been released as a commercial product; we followed O. J. Simpson down the L.A. freeway; we were treated to testimony about our president's extramarital sexual activity. The global media now have the ability to bring horror into our living room in real time, whether it is the image of a bomb making its lethal descent down a chimney in Iraq or of Elián González being grabbed by a flak-jacketed, helmeted government agent armed with an automatic rifle. The line of appropriate and acceptable coverage is gradually moving. And this expanded media coverage is increasingly being paid for by what *Advertising Age* columnist Bob Garfield calls "advertrocities"—Benetton's dying AIDS patients and dead Bosnian soldiers and the heroin chic of Calvin Klein ads. We know more, we see more. As cultural critic Kalle Lasn notes:

> I think these ads are operating on a deeper level than even the advertisers themselves know or understand. Their cumulative effect is to erode our ability to empathize, to take social issues seriously, to be moved by atrocity. They inure us to the suffering (or joy) of other people. They engender an attitude of malaise toward the things that make us most human. We pretend not to care as advertisers excavate the most sacred parts of ourselves, and we end up actually not caring.[15]

Faced with this onslaught of information and commercial imagery—much of it of questionable validity and taste—what are we to do? Simply put, we tune out. We are simultaneously better "informed" but less aware. We are becoming both cynical and confused. As media critic Neil Postman, author of *Amusing Ourselves to Death: Public Discourse in the Age of Show Business,* notes:

> Information has become a form of garbage. It comes indiscriminately—directed at no one in particular, disconnected from usefulness, we are swamped by information, have no control over it and do not know what to do with it. And the reason we don't is that we no longer have a coherent conception of ourselves, our universe and

our relation to one another and our world. Our defenses against the information glut have broken down; our information immune system is inoperable.[16]

What do consumers want in this environment of information overload? *Clarity, ease, certainty,* and *trust.* We need someone we can trust and rely on to clarify our options, to simplify our choices, to allow us to feel satisfaction with our decisions. Once again, this presents an opportunity for businesses to redefine value by recognizing the importance of values, to change the game for the mutual benefit of their customers and themselves.

The pursuit of commercial excellence is difficult even in settled times. Today's environment, with its radical time compression, increasing personal pressures, stress, ever-intrusive media, nonstop parade of technological and communication innovations, and lack of clearly communicated institutional values, has birthed a new consumer, a consumer we call the "instavidual." Instaviduals define value in direct relationship to a moment of personal need. Their need sets vary from day to day and even from hour to hour. Instaviduals demand that businesses be relevant to them, but their attribute preferences change as frequently as the weather. Catch this consumer at 7 A.M. and an acceptable product may take the form of an Egg McMuffin. But catch that same instavidual at 7 P.M. and an acceptable meal looks like a filet mignon and a double extra-dry martini at Morton's of Chicago. While most businesses insist on putting customers into traditional boxes suitable for longitudinal studies, instaviduals either defy definition or meet multiple definitions.

The convergence of these myriad forces has also created a new market in its wake, a market characterized by the emergence of a new consumer need set—one never seen by business and therefore consistently not addressed. We're not arguing the need to address the social issues raised in this discussion. These issues have been identified and potential remedies covered exhaustively in books such as Robert Putnam's *Bowling Alone: The Collapse and Revival of American Community* or Robert William Fogel's *The Fourth Great Awakening and the Future of Egalitarianism.* The purpose of this book is to define and articulate a coherent strategy for creating enhanced consumer value, and to put forth a methodology for implementing operational changes to allow that new strategy to come to life.

As we see it, the situation can be summarized as follows:

SOCIETAL SITUATION	HUMAN CONDITION	HUMAN NEED
Societal devolution	Inability of traditional institutions to adequately reflect fundamental human values	"Fortify, reinforce, ratify my personal values"
Increasing inability to keep pace with daily life	Increase in stress, guilt, anxiety	"Help me survive psychologically and emotionally"
Proliferation of information and communication technologies	Informed and aware, but cynical and confused consumers	"Clarify my options, allow me to feel satisfied with my choices"

Because consumers' personal needs and values are not being fully addressed, they are potential defectors who will take their business to competitors quickly and often. How else can we explain the initial consumer attraction to companies like Yahoo!, Amazon.com, eBay, and Dell Computer Corp.? They created a business model more in tune with what customers want and need: "Make it easy for me to find what I want, save me time, provide reasonable price value, deliver it where I ask, give me the opportunity to interact if (and only if) I want to, allow me to shop exactly when I want to, show me that you pay attention, and learn more and more about my tastes and preferences as you do business with me."

These companies teach us an important lesson, one that ought to frighten traditional consumer businesses. Of course, this is both an opportunity and a threat. But for many businesses that have been operating against a different consumer need set for years, the cost of switching, in terms of dislocation and risk, is quite high. It is always difficult to abandon a business model that has been successful. But, as we've shown, times have changed. And for those companies that move fast and early, an opportunity exists to drive new business into the white space created by this shift.

The solution to meeting the new need set of today's consumer is embodied in our construct of Consumer Relevancy, which can be defined simply as driving top-line growth by aligning the commercial context with realized human values. Consumer Relevancy is based upon three foundations:

1. **Human values are the contemporary currency of commerce.** In an environment where fundamental human needs are being met less and less elsewhere, businesses that address these needs are well-positioned to take shares from their competitors. Amazon, for instance, moved rapidly into a white-space opportunity by creating a technology-enabled business model that overcame the time and space constraints inherent to traditional book retailing.

2. **Human values determine commercial value.** Historically, product features and functions were the primary determinants of value in business. Build a better mousetrap, and the world will beat a path to your door. Today, product quality is table stakes, the ante in a high-stakes game of poker. While inferior quality will not be tolerated by today's consumer, product quality alone is not enough. Most cars run today, and do so consistently. Refrigerators keep food cold, stereos sound good, detergents get clothes clean, hotel rooms are clean and quiet. Consumers in mature economies expect products to perform at a given level of quality. Today, it is the human values that are displayed during the provision of goods and services that provide the opportunity for extreme differentiation, branding, and building loyalty.

   For example, Tom's of Maine's product offering parallels its target consumer's values. None of the products are tested on animals, the external packaging is all from recycled materials, and the majority of the ingredients are organic. Each tube of Tom's of Maine toothpaste is packaged with a customer story. The cost of printing and marketing these consumer messages, direct testimonials reinforcing the values of the target market, are treated as a production cost. The values of the company's customers appear as an ingredient cost on the balance sheet, just like wintergreen and spearmint.

3. ***Values* are more important than value in the eyes of today's consumer.** There was a time when most people derived their sense of self from traditional institutions. When things were less hectic, when we weren't as well-informed (or overloaded), the worth of a commercial transaction was defined largely by the product or service itself. Of course, it mattered how it was delivered, but that paled in comparison to the attributes of the product or service. This is no longer true. Today, differentiation is found in the manner in which the product or service is rendered, viewed through the lens of human values.

These three foundations give rise to the central argument that anchors the concept of Consumer Relevancy, and is the reason this book is critically important to business and business leaders. Right here and right now, the convergence we have described has fundamentally changed the definition of value when consumers search for providers of goods and services. Context has overtaken content as the primary driver of consumer value. It is within the context of any commercial transaction that the representation of human values can be found. Consumer Relevancy defines the new competitive battleground and offers a blueprint for future success.

In the course of writing this book, we found many examples of how Consumer Relevancy can translate first into strategy and later into tactical execution. But moving from theory to strategy requires that a company listen to its customers, its potential customers, its management team, its line managers, and even its suppliers to understand where it—and its competitors—are in a market. Once that assessment has been completed, a company needs to decide on which attribute it will dominate and which it will use as a differentiator. Trying to be all things to all people, or at least marketing "excellence" across all five attribute areas, is one of the most persistent and chronic ills affecting modern business. This impulse—and all its attendant symptoms—is at the heart of the myth of excellence. Great companies intuitively understand the seductive dangers of the myth and go to great lengths to define their competitive position by clearly selecting one of the attributes and then demonstrating how they dominate on that attribute even when there is little actual difference in the physical characteristics of the products and services themselves.

Gateway and Dell computers, for example, are essentially the same machines. But Dell chooses to dominate on service, while Gateway has focused on enhancing the customer's experience. Wal-Mart and Target compete in the same channel, but where Wal-Mart dominates on price, Target chooses to dominate on product. Northwest and Southwest Airlines both fly from Detroit to Chicago, but Southwest successfully competes against Northwest by stressing price and experience against Northwest's more frequent flight schedule and increased access. Morton's of Chicago and McDonald's both sell beef, but Morton's does it by stressing the product and experience while McDonald's leverages access. Sony and Bose both make audio components and dominate on product. But where Sony differentiates in the access arena, Bose chooses to differentiate on experience. Each of these companies has assessed its market, analyzed its values, and selected what it believes are the most effective attributes to dominate and differentiate itself in the minds of its customers. Endgame never occurs, because customer values are a perpetually moving target. Even the most effective attribute domination and differentiation strategy today needs to be rigorously reexamined tomorrow.

So how does a company construct a values-based market offering? The first step is to look past the offering (the product or service) it is selling and to begin thinking on a customer's terms. Saturn, for example, understood that buying an automobile was relatively simple compared with finding an automobile company and dealer you could trust. Understanding that most people placed an increasingly high value on honesty, fairness, directness, and accurate descriptions allowed Saturn to essentially "reverse engineer" from a values platform to a market offering.

We can't swear to it, but we bet somebody at Southwest Airlines had spent more than one afternoon watching the faces of passengers marching past the relative comfort of the first-class cabin into the more utilitarian confines of coach. The customer's need to be respected and treated as an equal became a platform of the external face of Southwest. When a customer gets on one of their planes she knows that her seat is no better or worse than any other seat on the plane.

And perhaps the greatest example of values-based marketing occurred when Johnson & Johnson voluntarily recalled every box of Tylenol from retail sale in the wake of a tampering scare. The company understood the value of "walking the talk" of trust and concern for the customer.

Finding out what values you ought to embody is relatively easy: You just have to talk to your customers in their language and be open to what they're saying. And once you've got the message, it must form the cornerstone of everything you do that touches the customer—no exceptions, no sacrifices to a clever marketing idea du jour, no panic when sales drop in a quarter. Saturn always sells trust, concern, and respect. Southwest always sells respect, equality, and fun. And Johnson & Johnson has come to stand for the ultimate in respect and integrity no matter what the cost. But knowing what your customers' values are and building them into your offering is not enough. They need to be reinforced internally as well as externally every business day. To build values-based offerings, you must first build a values-based culture. And that is much easier said than done, especially in highly competitive industries.

The incorporation of values is the cornerstone of Consumer Relevancy, and in the next chapter, we'll take an in-depth look at the Consumer Relevancy model and see how you can apply the concept in your company.

CHAPTER 2

The New Model for
Consumer Relevancy

So what does successful Consumer Relevancy look like in action? Consider this story. When we were working on this book, Ryan was walking through the aisles of a Superquinn supermarket, just outside Dublin. Here's what happened:

> Executives in several industries had told us that Superquinn might just be the best example of a service-centric company in the world, and so I found myself in Ireland walking through one of their stores. I wasn't pushing a cart, or carrying a basket, or being escorted by a company official. I was just one more male shopper wandering through the store with the kind of lost-sheep look so common to men who find themselves in a supermarket. "American?" the young clerk stocking the cheese case asked as I passed her. "Yes, but how did you know?" I answered. "It's the shoes," she said. "The shoes always give you away.
>
> "So, what's your name?" she asked, introducing herself, "and what brings you to our store?" Trying to keep my research at least quasi-objective, I told her I was in Ireland on business and had

wanted to see as much of the country, and how people lived, as I could. "Do you like Irish cheese?" she asked. I said that I had only had a few Irish cheeses, and those were generally well-aged. "Well, Ryan, tell me, what kind of cheeses do you like?" she asked. "Bleu cheeses," I found myself responding. "Have you ever tried a Cashell Bleu?" she asked. "No," I said, "at least not a fresh one." Without hesitation, she reached into the case, grabbed a cheese, brought out a knife, and cut open the package so I could sample the contents. "Now, if you like a little sharper bleu, there's this," she said, grabbing a second cheese from the case. The second cheese was joined by a third and a fourth and a fifth. Our conversation was drawing a small crowd, as good conversations often do in Ireland.

"This is Ryan from America, here to do business and learn about our cheeses," the clerk said to any and all in earshot. "I've given him a bit of this one and that. Here, go ahead and try a bit yourself." Soon, there we were, a community of cheese eaters. No strangers here. We all knew each other's names and what we did for a living. I learned about their relatives in America, and they learned about the Irish branches of my family. It wasn't the cheeses or the store that brought us together, although they were important elements. It wasn't even the (justifiably) legendary sense of Irish hospitality. It was the ability of a retail clerk stocking a cheese case to notice something about me as an individual and parlay that observation into the beginning of a personalized relationship, reinforced by the presence of some of the best bleu cheese on earth.

This would be a good story if it stopped there, but it didn't. Later that week, Ryan sat with Patrick Campbell, chairman of Campbell Bewley Group, an Irish-based manufacturer of quality teas and coffees and an operator of a variety of foodservice outlets from full-line restaurants to coffee bars and kiosks. They were discussing Campbell's marketing strategy for his teas and coffees. "We're careful where we sell," he told Ryan. "That's why we're so pleased that Superquinn carries our goods. We think it says something about us that we're sold through their stores." We know exactly what he meant. Superquinn clearly dominates on service and just as clearly differentiates itself on product. Superquinn unconsciously embodies the principles of Consumer Relevancy. What our visits to Ireland, the Netherlands, Belgium, England, the Caribbean, and France confirmed was that Consumer Relevancy has global and not just U.S. application.

Why? Well, from the seller's point of view, the relationships between consumers and businesses haven't changed all that radically from the days of the nineteenth-century country store and its urban equivalent to the twenty-first century's cybersouk. After all, the country-store operator had perfect knowledge of his or her customers, often sold without the exchange of hard currency, and in many cases delivered—essentially the same goals of today's cybercapitalists. So if things haven't changed that much, why do consumers seem so upset? Part of the answer is that while the essential transactional infrastructure (the five basic attributes of commerce—access, experience, price, product, and service) appears the same over time, the covering of that infrastructure (the specific meaning of those attributes at any given point) has been radically transformed.

Let's look at what this means for each of the five attributes.

1. **The mythology of price: Business brags about cheap, but people value honest.** One of the reasons we initially thought the survey respondents must be wrong ought to serve as a wake-up call for all companies. Time and time again, in our phone surveys and face-to-face interviews, consumers—regardless of income level, geographic location, and/or education—told us they were less concerned with getting the lowest price than they were with getting a fair and honest price. What does that mean? It means they want a price that is consistent and that doesn't appear to have been artificially increased or decreased at the expense of other things they want to buy. We've found whole industries guilty of practicing Consumer Irrelevancy in their pricing practices. Exhibit A: the American telephone industry. Consumers want some assurance that they've selected a fair and honest rate plan. Instead, they're bombarded with dueling verbiage about minutes, caller networks, multistate plans, and meaningless

features and options. Most customers don't care that they can get the lowest price available for calling their great-aunt Sadie on Sundays after midnight provided they call Sadie from Ohio when she's in Alaska on the fourth Sunday of any month starting with "J"—they just want to be able to understand their phone bill.

2. **Setting the service bar: Walk your talk.** Time after time, we have seen companies falling over themselves to provide "value-added" services for consumers in one area, while failing to provide basic service in others. Perhaps it's the hotel that offers weary business travelers discounted weekend family packages but gives away guaranteed rooms or loses reservations. Or consider the do-it-yourself store that offers classes in Renaissance parquetry but won't let you return a wrong-sized washer. All those special services mean little if a company can't successfully serve customers' basic, everyday requests. No matter how much you try to pad an offer, any customer knows one size never fits all. They don't want to be buried under a pile of bells and whistles. They want to be recognized as individuals and know that the company they're doing business with is willing to customize its offerings to their individual needs. Options don't mean much if you can't find the basic service you want.

3. **Access: It ain't just location anymore.** Yesterday, access meant a right-hand turn into a bank's parking lot or having gas stations on all four corners of a busy intersection. Today, consumers care more about navigation—physical and psychological—than mere geographic location. They don't want to be confused or slowed down by clever and elaborate layouts or trapped by forced traffic patterns into a human imitation of sheep in a slaughter chute. Getting to a business is far less important than getting what they want once they've arrived. Offer too much in the way of selection or distraction, and you run the risk of making the most important aspect of access—the customer's ability to actually locate and buy—too high a hurdle. This helps explain the success of e-ticket machines in airports and

the growing popularity of "Fast Pass" systems at parks like Disney World.

4. **The real meaning of experience: Intimacy matters.** One of the assumptions we made—and, we believe, one that is made by many others—was to equate "experience" with "entertainment." However, consumers across the globe told us they were looking for something quite different from business. According to these consumers, entertainment doesn't even make the top 15 on the list of important issues. What *do* they want? They want respect, to be treated like a human being, and to be offered unique products or services. We believe this is the strength of high-tech manufacturers like Gateway, which routinely sells products configured to specific customer needs rather than pushing only the most expensive computer system available. This approach of treating customers like human beings rather than as human purchase orders stands in stark contrast to the proverbial and stereotypical car salesman who tries to trick people into buying far more car than they need.

5. **Product: Your best just isn't good enough.** There's bad news here for branders—especially mid-range branders. Just because you believe your products are the best doesn't necessarily mean they dominate a customer's consciousness. Despite our initial misguided belief about how consumers view price, we thought we understood what they wanted out of product. Naturally, we assumed everyone would want "the best" (recognizing that "best" is relative, subjective, and personal)—or, at the very least, something approximating the highest quality. Once again, we were wrong. While a few consumers—notably Internet shoppers—said they buy only the best they can find, the vast majority of consumers indicated that consistently good product was more desirable than a single best offering. A number of our direct interviews said they were unlikely to spend the extra money on top-of-the-line products if they perceived that a less expensive item is likely to be "good enough." The overriding

sentiment is that, at any given price point, there is a "band of accept-ability"—i.e., the quality of products or services must fall within a certain range to be acceptable to consumers.

It Doesn't Have to Be That Way: A Hierarchy of Interaction

Consumers are sending a clear message: "If you give me what I need (hon-esty, respect, and trust), I will give you what you desire from me (my loyal patronage)." Explain it using any sociological or psychological theory that makes you comfortable, but the simple fact is that people are so hungry for basic human values, values they're not experiencing in their day-to-day lives, that they will flock to a company that provides them. This need for trust is so strong that it transcends the boundaries of the physical store, the pages of a catalog, and the bandwidth of the Internet. It is fundamental to any successful consumer business, from the largest online bookstore to a local coffeehouse, from an airline to a bank, from a mom-and-pop restau-rant in Brooklyn to a national health-care carrier.

A consumer's interaction with sellers operates at one of three potential levels: accept, prefer, and seek (Table 2.1). There is also a negative level—one "below ground"—an area of deep distrust and loss of credibility, a space in which no company wants to operate. Ask consumers and they will tell you of those times when they suffered the disrespect, dehumanization, and lack of accommodation at the hands of companies—even entire indus-tries. Where a company falls in this "hierarchy of interaction" depends on how well it listens to its consumers, truly understands what they are look-ing for, and satisfies their needs.

How does a company solidify a relationship with its consumers and work its way up the hierarchy of interaction? Most of all, it requires a new way of thinking—in short, a new concept of Consumer Relevancy, one that allows for differentiation, without attempting to do everything at world-class levels. Understanding Consumer Relevancy begins with an understanding of the interaction that exists among consumer behavior, business strategy, and the resulting relationship at each of the three levels.

TABLE 2.1

Hierarchy of Interaction:
What Consumers Are *Really* Saying About How
They Want to Interact with Companies

Attributes

LEVEL	ACCESS	EXPERIENCE	PRICE	PRODUCT	SERVICE
III: Consumer Seeks the Company (Dominate)	Give me a **solution**; help me out in a bind.	Establish **intimacy** with me by doing something no one else can.	Be my **agent**; let me trust you to make my purchases.	**Inspire** me with an assortment of great products I didn't know about.	**Customize** the product or service to fit my needs.
II: Consumer Prefers the Company (Differentiate)	Make the interaction **convenient** for me.	**Care** about my needs and me.	Be fair and **consistent** in your pricing. I'm not necessarily after the lowest price.	Be **dependable** in your selection and in-stock position, so I can rely on you when I'm in a bind.	**Educate** me when I encounter a product or a situation I don't understand.
I: Consumer Accepts the Company (Operate at Par)	Make it **easy** for me to find what I need, get in and out in a hurry.	**Respect** me; treat me like a human being.	Keep the prices **honest**; don't jack them up or offer big savings when there are none.	Be **credible** in your product and service offerings.	**Accommodate** me; bend over backward sometimes to show me you care.
Consumer Underworld	Block my way, hassle me, keep me waiting, make it hard for me to get in and out.	Dehumanize me; disrespect me; ignore my needs.	Be inconsistent, unclear, or misleading in your pricing.	Offer me poor-quality merchandise and services that I can't use.	Give me an experience I'd just as soon forget; give me a reason to tell my friends and relatives to stay away.

Level I is the threshold at which the customer says, *"I accept you. I trust you enough to buy your products and services and to consider coming back."* A basic level of *acceptance*—representing *par* for a particular market or business—needs to be established in customers' minds before they even consider a company as a default choice. If they find honest pricing, credible products, accommodating service, easy access, and the respect they believe they deserve, chances are that an opportunity exists for you to establish a comfortable interaction with a consumer, one that can lead to stronger ties and some degree of loyalty. Sounds obvious, until you remember the bank branch that never seems to have fewer than twenty-five people in line, or the website that seems to take days to move from page to page, or the thousands of stores across the country that are happy to sell you something but make you feel invisible if you try to bring it back. We could go on, but—based on your own experience—you probably get the picture.

In a Level I relationship, consumers are willing to make their *routine purchases* from the company. At this level, the relationship is transactional: The consumer needs something, the company carries an acceptable offering, and the exchange of cash for goods or services is made. This level conveys little sense of loyalty either way. The consumers may never buy from that company again, and the company doesn't necessarily care.

At *Level II,* you have an opportunity to serve the consumer, who says, *"I prefer your store, products, and services, and—all things being equal—I will probably make my purchases there."* Once the door is opened to doing business with a consumer, the next hurdle is to get that customer to *prefer* doing business with you. In the vocabulary of the instavidual, what can be done to encourage the consumer to drive the additional half-mile through heavy traffic to your store, wait patiently in line to be served by employees he or she has come to know and like, and look to your company as providing consistently good values and fair prices? At Level II, consumers actually prefer one store or brand over another. This happens when the company makes access to its facilities, product, or website convenient, shows respect on a personal level, clearly presents consistent prices, offers reliable, good-quality products, and is able to educate a consumer on how a product or service works.

To hit Level II, you must find ways to *differentiate* yourself from your competitors. Think for a minute about how you view your own suppliers or how you, as a consumer, relate to the companies competing for your business. Now try to see consumers as purchasing agents for their own lives, and think about how you could become one of the two or three "preferred vendors." What would your criteria look like? How would you bid a household's needs? There are plenty of options: Consider Blockbuster Video's promise to never let a customer go home disappointed because she wasn't able to find the video she came to rent. Or it may be a pledge like Burger King's to let customers have a Whopper any way they choose. That pledge was so compelling that it forced McDonald's to eventually follow suit by offering custom-built Big Macs. Or it could take a form such as AT&T's introduction of the Digital One program, which broke new ground in the cellular-phone industry by being the first to offer flat-rate pricing with no long-distance or "roaming" charges. Or think about Sears' commitment to buyers of Craftsman tools to unconditionally guarantee the products for the life of the tool, even if that exceeds the life of generations of owners.

Level II companies have distinguished themselves from market competitors and built a degree of trust sufficient to cause consumers to prefer doing business with them. There is an *affinity* between consumer and company that causes the consumer to recall the company's name or products at his moment of need. The consumer may also think of two or three other companies offering similar or even identical products, but they're rejected as quickly as they're recalled.

At *Level III,* the consumer says to the company, *"I trust you so completely that I will not only seek you out among all the other options, but I will also give you the authority to edit my options for me."* This is the ideal state, in which the consumer not only prefers one company over another but also will actively *seek* out the company of choice. At this level, consumers will gladly wait six months for delivery of the new-model BMW, will refuse to buy kitchen gadgets at any store but Williams-Sonoma, or won't drink coffee not brewed by Starbucks.

Of course, all consumer businesses want to find some way to differentiate themselves from their competition. That's more or less the first commandment of business: Unless thou hast something better or different to offer, keep it to thyself. The most successful companies, though, don't stop at just differentiating themselves. They find ways to *dominate,* to further separate themselves from the pack, causing them to be the one choice that pops into the consumer's mind at the moment of need. Successfully transforming differentiation into market domination, these companies become the definitive source of goods and services. For example, by offering easy access to a range of products and services that no other bookseller had before, Amazon became, in the minds of millions of consumers, the default retailer of books on the Internet. The Home Depot has grown to be the largest home-center retailer in the United States, providing an impressive array of products backed by a strong service orientation.

It is at this level that a company has the opportunity to move consumers to *lifestyle* relationships. Level III companies capture consumers' imagination so completely that those shoppers no longer even think about other options. In Level III relationships, the company becomes the source that customers appoint to make all the right decisions in light of their unique lifestyles.

Getting to Level III doesn't just happen. Companies achieve this degree of authority only through constant monitoring of consumer interactions at a level of detail that other companies find too granular. Of course, a number have done it, including Wal-Mart, America Online, Southwest Airlines, Lexus, Eddie Bauer, Citibank, eBay, Nokia, and Dell. These companies understand the new definitions of consumer value.

Naturally, the goal for any consumer business interested in long-term growth and profitability is to move up the levels as much as is practical and desirable. Few companies turn away the occasional shopper, but a company can't rely on "accidental" customers to increase market share over the long haul. Even at the preference level, where a particular business is one of a few options a consumer would consider, there's the risk that the company won't be chosen most of the time. While being a "preferred vendor" gives you a leg up, it doesn't guarantee growth.

The only way to ensure the strength and viability of your company for the foreseeable future is to fully dominate your market and build a lifestyle relationship with consumers who seek you out. If you sell "business casual" clothing, such as Eddie Bauer, you want to be the only place consumers go for slacks, blazers, and sweaters. If you are a purveyor of fine automobiles, like BMW, you want to capture all of your target consumers' vehicle purchases over the course of their lives. And if you're a provider of cellular-phone services, like AT&T, you want there to be no other options for cell-phone users—ever. At this level, you want your brand and products to be so closely defined with how consumers live their lives that the individuals wouldn't be caught dead wearing, driving, eating, drinking, or using anything else.

Creating a Consumer-Relevant Company

So how do you find the road to this commercial Promised Land? It starts with being seen as relevant by the consumer on his or her own terms and ends only when that relevancy translates into a lifestyle relationship. As we stated in Chapter 1, perhaps the most significant insight to come out of our research concerns the myth of excellence. Truly consumer-relevant companies don't attempt to dominate in every customer-centric category— price, service, access, experience, and service. Great companies learn to overcome the constant temptation to strive for universal excellence. You must decide on which attribute you want to compete.

In addition to choosing a primary attribute, companies that are highly relevant to consumers select a second attribute that serves as a strong complement and helps them further differentiate themselves from competitors. This kind of pairing explains how Target has been able to successfully coexist with Wal-Mart.

Finally, the most successful consumer businesses recognize that regardless of how well they perform on their primary and secondary attributes, they cannot fall below industry par on the other three. Many companies often overlook this critically important point. For instance, a retailer that has the best service and a broad selection of products will ultimately fail if its operating hours are too short, its stores are too hard to locate, or its prices are too high. Similarly, a restaurant where "everybody knows your name" and does a good job of satisfying special dietary preferences will struggle if its food quality is not up to snuff. Catalog retailer Lands' End has fallen into this trap. One of the most successful apparel merchants through the 1980s because of its superior service and ability to offer honest, consistent pricing, the company has fallen on hard times recently because of its "unexciting inventory" and "unattractive merchandise."[1]

The overriding message here is that successful companies understand that value, in consumers' minds, is the intangible "sum total" of a business's performance on all five attributes. There is an aggregate minimum threshold that every company must meet across the board to be successful. This threshold, though, is not the same for all companies. In mature markets or industries, the value threshold is much higher than in emerging industries or among companies with innovative business models.

The traditional retail grocery business, for example, is one of the most mature industries in the country. Because of their years of experience in shopping at supermarkets, consumers have high expectations for grocers in all areas of operations and have little tolerance for slippage. They expect competitive prices, ease of shopping and checkout, a wide selection of fresh products, friendly service, and a pleasant shopping experience. But that doesn't mean that grocery retailers must excel in all five areas; rather, it means that the bar for what constitutes the minimum acceptable performance in those areas is significantly higher than it is for, say, online booksellers. In this emerging market, consumers are more apt to give merchants some leeway in their performance because they recognize that the novelty of the business model carries some inherent challenges that will take time to address. This helps explain why the same consumers that do not tolerate inattentive or surly grocery-store employees put up with less-than-stellar customer service from their favorite online retailers.

But no honeymoon lasts forever, and even online companies have learned that ecstatic abandon has left the love affair that consumers initially had with Web retailing. The holiday shopping season of 1999 will be remembered as the beginning of the end for many Internet companies that—literally—couldn't fulfill their promises to customers. Thousands of consumers were furious when the presents they ordered from online merchants failed to make it under the tree by Christmas morning. Many of those who did receive their orders and found that they weren't quite what they wanted faced a daunting task in returning the merchandise to retailers that lacked a clear and easy-to-follow return policy. The point is that while consumers could overlook shortcomings in service among Web merchants in the early days, they now believe companies have had enough time to shake the bugs out of the system.

The Attribute Value Matrix

To illustrate the interplay among the five value attributes, and to demonstrate how a successful company can use these attributes to create unquestioned value for its target consumer, we have assigned a numerical value to each of the attributes. These values represent a company's allocation of resources and operational efforts to achieve either a threshold level of acceptance at which it seeks to meet market competition on an attribute (a 3), a level of differentiation where the company hopes to use an attribute to persuade consumers to prefer its products or services (a 4), or a level of market dominance where the consumer refuses to buy anywhere else (a 5).

When applying the model, there are four simple rules to keep in mind:

1. A perfect score across the five attributes is 5 (domination) on one attribute, 4 (differentiation) on a second attribute, and 3 (acceptable) on the remaining three.

2. Anything less than a 3 on any attribute is not sustainable and will cause brand damage.

3. Domination or differentiation on more than one attribute is excessive and is not economically optimal, resulting in companies leaving money on the table.

4. The definition of a 3 (acceptable) as it relates to any of the attributes can continually change, as consumer expectations change. Failure to keep pace and perform to the level of these changing expectations can cause the score to drop below 3.

Let's look at some real-world examples of how successful companies have used various combinations of the value attributes to compete in very different ways. We constructed a table (Table 2.2) in which the primary attribute is located on the horizontal axis and the secondary attribute on the vertical axis. We have placed leading consumer companies and brands at intersections in the grid to paint a picture of the competitive landscape. In actual client work, we've found that some of the most enlightening discussions occur when a company's executives sit together and try to place themselves and their competition on a blank version of this chart. In our experience, it almost always raises some interesting executive-alignment issues.

We've also asked groups of employees (executive office, middle management, and front-line troops) to perform this same exercise independently of one another, and then we've compared the results. Invariably, we've found that they appear to be working for several different companies and competing across several different markets—a signal that the company has critical internal communication and policy issues.

The point of the grid is not to be definitive about a particular company's strategy; it is to show how the pairing of certain primary and secondary attributes can give a company a commanding lead over its competitors. These placements represent values consumers believe the companies are offering (which *should* correspond with what the companies think they provide). By the way, whether we're right about all of our placements, and whether you agree with those placements, is not the issue. In fact, we may be wrong about some of them. The crucial point is that the people who matter—customers and consumers—have definite opinions, and our work to date tells us that many executives are ignorant of how their companies are perceived, how their competition is perceived, and what to do to create needed differentiation in a crowded, competitive field.

Wal-Mart, for example, was seen by most consumers in our survey as a retailer that primarily offers consistently low prices, a quality mirrored by the company's longstanding marketing slogan, "Always low prices. Always." Secondarily, the company prides itself on carrying a wide assortment of brand-name products—not necessarily the best products available,

TABLE **2.2**

Primary and Secondary Attributes of Selected Companies and Brands

		PRIMARY ATTRIBUTE				
		PRICE	**SERVICE**	**PRODUCT**	**EXPERIENCE**	**ACCESS**
SECONDARY ATTRIBUTE	**PRICE**		Geico, Lands' End, Dell, Gold's Gym	Target, Staples, Kohl's, Dixons, Mazda, Honda (car), Maytag	Chuck E. Cheese, Ikea, Club Med, Gateway, Southwest Airlines, Gourmet Garage	Avon, E* Trade, Tide
	SERVICE	AutoZone, Tesco, Craftsman tools, Saturn		The Home Depot, Ferragamo, Gucci, Record Time	Four Seasons, Kraft, Peapod, Canyon Ranch	McDonald's, Webvan, Progressive Corp., Circles, Gerber
	PRODUCT	Wal-Mart, Ames, Costco, Red Roof Inns, Zara, Suave	Circuit City, Citibank, Allstate, Boots, Superquinn, Chevy Trucks, Continental Airlines		REI, Midwest Express, Nike Stores, The Disney Store, Harrods, Bewley's, BMW, Rolex	Amway, Walgreens, Yahoo!, Amazon.com, Coke, Kodak, CNN, Gatorade
	EXPERIENCE	Honda Goldwing motorcycles	Nordstrom, Singapore Airways, Hong Kong Suits	Williams-Sonoma, Best Buy, Pier 1, Tumi, Tylenol, Bose		AOL, Hallmark
	ACCESS	Dollar General, Family Dollar, Charles Schwab, Priceline, Visa, Carrefour, Casio	Dell Computer, American Express, M&M Mars (online)	Sony, Frito-Lay, 3M, Eddie Bauer, Chase Bank, Whirlpool, Lowe's	iVillage.com, Starbucks, Marlboro	

but ones that consumers consider desirable and important. On the rest of the attributes, Wal-Mart performs as people would expect any mass merchandiser to perform.

Recognizing it would have a difficult time competing directly against Wal-Mart, discounter Target—which operates in approximately the same arena—has chosen to do something a little different. One of the few companies that has managed to stand up to the challenge of the Arkansas juggernaut, Target, like Wal-Mart, emphasizes the same two attributes—price and product—but Target focuses primarily on product and secondarily on price. Yes, Target's prices tend to be lower than specialty stores, but they aren't as low as Wal-Mart's. However, its product assortment tends to be much more trendy than that of Wal-Mart, attracting a shopper who's a bit more stylish and fashion-conscious.

According to Robyn Waters, vice president of trend merchandising at Target, the company's ability to combine "hip design with value pricing" is what sets the retailer apart from others. "We are very focused on making the budget dress or the budget glass the best it could be—in its style, quality, merchandising, and marketing—or we don't bother," she noted. Added Roger Goddu, a former Target executive, "It all comes back to trend merchandising. [Target] is viewed as a vogue place to shop for fashion at value prices. Their customers are more into fashion trends than Wal-Mart's, and they can coexist with Wal-Mart on this basis."[2]

A similar contrast exists in the do-it-yourself home-center arena, where The Home Depot is the reigning champ and Lowe's the strong challenger. Early in the game, The Home Depot staked out its competitive ground by focusing primarily on a broad assortment of nearly every type of hardware, lumber, and gardening product one could need, and secondarily on offering superior service. While initial advertising promoted low prices, The Home Depot quickly set the bar for service in this segment, with its hiring of associates who actually knew something about the products sold (or training them well if they didn't); its policy that any shopper asking for the location of an item should be led, not pointed, to the spot by the associate; and the offering of in-store seminars and workshops for customers on myriad home-improvement topics.

Lowe's, on the other hand, has chosen to emphasize access over service, while maintaining the same primary focus on products. The product assortment at a Lowe's store is similar to that at The Home Depot. But the company stresses the fact that it is easy to find those items, thanks to clear, visible pricing and wide aisles—the key characteristics of access.

Striking the Balance

Finding the right combination of access, experience, price, product, and service is not only critical, but it's also extremely difficult to achieve. However, as we explore later in the book, many successful businesses, such as Gourmet Garage, Dollar General, Best Buy, and Irish grocery chain Superquinn, have achieved that delicate balance. Each has elected to excel in one attribute, differentiate in a second, and maintain an acceptable level of performance in the other three. Their success hinges on building and maintaining a rock-solid relationship with consumers, one grounded in trust and mutual respect.

Wal-Mart: Theory into Practice

When you take a closer look at what consumers consider important, you begin to see an emerging pattern of basic and, one might argue, essential human values—which serves as the foundation of our new model for Consumer Relevancy. So who does it right? Our research tells us the answer is a resounding "Wal-Mart." This mega-merchant is a classic price/product retailer, with a 5, 4, 3, 3, 3 profile across price, product, service, access, and experience.

As part of our survey, we asked consumers to name their favorite retailer in five principal segments (grocery, general merchandise, drug and convenience, specialty, and consumer direct). We also asked them to vote for the best overall retailer in America. It shouldn't be much of a surprise that Wal-Mart dominated the general merchandise channel, but what was most interesting was the chain's ranking in other segments. Wal-Mart placed first in three categories—grocery, general merchandise, and overall—second in the specialty retailer category, and third in the drug and convenience segment. The votes weren't even close in the overall category, with Wal-Mart outdistancing its nearest competitor by nearly 400 votes.

There are many potential reasons for Wal-Mart's dominance in our survey, not to mention the real world. One could credit its highly effective supply chain, the breadth and depth of its databases, or its phenomenal clout and buying power, to name a few. Of course, the consumer doesn't see most of those things, and since we asked *them* to rank Wal-Mart, we believe the company's real "secret" is essentially quite simple. Wal-Mart has risen to the top of the retail world because it knows what today's consumers value—as reflected in the new definitions of the value attributes—and understands the implications those new definitions have for the company's operations. In other words, Wal-Mart knows that consumers don't necessarily want the *lowest* prices all the time, or the absolute highest-quality products, or a store on every corner. Wal-Mart executives know that experience is, at its essence, courteous and friendly store employees, and that service means gladly and quickly accepting merchandise returns, no questions asked.

And because the company understands these definitions, Wal-Mart has made smarter decisions that have a major impact on all facets of its operations. Put another way, because Wal-Mart understands what consumers value and why, it has succeeded—like no other retailer in history—in consciously exhibiting honesty, treating customers with respect, and gaining consumers' trust. And as a result, consumers have rewarded Wal-Mart with their fierce loyalty and rabid patronage.

And just how does Wal-Mart know these things? No secret Arkansas mojo here—it talks to its customers. This is the enduring legacy of Sam Walton, who set the tone early in his career and carried it with him until the day he died. Perhaps even more important than setting the tone, Walton ensured that everyone in the Wal-Mart organization—from the executive suite to the loading dock—understood why it was important to continually talk to customers and actually listen to what they were saying. Wesley and Jimmy Wright, brothers who spent a good portion of their careers with Wal-Mart capped off with stints as vice president of merchandising and vice president of distribution, respectively, told us how Walton led his troops quietly and by example.

"Here's a typical Sam visit to a Wal-Mart store," recalled Wesley Wright. "First off, nobody at the store even knew he was coming. He flies in—doesn't have anyone pick him up—and when he gets to the store, he just walks around and talks to the associates. It sounds amazing, but he knew everything about all of the associates in the stores. When he talked with one of the cashiers, he knew her name and how much in sales she rang last month. He'd ask her how much she did this month so far, and how things were going. He showed a genuine interest in her and her job. And when it was time for lunch, he'd just grab a can of tuna and some crackers and sit in the employee lounge and talk with the associates. After lunch, he often would get on the PA and announce to the store, 'Folks, this is Sam Walton, founder of Wal-Mart. Could I get all of you to come up to the front of the store for a second—even the customers?' Then he'd sit on the floor and ask everyone, 'Tell me what's going on in the store. If this was your store, what would you do to improve it?' And he'd be there with his yellow pad, taking notes. And you know that he would make sure that what was on that notepad got taken care of, whether it was the responsibility of the store manager, merchandising, distribution, or HR."

Added Jimmy Wright: "Sam never lost touch with the consumers and the associates, no matter how big Wal-Mart got. He created a culture of unity, support, and alignment—everyone from top to bottom had the same goals. Because of the commitment to employee training and Sam's leadership, that culture continues to this day. Sam's focus was on three things—take care of the customers, take care of the associates, and have name-brand products at everyday low prices—and that focus never wavered in the twenty years I worked for him."

CHAPTER 3

Would I Lie to You?

The Overrated Importance of Lowest *Price*

ROCHELLE PUSHED BACK FROM her computer and surveyed the tiny office created by the hasty imposition of some sheets of drywall and a few two-by-fours to what would have been extra backroom space in a Speedway gas station in Eastpointe, Michigan. We thought she would be the poster child for the model "price shopper," and in some ways we were right, but in at least one critical respect we could not have been more wrong. After all, the Detroit native is a single mother of eight children, ranging in age from five to twenty, and works as a Speedway service-station manager. And with nine mouths to feed on a regular basis, not to mention a small but growing army of grandchildren and assorted relatives dropping in, price is clearly important to Rochelle. What surprised us, though, is that price is not always her primary shopping motivation.

"If the product is good quality, I will pay the price," Rochelle said. "If it is poor quality, I don't care what the price is. I won't buy it. If I get bad meat, you can guarantee I won't go back again."

What does matter to Rochelle—and to plenty of the other consumers to whom we spoke—is honesty and fairness when it comes to price and pricing policies. She related a story to us that is representative of the kind of frustration many shoppers expressed. "I went clothes shopping to buy uniforms, and they had the price in the store marked as one amount, and the advertised price was a different amount," Rochelle said. "It was advertised at $9.99 and the price marked was $14.99, and when you are buying two uniforms each for five kids, that is a lot of money. And I'm arguing with the cashier, saying this is your advertised price and you have to sell it at that, it's the law. We argued for about ten minutes before she got her boss."

What finally happened? "Her boss said, 'This is what it says in the paper, evidently it was overlooked, so give it to her at that price,'" said Rochelle. "But I won't go back to that store."

Price is perhaps the attribute most commonly abused by companies chasing the myth of excellence. Believing that price is the ultimate consumer siren song, too many businesses offer gratuitous discounts on items or services that consumers would be happy to pay full margin for. Often these unexpected—and fundamentally unwanted—price reductions come into direct conflict with fundamental customer values. Customers trust prices they believe are fair and honest, often distrusting promises of "lowest possible cost." A Neiman Marcus shopper, for example, is looking for both superior products and superior service. Offering those products or services at "40 percent off" appears disingenuous. The same holds true for mass offerings from supermarkets to drugstores. Consumers routinely told us they thought that this week's "special" was either being subsidized by other products or would result in an inflated price being charged for the discounted product when it went off sale.

As we worked our way through the research data, we encountered what at first appeared to be a paradox: Price is seemingly the easiest attribute to define and yet the hardest to accurately describe. This paradox makes price the easiest attribute to mis-define. It's all too tempting to fall into the trap of defining price in a traditional way—as the absolute cost (generally low) charged for a good or service. But the message from consumers is clear: Dominating on price doesn't necessarily mean having the absolutely lowest cost—it means consistently offering customers fair and honest prices.

This new definition ought to shatter some very basic beliefs about what it means to be a price operator and serve as a wake-up call for many, if not most, companies. While most consumer businesses appear happy to compete ferociously on the basis of cost of goods or services, content that consumers really want the lowest prices available, they're just flat wrong!

Time and time again, in our phone surveys and face-to-face interviews, consumers—regardless of income level, geographic location, and/or education—said they were much less concerned with getting the lowest price than they were with getting a fair and honest price. What does that mean? It means they want a price that is easily visible and consistent and that doesn't appear to have been artificially increased or decreased at the expense of other, related items they need to purchase. You don't have to offer these consumers a sale, but if you do, it had better be a real sale, not some predictable, inventory-reduction marketing ploy. If an item is advertised at a particular price, you'd better honor that price at the point of sale. The topic of "lowest prices" never even surfaced in the face-to-face interviews unless we brought it up, and, in most cases, the whole topic of pricing tended to take a back seat to discussions of product quality, shopping ease, and service.

Fundamental societal change has taken place when it comes to price. Absolute lowest price may continue to be important to some segment of the population, but it will be just one factor in the purchase-decision process for the vast majority of consumers. And, in many cases, price will actually be a less significant factor than it has been, because people today—and tomorrow—are more rushed and more time-starved than ever before.

Most consumers told us that they value honest pricing because they don't have time to comparison shop. Time-strapped consumers hurrying down the aisles of the local Kmart store are less likely to question whether the price of a 100-ounce bottle of Tide liquid detergent is higher or lower than what they might find at the local Winn-Dixie, Kroger, or Target store—because it would be impractical to drive to all four to find out and too time-consuming to compare prices in ad circulars.

At the same time, however, our research indicated that there is a crucial difference between price and the other four attributes, because price is the one that requires the consumer to give up something—namely, money. A business can provide access, create the experience, and offer the product and service. But, ultimately, a company can only set the price; it's the consumer who provides the cash.

Which may help explain why consumers are particularly suspicious when it comes to prices. Today's sophisticated shoppers know that each pair of hands that touches an item means an increase in the price to them. But how much of a markup is taken? Are the manufacturers' discounts really passed on to consumers, or is the company taking a big cut for itself? The real problem with the traditional high-low method of pricing is that consumers simply don't trust it. They don't feel they're being rewarded at the lower sale price but, rather, that they're being screwed at the higher regular price.

The seeds for such suspicion were sown in the 1960s, when retailers of all sorts, but chiefly department stores and grocery chains, developed a pricing strategy they hoped could help them take advantage of new or seasonal items by selling them at high prices. Seeing the latest fashion or encountering an item for the first time, consumers, who were not particularly price-conscious, would buy the item without questioning its price. It was not so much a matter of socioeconomic status as a mind-set: The very wealthy as well as the poor sometimes ignored a price tag if the item carried a lot of value and dependability for them. If a new fashion didn't sell immediately, a company could always lower the price later in the season to draw price-sensitive customers into the store. Then, through promotions and special sales, merchandise could be sold even at a loss if that meant customers bought other items at their regular high prices. This high-low pricing strategy, moreover, could take some of the worry out of inventory control, because a "hot" item would sell out in a hurry whereas a less popular one might be sold during a special promotion.

Wal-Mart changed all that when it popularized the EDLP philosophy—everyday low prices. With EDLP, the company could sell in large enough volume to have firm control over suppliers, keep prices low, and still clear a sizable profit without having to worry about sales and promotions. Moreover, the EDLP strategy would enable the company to defuse some of the distrust and confusion that high-low had engendered among consumers. With EDLP, the thinking went, consumers would understand that they get one low price consistently—maybe not the *lowest* price, but a fair price on the items they want, when they want them, without having to clip coupons or drive all over town searching for the best bargains.

What Wal-Mart understands—but most consumer businesses don't—is that price has become a multidimensional attribute that goes far beyond the simple notion of lowest price. Those dimensions consist of honesty, consistency, fairness, reliability, a range of acceptable prices, and price impression.

As we spoke with individual consumers, the following three price-related issues (listed in descending order of importance) emerged as the most critical to consumers of all demographics who shop primarily in physical stores:

- They feel that they are getting an honest price, one that hasn't been artificially inflated.
- During sales, they save significant money on their purchases.
- The companies they frequent offer leading brands at lower prices.

Few people we spoke to stressed the need for the lowest prices they could find. And when they did discuss price, most consumers listed it second or third—behind product quality and physical plant access—when identifying what makes them want to buy. "I shop at Banana Republic because they have decent prices, but also great-quality clothing," said twenty-five-year-old Oscar. Similarly, Vickie, a twenty-seven-year-old consultant, said, "The quality of the products determines where and what I buy. The price should match the quality." And Mary, fifty, noted, "I do look at prices, but that's not always the best gauge of the value of the product. It's not critical that the price is really cheap; it's just got to be reasonable."

It's this last notion—that prices just have to be reasonable—that came up again and again in our face-to-face interviews with consumers. This led us to conclude that there are many effective ways to compete against strict lowest-price businesses, a valuable lesson for companies without the size, operating scale, or margins to compete on lowest price. Prices that fall within an acceptable range tend to be viewed as "honest" by consumers, keeping in mind, of course, that this range will vary depending on factors such as product category and region of the country.

What does this mean for consumer businesses? It's very simple: High-low pricing growth strategies are dead-end streets. Price plays *might* work in the short term by increasing sales and share. But based on what consumers told us, it's a position that can't help any company create either a loyal customer base or a sustainable competitive advantage over the long haul or at scale. Why? The high-low strategy fails because it teaches consumers to distrust the business, and, ultimately, causes a business to lose share of mind and share of consumer.

In fairness, the Internet appears to be an interesting exception to the new definition of price. Online shoppers don't mind spending extra time surfing the Web for the best bargains, as evidenced by the fact that the top price-related issue among our cybershopper respondents was "Feel you are getting the lowest price available." For the time being at least, the online shopper sees the Internet as one big global bazaar. Priceline.com and its "name your own price" mantra, eBay with its frenzied auctions, and the promotional din of Web booksellers like Amazon, Barnes & Noble, and Borders have conditioned online shoppers not to settle for "paying retail." This conditioning, combined with consumers' knowledge that comparison shopping was just a few clicks away and that shipping costs would bump up the final price made the Internet a free-fire zone for low-price operators—until the second- and third-round financing fell through.

Lowest price might be the key price-related factor in the wired world, but in the physical world, a consumer business attempting to dominate on price today must recognize the multidimensional aspects of price. Even operators that intrinsically appear to be only about flat-out lowest prices understand that, in fact, it takes more to attract customers. Consider the dollar-store retailers, for example. There is a temptation to classify these stores as a channel unto themselves, with different rules than would apply to other types of consumer businesses. After all, lowest prices is what they're all about—and it's *all* they're about, right? Don't their names say it all? Dollar General, Todo a Peso, The Dollar Store, Family Dollar. You can't get much cheaper than a buck.

But, in fact, the different dimensions of the price attribute apply to these businesses as well. Consider Dollar General Corp., a Nashville-based retailer that caters to low- and fixed-income consumers. While the company's stores clearly dominate on price, they are also a paragon of pricing consistency. "There's way too much inconsistency in pricing out there today," Bob Carpenter, the company's president and chief operating officer, told us. "Our customers need to know that they can count on us every day to give them the value for their dollar that they need. So we don't have sales or specials—just consistent, honest prices on everything in the store, no matter which store you're in, no matter when you shop."

These pricing attributes don't appeal just to lower-income consumers. Dollar-type stores also populate the landscape of suburban malls, for instance, where income levels can run the gamut. "I buy arts-and-crafts supplies for two hundred kids in the Just a Buck store because I know I won't get screwed on the prices," said Barbara, who runs a suburban Connecticut day-care center.

Perhaps no consumer business understands the new definition of the price attribute better than Wal-Mart. Through its consistent, honest pricing, the giant retailer has succeeded in setting the lowest-price impression among consumers and has become a trusted purchasing agent for those shoppers. In other words, people automatically think of Wal-Mart as the price leader.

But is the impression of lowest prices reality? While most consumers believe that Wal-Mart always has the lowest prices, a market-basket comparison that we conducted proved otherwise. Our research, in which we compared the prices charged by Wal-Mart and its three major competitors in eighteen U.S. markets on a list of common items, showed that Wal-Mart was not always the lowest-priced player (Table 3.1).

On average, Wal-Mart's prices were higher than those of its competitors on one-third of the items checked. On those items for which its prices were lower, consumers could expect to save anywhere from $0.14 to $1.62 per item, although the average savings were about $0.37 per item. However, in about a third of the instances where Wal-Mart's prices were lower, the savings amounted to only $0.02 or less.

TABLE 3.1

Market-Basket Comparison of Wal-Mart Versus Major Competitors

MARKET	NUMBER OF ITEMS WHERE WAL-MART IS LESS EXPENSIVE	AVERAGE SAVINGS	TOTAL NUMBER OF ITEMS COMPARED	PERCENT OF ITEMS WHERE WAL-MART IS LESS EXPENSIVE	WHERE WAL-MART IS LESS EXPEN- SIVE, PERCENT OF ITEMS WHERE SAVINGS IS $0.02 OR LESS
Houston	11	$0.22	18	61%	36.4%
Chicago	16	0.20	22	73	37.5
Detroit	8	0.19	23	35	14.0
Salt Lake City	10	0.44	16	63	40.0
Philadelphia	13	0.45	18	72	30.8
Washington, D.C.	11	1.62	13	85	9.0
Tampa	13	0.25	22	59	30.8
Overland Park, Kan.	13	0.24	20	65	23.1
Richmond, Va.	17	0.59	19	89	6.0
Seattle	12	0.25	19	63	41.7
Charlotte	14	0.41	20	70	17.0
Phoenix	14	0.22	20	70	28.6
Denver	12	0.14	18	67	33.3
Dallas	12	0.18	18	67	25.0
Los Angeles	16	0.21	22	73	25.0
North Brunswick, N.J.	7	0.56	11	64	14.0
Atlanta	8	0.17	14	57	50.0
Minneapolis	11	0.33	19	58	18.2
Average	**12**	**$0.37**	**18**	**66%**	**32.3%**

In some cases, we found a wide disparity in the prices that Wal-Mart charged for the same product in different areas of the country. A Wal-Mart store in Houston, for example, sold a 100-ounce bottle of Tide detergent for $7.32. The same product went for $6.27 at a Wal-Mart in Chicago, $5.62 in Salt Lake City, and $4.48 in Detroit. But the critical point is that consumers have come to *perceive* the prices at Wal-Mart to be the "lowest," even when that is often not the case. Wal-Mart has done such a good job of winning the consumer's trust that the company has become, in effect, the pricing authority, because its EDLP focus reassures customers that no pricing games are being played. And it's not just consumers who have this impression. Time and again, groups of business executives to whom we've presented our research said that when they think of lowest prices, they think of Wal-Mart.

Now, this doesn't mean the company has high prices. You have to have *low* prices to create the impression of *lowest* price. But the bottom line is that consumers simply feel they won't get ripped off in Wal-Mart, lending credence to our belief that price impression is, in fact, more important than price itself. How did Wal-Mart get to that place in consumers' minds? It didn't get there with price—at least, not initially. After all, Sam Walton started off with just one Ben Franklin store in the middle of Bentonville, Arkansas—no scale, no way to leverage price. Instead, the company listened to consumers, delivered what they wanted, and, in the process, established a relationship based on trust. Only then was Wal-Mart able to leverage that relationship to become viewed as the price leader.

Applying the Conceptual Model to Price

Because every company's position in its industry is unique, each having operations and processes that demand a solution tailored to the company, we cannot offer a generic, cookbook approach to building a successful strategy for competing on price (or any other attribute, for that matter). Rather, the model in Figure 3.1 is based on what we believe represents a realistic response to consumers' concerns.

FIGURE 3.1

Competing on Price

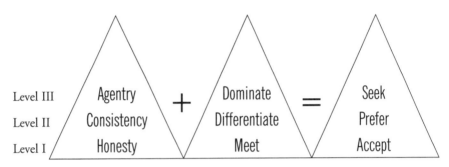

In our conceptual model of the consumer-company relationship, Level I represents the threshold of competing by offering honest, fair prices—the level at which consumers will *accept* you. Those prices must be viewed as competitive in the market, leading a consumer to say: *"If you don't shock me with your prices, I'll shop you."* This is the least you can offer if you want to compete on the attribute of price. Remember that customers at a brick-and-mortar store, as opposed to those shopping online, are likely to have a wider "bandwidth" of acceptable prices that they are willing to pay for a given item, but that proposition should not be construed as a license to soak customers on price. A 4.6-ounce tube of Colgate toothpaste, for instance, might range from $1.25 to $2.25, depending on the retailer, but even the most price-clueless shopper might interpret anything above that as greedy and unfair.

The success of companies such as Men's Wearhouse speaks volumes about consumers' interest in honest pricing. Men's Wearhouse, which features well-known name-brand men's apparel and accessories at prices 20 percent to 30 percent below those found on the same items at specialty and department stores, has been on a roll. The company's annual revenues have more than doubled in the past few years, to $1.187 billion in fiscal 1999. Patrons of Men's Wearhouse are not necessarily standard-issue price shoppers; rather, they are generally fairly affluent professionals who believe that department-store and boutique markups on suits, sport coats, and sweaters are unreasonable, and that Men's Wearhouse prices more accurately reflect the "real" prices of such garments.

If you are an online business, however, you have to offer prices that are lowest as well as honest. Internet-savvy consumers have too much power at their fingers to let a company get away with charging anything less than the lowest price. Such power, in fact, has gone a long way toward transforming a number of industry segments, perhaps none more so than the auto industry. Never before have consumers had the kind of pricing information at their disposal that they do now through websites such as Edmonds.com, Autobytel, and others. In the past, the sales rep at the car dealership held all the cards, but today a click of a few buttons on the Edmonds site can give car buyers complete information on what the dealer paid for the car and its options. If a dealer chooses to inflate the price of the car or an option, consumers know the percentage of inflation and can make their own decision about whether it's a reasonable profit for the dealer or blatant gouging.

At Level II, a company has to offer not only honest and competitive prices but also consistency. If you're perceived as having consistently competitive prices, consumers will *prefer* you. Consistency is the feature consumers said was more important than deep cuts in prices one week and a return to high pricing the next. Pricing consistency is a hallmark of online brokerages such as E*Trade, Schwab.com, and Quick & Reilly.com, where the price of buying or selling stock is a flat fee.

In essence, the assurance that prices will remain stable and predictable is enough to bring consumers back to your company when they need your products and services. If you offer consistent prices, consumers will come to see you as their preferred retailer.

We call Level III "agentry" to indicate that if a company goes beyond honest, consistent pricing and establishes a lasting price impression and a relationship with consumers based on trust, then consumers may abdicate to that company all responsibility for making purchases. In such a situation, consumers' faith runs so deep that they are willing, in effect, to say to the company, *"I trust you to anticipate my needs and make for me the pur-*

chases I need in your category." From the consumer's point of view, the relationship goes beyond the mere preference of Level II and assumes the quality of *this company and no other.* A company operating at Level III becomes the *pricing authority,* the company that essentially sets the price standard for its industry or segment.

If a company is perceived as the standard for low prices, consumers will *seek* out that company. This can occur even when there may be empirical evidence to prove that another company, in fact, offers lower prices. It's clear that when it comes to price, consumer behavior does not necessarily follow linearly across the attribute. As discussed earlier, Wal-Mart does not have the lowest prices on all items it carries. However, the company's customers believe that the Wal-Mart price is the *real* price, and that anything lower is just a short-term ploy by another company to entice shoppers and that ultimately it won't be sustainable.

Similarly, Dollar General has assumed the status of trusted agent among its customer base. "We've been in business for sixty years—we invented the dollar-store concept," said Bob Carpenter of Dollar General. "Our customers trust us because we have proved day in and day out that we will strive to bring them value. They know that the price we offer on an item is the absolute best we can do. And we try to never violate that trust."

The success of Dollar General offers a powerful argument for the EDLP strategy. Like Wal-Mart, Dollar General can trace its success to low and consistent prices. But, while Wal-Mart emphasizes *product* as its secondary attribute, Dollar General focuses on *access* to help differentiate its stores from the 100,000-square-foot-plus facilities operated by the Arkansas giant and other discounters. As you will see in the following case study, the results have been stellar: Revenue, gross profit, net income, and earnings per share are all up substantially since 1997, due in large part to the company's in-depth understanding of what its customers want and unwavering commitment to meeting those needs.

Case Study

Dollar General: "Value for Your Dollar"

Flannel shirt: $5. Bottle of dishwashing detergent: $1. Cotton khakis: $10. Box of presweetened cereal: $2.50.

Unbelievably low prices? You bet. Poor quality? Not at all. The flannel shirt is all-cotton and well-constructed. The dishwashing liquid is Dawn, one of the best-selling and best-known brands in the world. The cereal? Kellogg's Frosted Flakes. And the khakis? All-cotton as well, and made to the exact specifications of Levi's popular Dockers brand chinos. For most retailers, prices like these are unheard of even during sales with the deepest discounts. But for Dollar General, it's business as usual.

"You could say that we're a retailer focused on low prices, but that's really not the whole story," said president and COO Bob Carpenter. "A low price doesn't mean a thing if what you bought is cheaply made. Our customers can't afford to buy cheap things. They have to make their dollars stretch better than anybody else, so they need things that last. And that's what we give them: good quality at low prices, which we think equals value for your dollar."

It's a message reinforced by Dollar General's mission: to use its position to create a better life for everyone, many of whom rely heavily on Dollar General's ability to get them life's basics at prices that are within their budgets. "There's a real ministry when you're dedicated to selling toilet paper and bleach cheaper than anyone else in the business," said the company's CEO, Cal Turner Jr.[1]

Dollar General's growth in the past five years has been nothing short of phenomenal. Targeting the largest segment of the U.S. population—consumers with annual incomes of less than $25,000 and seniors on fixed incomes—the chain has more than doubled its number of stores since 1995 and has grown at an average rate of 20 percent to 25 percent a year. Now operating more than 5,000 outlets in twenty-four states, Dollar General generated more than $4 billion in sales in 1999—up from $2.6 billion in 1997. This would be considered a strong performance for any business, but it's especially impressive for a company that sells half its products for $1 or less and whose average register ring is $8.

The prospects for continued growth look positive, given the state of the company's target market. In fact, Carpenter believes that Dollar General has only scratched the surface of its potential customer base. "More and more people are living paycheck to paycheck these days," he said. "And it doesn't matter what the size of the paycheck is. Whether you're making $25,000 or $40,000, if you don't have a lot of extra money, you have to get real value for your dollar. Plus, as everyone knows, America's population is getting older, they're living longer, and people are retiring earlier. That means there will be more people on fixed incomes—for a longer period of time—who have to really stretch their incomes."

That's not the only factor in the company's success, however. Dollar General succeeds, first of all, because it is highly tuned to what its customers really need and operates predominantly in areas that are off the radar screen of other retailers—namely, small cities and towns in rural America. Approximately 75 percent of the company's stores are in towns with populations of fewer than 25,000 people—too small, according to Carpenter, to support the large discount chains such as Wal-Mart and Kmart. (The remainder of its stores are in urban neighborhoods that many of the major mass discounters ignore.) But most important, the company owes its success primarily to its combination of price leadership and accessibility. Dollar General dominates like no other on the value attribute of price and supports its pricing authority with a strong secondary emphasis on access.

Dollar General operates at par in terms of service and experience largely because labor cost in the channel is a significant leveler. However, the company is positioned slightly above par on product. Most of the players in what's come to be known as the "price-defined" channel have natural restrictions in the products they offer. They must be able to sell items at $1 and still maintain an acceptable margin. Of course, within that band of products, there are items with higher margin potential than others. Dollar General operates at the top end of that band due to its strong emphasis on product quality.

Consistency and Honesty in Pricing

DOLLAR GENERAL'S FORMULA FOR SUCCESS

PRIMARY ATTRIBUTE: PRICE

- Accepts only cash to eliminate credit-card fees and technology expenses.
- Does not advertise regularly, except to announce the opening of a new store.
- Features limited price points to make shopping easier for customers and accounting and inventory easy for employees.
- Carries predominantly house and private-label brands for lowest consumer prices and maximum margins.
- Focuses on fast-turning consumables to drive inventory volume.
- Operates "no-frills" stores with inexpensive fixtures and displays.
- Uses its network of district managers to help determine where to open stores and a small cadre of real-estate professionals to close lease or sale transactions quickly.
- Signs low-rent, short-term leases to minimize real-estate costs.
- Uses only basic technologies that help boost operational efficiency.
- Locates stores as close as possible to distribution centers to minimize transportation costs and reduce replenishment time.

Nobody does consistent and honest pricing better than Dollar General. At Dollar General, you won't find sales. In fact, Carpenter said, the company embraced the concept of everyday low prices well before Wal-Mart did. "We don't believe in sales," he said. "We believe in integrity in pricing, and that means that we'll guarantee that we'll offer you an item for the best price we can, given our margins—which are very small—and that every time you come into the store, you're going to get that price. Period."

What's more, he noted, "We don't play the $0.99 game with our customers. We go with even dollar price points. Our customers are smart enough not to be fooled by the sound of a supposedly cheaper price."

By taking the guesswork out of buying and, in the process, earning customers' complete trust, Dollar General has become the purchasing agent for many of its shoppers. In fact, the company considers its buyers "customer representatives" whose job it is to wrestle with suppliers for the best-quality products that the company's customers really need.[2]

Dollar General's price philosophy is rooted in ten crucial factors:

1. **Cash and carry.** Dollar General operates on a strict "cash and carry" basis, which means the company doesn't have to pay the 2 percent to 6 percent fees charged by credit-card companies. This policy also eliminates the need for credit-card verification systems (not an incidental expense when you're talking about two or three registers in each of its 5,000 stores). Besides, with an average ring of $8, there's no real need to accept credit cards.

2. **No advertising.** You'll never see a Dollar General sales circular in your mailbox or a product-oriented ad in your local newspaper. That's because the company limits its promotional spending to one special occasion: the opening of a new store. "For many retailers, their promotions account for 3 percent of their overhead costs," said Carpenter. "Not us. The only time you'll ever see an ad from Dollar General in your newspaper is when we do a grand opening for a store, to let people know that we're going to be open in a certain town at a certain location. That's it. We don't do TV, we don't do radio, and we don't advertise our products."

3. **Limited price points.** To keep things simple for customers, and for the company, Dollar General features only fourteen price points. This practice greatly reduces accounting and inventory time, not to mention headaches.

4. **Mixing of brands.** In its early days, Dollar General served as a clearinghouse for closeouts and "irregulars" from regular-price

retailers. Then, in the mid-1980s, seeking more consistency in its assortment, the company moved to only first-quality closeouts. But that still didn't allow the company to operate with the consistency it desired, and the model was changed to only first-quality items at everyday low prices.

Today, Dollar General features a mix of brands that enables the company to provide consistently good quality while keeping prices as low as possible. Approximately 10 percent to 15 percent of its items are well-known national brands, primarily in the grocery and health and beauty areas. According to Carpenter, these brands are essential to the store's mix because for certain items—toothpaste and laundry detergent, for example—consumers clearly prefer a recognized brand.

An equal portion of Dollar General's assortment consists of the DG Signature label. This is the company's house brand, and it appears primarily on grocery goods for which a national brand is not critical. The remainder of the products—about 70 percent—consist of various labels exclusive to Dollar General that, while not carrying the signature guarantee of the DG brand, still meet the company's high standards for quality. The all-cotton khakis, for instance, are sold under the Crossbow label.

The bulk of the company's private-label goods are bought directly from the manufacturer to eliminate the costs associated with distributors. Carpenter said that nearly 30 percent of these goods are sourced from outside the United States, particularly China. "With the volume we do, we can be very aggressive on pricing and specifications with our suppliers," he said.

Interestingly, the merchandising of the three brand types in the store does not follow the usual retail philosophy. "We don't set up private labels right next to every one of our national brands just to make the private label's price look better," said Carpenter. "That's how 90 percent of retailers operate, but not us. We just put the private label in where we think consumers will be accepting of something that may not be a household name, but the quality is good and it's a good value. We want to be honest with our customers, and when we think we have found a great value for them, we put it out there."

5. **Tight focus on assortments.** Carpenter notes that Dollar General features an assortment geared toward fast-moving consumables: food, health and beauty supplies, household goods—things that people use up and must replenish. This is critical in a business where volume is relied on to offset low margins. Dollar General avoids heavy exposure in apparel—it turns too slowly—but when it does offer soft lines, it sticks to the basics.

6. **Simple, no-glitz stores.** No one would mistake a Dollar General store for Neiman Marcus or even Target. But the decidedly unglamorous stores suit Dollar General customers just fine. "Our customer doesn't come to us because we have an upscale place," Carpenter noted. And keeping in-store displays and fixtures simple makes it easy for the company to outfit its locations without disrupting its margins.

7. **Quality labor force.** Like any retailer today, Dollar General is continually challenged to find the best employees it can at the most reasonable wages. Earl Weissert, the company's executive vice president of operations, said that one of the keys to getting solid employees is tapping the company's own customer base and leveraging its stores' locales. "We're primarily in rural, small-town America, and there are a lot of people in the towns we serve who need a good job," he said. "Single mothers in their thirties and forties, in particular, are a good fit for us, especially in the store-manager position. They're used to running a home, cleaning up after the kids, balancing budgets—doing all the basics around the house. Our business is so simple that it's just like running a home."

Unlike other retailers, which typically have a variety of levels of store employees, everyone working a Dollar General store "does windows." There's no sense of hierarchy; rather, everyone pitches in to do what needs to be done—whether it's ringing the register, unloading the truck, or cleaning the storeroom. This enables the company to operate a busy store with an average of just seven to nine people and, in the process, keep its labor overhead low.

8. **Innovative real-estate operations.** Most, if not all, $4 billion retailers have a large real-estate department with scores of highly paid professionals who use elaborate formulas to determine site selection. Not Dollar General. While the company has approximately twenty full-time real-estate professionals who consummate building-purchase and lease transactions, the bulk of the work in choosing store locations rests in the hands of Dollar General's 250 district managers (DMs). "If I'm a DM, and I grew up in the town, then I know the people, the population, the best streets in town," Weissert explained. "Since I'm on site, I'll know when a certain store might be going out of business and when its location would be available. And all of our DMs know the criteria we look for in locations— like being near a supermarket and being on the key roads in the city or town. The DMs are our field people in real estate, and they send us only the best leads to check out. So when our real-estate people go out to follow up, they're not wasting their time looking at dozens of places that wouldn't be appropriate for us."

Because the company is not looking for a huge footprint, it can be flexible in the types of spaces it takes on. While 7,000 square feet is ideal, Dollar General can be effective in a location between 5,000 and 8,000 square feet, because its planograms can accommodate numerous sizes and configurations. In one instance in West Virginia, the company converted an old school gymnasium into a store. "We didn't change the floor. We just put in some ceiling tiles and some fixtures, then brought in our merchandise," Weissert said. And, he noted, in the markets Dollar General is interested in, turnover in sites of the appropriate size is continual, providing a substantial supply of potential locations.

When a site is decided upon, the deal is closed quickly. Dollar

General usually signs leases for three to five years to keep the terms simple and to avoid locking the company into a long-term obligation on a site that may not pan out.

9. **Judicious use of technology.** For many retailers, the Internet represents a huge opportunity to reach new markets and enhance the way they interact with their customers. In the halls of Dollar General's corporate headquarters, however, e-business—at least the business-to-consumer variety—garners little excitement. "Our customers buy at the moment of need," noted Bruce Ash, vice president of information services. "They can't wait two or three days for toilet paper or cereal to be delivered to them." Instead, the company focuses on what some may characterize as mundane technologies but what Ash considers keys to Dollar General's ability to accomplish its mission. "We have to keep our investments in IS really in line with the business model, to make sure it's relevant and appropriate to our business concept," he explained. "We don't have huge margins, so we're very conscious of costs. We only invest in what we really need to run the business."

For example, the company uses a basic technology infrastructure that features a main data-processing facility at headquarters connected to the company's six distribution centers (DCs) via a wide area network (WAN). The WAN enables headquarters to have online access to all the operations in the DCs to keep tabs on the heart of the business. To keep the business running smoothly, Dollar General uses a few basic systems: warehouse management, transportation scheduling, merchandising, and financial. "The combination of these systems really ensures that the whole cycle of goods moving from the vendors, through the DCs, and to the stores works," Ash said.

The warehouse-management application plays a particularly critical role in Dollar General's operations, as it ensures that the company maintains maximum velocity of its products. Using the data captured by the warehouse system, the company's merchants can understand such things as what products are available, where they're located, and what's being damaged in shipment. And the company's checkout scanners feed critical product-movement data into the merchandising systems, giving decision-makers detailed information on what products are selling, how often, and in which stores.

Interestingly, there are a few applications missing from Dollar General's technology portfolio that most retailers today couldn't live without—namely, those used for customer data collection and forecasting. Because Dollar General does not run specials or sales, and because most of the company's customers are "regulars" who live within two or three miles of the store, there's no reason to collect in-depth shopper information. "We're not like a department store, which wants to use your purchase data to give you preferred notification of sales or special offers," Ash said. "It's only important for us to know that an item was sold; we really don't need to know who bought it. I can't think of anything that we would do differently if we had that kind of information. We certainly wouldn't give them offers to buy goods at a lower price. We're doing that already."

Similarly, because the company stocks only fast-turning basics, there's no need for a sophisticated forecasting system to help predict trends and buying patterns. There's little variability in sales profiles from store to store, and there's not much volatility in the company's product mix. "We're not in a highly seasonal, fashion-oriented business," Ash noted. "If we make a mistake and buy too much soap, yeah, it's wrong, and it's an inventory bulge. But we won't have to mark it down, because eventually it will sell. While a mistake like that on sweaters in a department store might be trouble, in our model it's not the end of the world."

In addition to being frugal in its technology investments, Dollar General employs a lean staff of technology professionals. There are only seventy-five full-time professionals at the company—forty-five of whom are focused on applications (programmers, systems analysts, and project managers) and thirty of whom are responsible for

IS operations, keeping the computers running, monitoring the net-works, etc.

10. **Highly efficient distribution.** Without a doubt, a major contrib-utor to Dollar General's ability to offer consistently low and honest pricing is its efficient distribution operation. The company operates six highly automated DCs—ranging in size from 850,000 square feet to 1 million square feet. Each DC serves approximately 700 stores, shipping more than 1 million cartons a week. Emulating Wal-Mart's early hub-and-spoke strategy, Dollar General concen-trates on opening stores close to existing DCs to minimize trans-portation costs. For instance, in 1995 the average distance between a store and a DC was 600 miles. It's now about 300 miles, and is expected to drop to 250 miles in a few years.[3]

To increase DC efficiency, Dollar General recently embarked on an ambitious measurement program designed to help the manage-ment team identify areas in which the company can improve its per-formance—and, along the way, take more costs out of the system. Jeff Sims, vice president of logistics, said the company now is "basi-cally measuring everything that moves. We're getting into quantified measurements in a big way, looking at things like carrier stock out, vendor stock out, DC stock out, imports per day, bills processed per hour. Some of our measurements are ugly. But that's the only way we're going to be able to understand where we need to improve."

The company's logistics strategy has helped fuel its growth to this point. But, according to Sims, Dollar General has only scratched the surface of what it can do in the future. "These DCs, as constructed, can serve well beyond 1,000 stores each," he explained. "Today, they do about 700. We've got top-notch material-handling and IT sys-tems that can handle much more throughput and that we really have to leverage. It's like having a high-performance engine in a sports car with a single-barrel carburetor. It's not the size of the engine that determines how fast you go. It's the controls. It's the precision with which you flow the fuel through the engine that wins the race."

Easy Access Brings the Traffic

DOLLAR GENERAL'S FORMULA FOR SUCCESS

SECONDARY ATTRIBUTE: ACCESS

- Store size makes it easy for customers to get in, around, and out quickly.
- Displays nothing above eye level, so customers can see the entire store.
- Uses high-speed laser scanners and avoids overmerchandising the checkout counter to speed customer processing.
- Has item prices preprinted or labeled by the manufacturer directly on each product to eliminate consumer searching for prices.
- Features the same layout, flow, and product mix in each of its 5,000 stores.
- Holds its SKUs to 4,500 to avoid crowding the stores and confusing customers as they shop.
- Locates stores on major roads in the heart of small towns or on major public-transit lines in urban neighborhoods.

To ensure that its value proposition is impossible to beat, Dollar General pairs price with a secondary focus on ease of access. As Bob Carpenter puts it, the size and layout of the company's stores give Dollar General an additional leg up on the competition and help strongly differentiate the company's stores from those of the larger discount chains. "We don't mind Wal-Mart—in fact, we try to locate near them as much as possible," he explained. "Our customers don't have the time, or physically don't have the energy, to wade through a 200,000-square-foot store. They want to come in, find what they're looking for quickly, and get out and on their way. That's not possible at Wal-Mart, and our customers know it. In reality, we're a convenience store without the higher prices."

Dollar General has identified seven factors that help keep its stores accessible to busy families and older customers alike:

1. **Small footprint.** At about 7,000 square feet, the typical Dollar General store is smaller than competitors' outlets.

2. **Eye-level focus.** In every Dollar General store, nothing—fixtures, signs, merchandise—is above eye level. This, according to Carpenter, is a crucial element of the company's store layout. The uncluttered "airspace" enables customers to stand at the store entrance and have an unobstructed view of every area of the store—thus making it easy for them to see where everything is without wandering around the building.

3. **Streamlined checkout.** To keep the checkout lines moving, Dollar General has installed new flatbed laser scanners that allow cashiers to ring up items more quickly than with the previous handheld models. In addition, the company recently removed impulse-buy items such as gum, candy, and tabloids from the front-end area. "Our buyers are giving us a hard time about that, but we think that we're right in the long run because our customers will appreciate our help in getting them out more quickly," said Carpenter.

4. **Clearly marked prices.** One of the basic tenets for competing on access is clarity and visibility of item prices. At Dollar General, the price of every product is clearly marked right on the item. In some cases, the manufacturer preprints the price on the label; in others, it's printed on a sticker that the manufacturer affixes to the label before shipping. With this program, there's no need for large price signs either on the shelves or hanging from the ceiling.

5. **Clean and well-arranged stores.** Dollar General also excels in making it as easy as possible for shoppers to navigate its stores. All the stores are clean and well-maintained, with no dirty floors or boxes

or crates strewn in the aisles. Furthermore, every store features the same layout and traffic flow: food on the left, household products and apparel in the back, and health and beauty products on the right. And, as a further nod to consistency, approximately 95 percent of the products are carried in every store (in the same location in each store), with the remaining 5 percent comprising geographically specific add-ins (such as suntan lotion and floats in a beach town or more health-care items geared toward older consumers in a store near a retirement community).

6. **Limited choices.** The company keeps a tight rein on its SKUs, limiting itself to just 4,500 (compared with about 35,000 SKUs offered by Wal-Mart). For one thing, the size of the average Dollar General store simply can't accommodate a large number of items. Second, adding more SKUs would crowd the look of the stores, making them feel less inviting and accessible. In addition, most of the company's customers really don't want—or have the time—to wade through fifteen different types of a single item (like toothpaste). Carpenter said the company knows what 75 percent of Americans buy, and sticks to those items for its stores.

7. **Convenient location.** Although access today is more about internal navigation, a nice store means nothing if consumers can't get to it. That's why Dollar General tries to locate its units in the heart of small towns or on major public-transit lines in larger cities.

Driving It All: Simplicity and Values

Dollar General's success seems amazingly simple. And, in fact, it is. *Simplicity* is one of the two critical success factors that the company's management point to over and over. In the stores, for instance, a store employee with a simple, handheld scanner does replenishment ordering: Scan the items that you need, indicate how many of each you want, and it's done. The consistent layout of the stores makes it easy for store employees to stock the shelves when inventory comes off the truck. And the cash-only policy makes running the register a breeze: Scan the items and take the money. "Our stores are so simple and easy to learn," said Earl Weissert. "So compared to other retailers, who have a bunch of policies and procedures that tell everyone how to work the store, we have almost nothing. Just some basic notes about attendance, vacations, and holidays."

According to Weissert, the simplicity of the company's operations also makes it easier to find employees to do the job, and employees are happier because they are empowered to make decisions for themselves. "Keep the work simple, the tasks easy, have a plan, and people will perform based on the guidelines we've given them," he said. Plus, the company doesn't have to spend a lot of time and money on training. Weissert noted that a person can learn how to run a Dollar General store in up to four weeks. "It is easy to teach anyone how to count the money, order the merchandise, unload merchandise from the truck, and put it out following the planogram," he said.

The other bedrock of the company's operation is its strong emphasis on values put into action. Each employee carries a card imprinted with the company's guiding mission and principles. Among the values:

- Building a company with people who are committed to moral integrity
- Leadership that encourages team spirit and empowered employees
- The dignity of work and others
- Emphasizing strengths in a positive environment
- Mutual gain

Company executives believe that these values distinguish Dollar General from any other company and provide a competitive advantage. "Our operations at Dollar General are nothing special," Weissert noted. "The only things unique to Dollar General are our culture and the values of our people. Our CEO tells our competition all the time what we do, and he knows that they can't duplicate our success because it's based on having the right values. Everyone just smiles and says, 'Right.' But it's true."

Added Jeff Sims: "I've heard a lot of lip service about culture and values in my career, but I hadn't actually seen it. Here, the positive attitude and culture literally ooze around the hallways in the company."

These values drive Dollar General's hiring policies. The belief is that if you hire someone with the right values, the rest will take care of itself. "When hiring, we certainly look at a person's morals and values," said Weissert. "That's critical, because we can teach people the technical stuff, but we can't teach values. If we see someone who has pride in their work, wants to treat coworkers and customers fairly, and understands that we are truly going to treat them fairly, they'll be a great fit."

From a management perspective, the emphasis on values has a major impact on problem resolution. According to Weissert, if there's a problem at hand, the typical reaction in most companies is to affix blame. At Dollar General, however, the underlying belief is that no one intentionally comes to work trying to figure out how she can mess things up. So, instead of pointing out what somebody did wrong, Dollar General management strives to always help the person understand what she needs to know to do it right.

"At Dollar General, it's okay to make a mistake," said Weissert. "We applaud people making mistakes, because you learn from your mistakes. But it's not okay to break one of the values. The only thing that will get you in trouble at Dollar General is breaking one of the values."

Challenges for the Future

The company's management believes the future is bright for Dollar General, as its target customer base is growing exponentially. But, they note, there remain a few issues that must be addressed. First and foremost, the company must maintain the culture and values that make it unique. Remarkably, Dollar General has been able to keep its sense of values as it has grown from a few hundred stores to more than 5,000. But, as we have learned in our research, culture is difficult to scale. Will Dollar General look and feel the same when it reaches 7,000, 9,000, or 10,000 stores? Time will tell.

Second, to maintain its leadership position in the industry, the company must remain nimble and able to respond to the advances of new competitors. No one at Dollar General is naive enough to believe that the company can't be beat. Weissert, in particular, sees the potential for someone to come along attempting to become the "new" Dollar General.

"We all know that competition changes," he said. "We don't expect it to be this easy forever. As people see the success we've had, some will try to figure out what we've done and try to duplicate it. As the old saying goes, 'Imitation is the sincerest form of flattery.'"

SELF-DIAGNOSTIC: PRICE

- If you choose to dominate on price, does your customer communication on pricing stress fairness and honesty?
- If you're not competing on price, are you meeting the prices of the competition, or are you just blindly matching the lowest prices in your category or market?
- Consistency matters, no matter what price strategy you adopt. Would a customer conducting business with you today recognize your pricing policies from six months ago or six months in the future?
- Ask your friends if your company's pricing claims appear to them to be clear, simple, and intuitively correct, given your products and/or services.
- If you aren't chasing the bottom of your market but rather trying to match competition, how often—and objectively—do you review your competitors' pricing positions?

CHAPTER 4

I Can't Get No Satisfaction

Service with a Smile?

IT WAS THE KIND of July afternoon anyone who knows Detroit knows too well—too hot, too humid. The westbound traffic on I-94, which on a good weekday afternoon flows through the city like blood circulating through the veins of an eighty-year-old cholesterol junkie, had come to a stop, thanks to an impromptu exercise in spontaneous highway closing by the Michigan State Police. Then the rain came, making visibility difficult and traffic impossible. Hundreds of people fought their fellow travelers for a car-length advantage in the crawl to the airport.

A lot of people were late to Metro Airport that day, and maybe the man in seat 1C was one of them, maybe not. At any rate, the inbound equipment was delayed, so that if you were late, you could still make the flight to Atlanta—assuming, of course, that it ever took off. Eventually the plane began to load, but even as the clouds lifted off the fields, new storm clouds began forming in the cabin. The rain hadn't helped either the temperature or the humidity. By now, the passengers, who half an hour ago would have missed the flight if it hadn't been delayed, were cursing the airline for the delay in takeoff.

Mr. 1C made a fatal mistake for first-class passengers out of Detroit: He showed up five minutes into the boarding, which meant he sacrificed any hope that both he and his bags would be flying in first. "But I have a first-class ticket," he said, wandering from overstuffed overhead to overstuffed overhead. "Sorry, sir," the attendant said, "but since you're in a bulkhead row, you'll just have to stow your bags in the back of the plane." "But that means I'll have to wait for the whole plane to empty out before I can get my bag," Mr. 1C said. "I'll be happy to check it for you, sir," the attendant said. Mr. 1C then uttered a spew of unintelligible words in what may or may not have been some Eastern European dialect. The tone was generally pleasant enough, but the meaning seemed clear. "Look," the attendant said, "I don't know what you said, but you can't say that to me."

Mumbling, Mr. 1C wandered back to the exile of coach to find a place for his blue cloth backpack. Returning to his seat, he fell into his chair with a motion clearly intended to convey his world-weariness and radical ennui. Almost immediately, he leapt out of the seat, screaming a word clearly understandable, albeit inappropriate in a business book. "I've ripped my pants," he bellowed, and indeed he had. Thanks to an errant seat spring, a fierce, ugly rip had separated the attractive green microfibers from roughly mid-pocket to mid-calf, settling (for any or all interested) the boxers-or-briefs question once and for all. "I demand to see a customer-service agent at once," Mr. 1C said, his voice suddenly as ragged as his trousers.

His fellow passengers issued a collective sigh. If 1C got his wish, the flight, already an hour late, might be postponed indefinitely, if its departure depended on the airline's historically demonstrated pattern of customer service. But less than ten minutes later, a vision of command-and-control strolled into the first-class cabin with the élan of Mike Tyson leaving his corner to answer the first-round bell. Customer Service was an imposing woman, well over 6 feet tall and well north of 225 pounds. She towered over 1C, glaring down at him. "Yes, sir, I heard you've got a problem," she barked. 1C's own bark had become a tremulous whisper. "I ripped my pants," he said, like a naughty schoolboy confessing to an evil stepmother. "Where did you rip them?" Customer Service demanded. "You want to see?" 1C asked submissively. "Of course I don't want to see,"

Customer Service countered. "I don't care where they are ripped, just where you ripped them." "I tore them sitting down," the contrite 1C answered. "That would be on the plane?" Customer Service said. "Yes," 1C confessed. "Well then, I can't help you—you'll have to file a complaint in Atlanta." "But my pants are torn," 1C moaned. "But I just told you I can't help you. Customer service in Detroit doesn't have anything to do with anything that happens once you get on a plane," she said. "But my pants are torn," 1C repeated. "Sir, did you understand me?" Customer Service asked. "This plane is going to Atlanta. You ripped your pants on the plane; therefore, you have to file a claim in Atlanta."

1C stared at the floor. "But I don't understand," he stammered. "I'm sure you can see I just want someone to help me." Customer Service swelled to her full height and stared right through 1C, speaking in clipped, measured, deliberate tones. "Look, I think I've explained this to you, sir," she said. "I'm a customer-service agent. What exactly do you expect me to do for you?"

As our unfortunate fellow passenger discovered, service is all about people. In fact, it is the element of human-to-human interaction that most clearly defines the service attribute. Unlike product or price, service is a living, breathing dynamic, characterized largely by emotion. Service is experienced in a very personal way, and, therefore, the mechanisms that companies use to motivate their employees are a critical part of how their customers experience service.

But with the right motivation, employees can make a huge difference. Consider the case of Continental Airlines, which underwent an astounding turnaround in the 1990s. In the late 1980s, when the U.S. Department of Transportation began keeping score of the airlines' performance, Continental ranked at the bottom of the list on matters such as on-time departures and arrivals, lost luggage, passenger comfort, cancellations, and overall customer service. When Gordon Bethune took over as president and COO of Continental in 1994, he inherited a company deep in the doldrums. Employee morale was at a low point, flights were assigned to unprofitable routes, and customers were complaining louder every day. As CEO (also since 1994), Bethune has reenergized the company by rewriting the rules of its culture, improving employee relationships, and satisfying both customers and stockholders.

In its study of airline passengers' satisfaction, J. D. Power and Associates and *Frequent Flyer* magazine have ranked Continental first in customer service for three of the last four years.[1] Moreover, Continental was selected by *Fortune* in 1999 as one of the 100 best employers in America to work for. And the company's frequent-flier program, OnePass, is routinely held up as the model of what a loyalty program should be.

In describing the new corporate culture, Bethune likes to use a football analogy: "It's not really all that complex. Eleven guys get a ball across that goal line. That's pretty much the whole strategy. How come so many people don't score? Because they don't have a clue how to get those eleven guys to want to do it better than those other guys. How do you get 48,000 people in one company to want to be a good airline? Knowing what a good airline is, is not the same as knowing how to get people to do it."[2]

The key, according to Bethune, is to get everybody to agree on what "success" means. Otherwise, the enterprise suffers from dysfunctional pushing and pulling toward myriad goals, which ultimately results in customer dissatisfaction. In addition to surprise meetings with employees at every level, from baggage handlers to ticket agents and airline pilots, Bethune believes in the power of teamwork and rewards. Since 1995, the company has offered employees $65 a month in bonuses every time they meet their on-time goals, and $100 in bonuses each time Continental scores a first-place finish ahead of the other airlines. Expenditures for the rewards program total approximately $3 million to date.[3]

Ideas on better customer service are welcome everywhere in the company, Bethune says. As the top U.S. carrier in Mexico and the second-largest U.S. carrier in Latin America, for instance, Continental has assigned Spanish-speaking employees to those flights and has instituted regional food rather than the universal bag of peanuts. According to Bethune, Continental is "a company of multi functions that has value when we all work cooperatively—pilots, flight attendants, gate agents, airport agents, mechanics, reservation agents. And not to understand that about doing business means you're going to fail. Lots of people failed because they don't get it."[4]

As Bethune sees it, great service means giving the customers what they want: "Customers don't measure winning or losing by our income statement or earnings per share," he says. "They measure us by how we get them to where they want to go with their underwear on time."[5]

As evidenced by Continental's success, employees—and accompanying issues like selection, hiring, rewards, measures, and training—represent a vital investment for any business that hopes to dominate on the attribute of service. Yet even with that investment, service can be the most difficult attribute to execute against consistently, for the very reason that a company must rely on people to perform that service—and the bottom line is that no business can truly control its people, certainly not the way it can control product or price, for instance. Human beings, after all, have good days and bad days; they have varying moods and are subject to the fact that the world around them is a highly variable, emotional, and, at times, difficult place. So while a company can train its employees to say "Hello," "Thank you," and "Have a nice day," it can't control *how* they say it or how a customer perceives the employee.

There's no question that today's tight skilled-labor market, with some of the lowest unemployment levels ever seen, presents obvious challenges to executives leading service-oriented companies. But even so, superior service can be achieved with hard work, great leadership, and a company culture that is dedicated, above all else, to serving customers—as the case studies later in this chapter demonstrate.

The critical role played by employees in the service equation was pointed to over and over again by executives we spoke with in the course of our research. Cathy Baum, executive vice president of Stanley Martin, a Washington, D.C., home-builder, emphasized the importance of the human element in the hypercompetitive residential home-building industry. "Why do people buy a home from one company rather than another? It all comes down to the salesperson," she told us. "It's about having the right information at the right time; knowing what to say when a question is asked; understanding human nature; and having a certain sixth sense about how to handle a customer when they walk in the door. It's a quality that goes beyond the price or the location of the property."

It's also a quality that carries over to many types of businesses in many countries. "Our customers really have an attachment to our butchers and fishmongers," said Cormac Tobin, a business manager at Superquinn, an Irish grocery retailer. "They love coming to the counter because the butcher can say, 'Oh, you're having the boss over for dinner? Well, here's the cut you need, here's how to slice and prepare it, here are some good spices for it.' A lot of the next generation coming up really like to cook, but it hasn't been taught how to do it. So we're helping to educate them and give them the confidence to try new things."

It became clear that there was another key difference between service and the other attributes. In most instances, a company builds the attributes and the consumer responds. A company can set price, a company can select products, and a company can establish access (we'll get to experience later). Service, however, is a highly subjective attribute, varying not just from person to person but often from day to day or even hour to hour.

One thing that's clear: While an absolute definition of the service attribute may be subjective, consumers are objectively growing increasingly dissatisfied. The 2000 American Customer Satisfaction Index conducted by the National Quality Research Center at the University of Michigan Business School found that customer-satisfaction rates for industries such as airlines, retailing, restaurants/fast food, gas stations, and banks have fallen to some of the lowest levels since the survey began in 1994. Service tales of woe are hardly restricted to the physical realm. By some accounts, as many as one-quarter of online shoppers during the 1999 Christmas shopping season said they would never shop on some websites again because of the poor customer service they encountered.

Clearly, service is not what it used to be—in conception or in practice. Moreover, consumers have come to redefine what service means or should mean, creating a disconnect: Consumers and companies often do not see eye to eye on this attribute. Many businesses, for example, believe that packing their offerings with what they consider to be "value-added services" will attract customers. This explains why dry cleaning and banking are available in grocery stores, and why coffee bars can be found in bookstores. The problem is that for most consumers, these services really take a back seat to some very basic competencies that many businesses have failed to master. Consumers made it clear that they are looking for fewer gimmicks and more delivery when it comes to service. If the service provided at the moment of interaction is deficient, all the value-added services in the world aren't going to help a business hang on to that customer. This suggests that businesses seeking to dominate on service would do better taking the money they have been putting into all those extra services and putting it into employee screening, training, measuring, and rewarding in an effort to provide better point-of-interaction value to the customer.

Service shortcomings haven't always been par for the course. Many can remember the "good old days" when service *was* important, when consumers' expectations for individualized attention was not considered out of the ordinary. In the late nineteenth and early twentieth centuries, "full service" dominated the business landscape. At the dry-goods store, a clerk cut the cloth to customers' specifications. The owner of the general store climbed a ladder and measured out however much flour or dried peas people asked for. The storeowner knew his customers and the needs of their families. These merchants had a degree of "perfect knowledge" of their customers, and could predict their buying habits and needs with relative ease.

But the notion of what constitutes service has changed over time. Take gas stations, which, you may remember, used to be called *service* stations, complete with human beings who would check your oil, wash your windshield, and pump your gas. Today self-service has become the service norm in the gas-station business.

In fact, lower levels of service have become the standard in numerous industries. In the airline business, for example, the hub concept has served to reduce competition and, in the process, has resulted in a lower service standard. If you live in Memphis or Minneapolis, you're a Northwest customer; if you live in Cleveland, you're a Continental customer; if you're in Atlanta, you're a Delta customer. It's possible to fly other airlines, but it's not nearly as convenient, so frequent fliers to or from hub cities tend to fly hub airlines whether service levels are excellent or poor.

The paradox is that at the same time that service levels have been dropping, consumers' expectations have been rising, due to their increased awareness resulting from access to media, technology, information, and knowledge of lifestyles and products. Consider, for example, the amount of information that some consumers bring to the home-buying decision. "Five years ago, no information about home building was on the Internet that people could easily access or understand," Baum told us. "Today there are dozens of sites that list homes. People research product information and appliances. We tell them we're using XYZ insulation, and they research whether there are any medical hazards related to the insulation. Or they go into a house and see some sap coming out of a piece of wood, and they'll go and research the structural integrity of wood and what the sap means."

Understanding consumers' expectations as they relate to a particular business is the key to creating a service formula that matches that level of expectations. Take the restaurant business. Let's say you have four kinds of restaurants: a buffet, fast food, a neighborhood place, and an upscale white-tablecloth establishment. What's the correct service formula for the buffet? None, with the exception of back-end service such as making sure the food is hot and in plentiful supply at the buffet line. In that case, a consumer wouldn't—and shouldn't—have high expectations for personalized service. With a fast-food restaurant, there should be a bit more service expected and delivered. Someone takes the order, assembles it, and hands it over to the consumer. In a neighborhood restaurant, the service expectations would be a little higher. Perhaps the owner comes by and says hello. Finally, in the case of a white-tablecloth restaurant where a consumer is spending $100 or more, a considerably higher level of service is expected.

As long as an establishment delivers what the consumer expects and lets customers know up front what level of service will be delivered, and assuming, of course, the company delivers against those expectations consistently, each service formula is successful for its particular business. But if a consumer spends $100 in an upscale restaurant and is treated as if he were in a McDonald's, then the company's got a problem. It all comes down to managing expectations and delivering against the ones you manage.

If it's true—and we believe it is—that lower service has become the accepted norm, what's the incentive for businesses to change? In the most practical sense, competition—or the threat of competition—can be a key driver of change. For instance, if enough consumers begin to use online grocery companies because of the convenience and service they provide, supermarket operators may be forced to rethink their service equations.

But there's an even greater incentive for businesses to take stock of their service offering. Based on our research, it's clear that service may actually offer businesses the greatest potential return on investment of any of the five attributes, simply because most companies are doing so poorly at providing good service. In fact, service may represent the richest untapped area for differentiation in the entire consumer goods and services industry. If you're a price or product operator, another company can come along and copy your price or product offering. But it's much more difficult to copy a service offering, as so much depends on employees and company culture. For that reason, service may actually provide a better measure of competitive insulation than the other attributes. So while clearly there are costs involved in terms of employee hiring and training, the potential benefit is significant.

What Consumers *Really* Want

Historically, companies have thought of service as something they offered to consumers. However, we posit a very different view of how consumers view service: as something a business *is* or something it *embodies.* Viewed through this lens, an element as seemingly simple as a hassle-free return policy takes on new meaning. For today's consumer, the return policy is an acid test of authenticity. It offers evidence that a business walks its talk. Consumers also made it clear to us that it's not enough to have the policy; it's the action that surrounds the policy that really counts. After all, everybody makes the same claim when it comes to their return policy, assuring consumers that returning an item won't be a problem. But when customers actually try to return something, they often find themselves crawling a mile on their hands and knees over broken glass with little hope of satisfaction.

For most consumers, the ability to return merchandise unconditionally, without hassles from rude or incompetent service representatives, seemed to be a baseline for acceptable service. This speaks to the importance of providing a warranty for your products and, by extension, your business. It also provides additional evidence that consumers today tend to be distrustful, wary, and cynical. If customers don't believe that a business stands behind its products, they will view that as an egregious, irrevocable service failure that will cause them to flee from the company.

Roberta, a forty-five-year-old accountant from Cleveland, told us about a shopping experience that left her seeing red: "I purchased an outfit that I thought was in good shape, but when I got home, I discovered it had a rip in it," she recalled. "Although I had just made the purchase thirty minutes earlier, I had to fight with the clerks to see if they could either take something off the price or let me exchange the damaged item. Even the supervisor wasn't really cooperative, and from that point I didn't want to go back to that store to shop. Eventually, I had to take it to the tailor and have it sewn up."

The survey responses left us with a question: If all consumers are really looking for is to return merchandise easily and not have their goods damaged, why do so many seem so unhappy? What we learned in our one-to-one conversations is that service really isn't quite as simple as those survey responses might indicate. In fact, it became clear to us that service is, in fact, a complex attribute.

Consumers differentiated among various kinds of service that a company can offer. They spoke about *pre-sale service,* signaled by a pleasant and sincere "May I help you?" and characterized by a knowledgeable salesperson capable of answering customers' questions. Then there's *transaction-level service,* which occurs at the time of sale and includes packing or gift wrapping as well as intelligent, helpful suggestions about compatible items on sale, special discounts, or company-sponsored perks. And, finally, consumers pointed to *post-sale service,* which usually takes the form of sincere and knowledgeable people who are committed to helping customers resolve various problems they may have with their purchases (e.g., defective or unwanted merchandise, product repairs, and product-usage assistance). Businesses seeking to dominate on the service attribute must master all three types of service.

Consider, for example, how important post-sale service can be for a service-oriented home-builder such as Stanley Martin. Cathy Baum related a story about a fire that burned a just-completed house nearly to the ground. "The house had been finished and, with the land, was worth about $1.3 million," she said. "The homeowners were due to move in to the house in about two weeks. When the fire occurred, we were on the site within twenty minutes. Did we have to be there? Maybe not. The people—not us—owned the house and the lot. But we're their builder. We believe it's our responsibility to take care of them. We talked with the fire marshal; we called the lender and the insurance company. My salespeople helped them find a place to stay, stopped the moving company, stopped the telephone service. We handled all those details. It was simply the right thing to do. Most companies might start to panic more about the cause of the fire and their legal liability rather than taking care of the human beings involved. For us, the service cycle starts from the time the consumer first calls us and then continues for years."

There's also an element of customer reward that enters into the service equation—something that industries like the airlines and supermarkets have failed to understand. In both cases, the "worst" customers are often the ones being rewarded while the "best" customers are punished. Consider the high cost of a ticket for the business traveler who has logged hundreds of thousands of miles on a particular airline but who needs to get from New York to Chicago tomorrow. Meanwhile, the vacation travelers who booked their flight two months in advance but fly from New York to Chicago just once a year got their ticket for what amounts to the tax on the business traveler's fare.

Now translate this to the grocery business. The cherry-picker who grabs a few of the below-cost loss leaders gets to zip through the express lane, while the loyal shopper who spends $200 every week in the store waits in line for half an hour to check out.

Signs of the instavidual we described in Chapter 1 cropped up frequently as we examined the dimensions of service. It became clear that the same consumer may receive an identical delivery of service in different ways. For instance, a person who's in a hurry one day may be perfectly happy to pick up a cup of coffee and hand over his money without worrying about whether the person on the other side of the counter said thank you. On that day, the consumer's perception may be that the service was fine. However, the following day that same consumer may not be so rushed, and the identical service may seem less than adequate because of the lack of human interaction. Same consumer, same employee, same product, same price, same delivery of service—but under a very different perception on the part of the consumer.

There is a close relationship between service and experience, in part because both are somewhat less tangible than the other three attributes. Access, price, and product are more about *what* you offer, while experience and service are about *how* you offer it. In fact, it's possible for the attributes of service and experience to be so closely intertwined that each becomes a part of the other. We experienced that intertwining one brutal February day when we were scheduled to fly from Detroit to Chicago on Southwest Airlines. Winter storms were raging at both ends, and the flying windows were minimal, but small windows out of Detroit and into Chicago were opening and closing seemingly without warning. The gate agent told us a takeoff might be possible, but only if the first person to board took the last seat on the plane. In other words, we were asked to forget our pre-assigned boarding order (there's no assigned seating on Southwest flights) and board as quickly as possible from back to front. As you might imagine, there was plenty of grumbling. The agent apologized and said that as a small token of appreciation they'd have some refreshments for everyone. No sooner had she said that when carts were rolled in filled with doughnuts, bagels, coffee, and tea. People were starting to feel better.

But Southwest wasn't done yet. The agent offered to give anyone a $50 travel voucher if they sang some karaoke over the gate microphone while we waited. People started to line up quickly, singing five or six bars, on average, before falling apart laughing. And, as promised, a flight window mysteriously opened. "Now," the gate agent urged us. Before you knew it, everyone had obediently boarded as instructed—back to front—without pushing, shoving, or complaining. The plane was soon on its way to Chicago.

Southwest could have simply offered the minimal level of service: "We'll get you to Chicago." But instead, the company said: "We'll get you to

Chicago, and we'll make sure that you're happy when you get there." It took the level of service up a notch, treated the customers as human beings, and made the whole thing part of the overall experience of flying with Southwest.

How does the service attribute play out in the online world? Our survey responses indicated that there are some differences but also some similarities between service in the physical space and in the consumer-direct space. Online shoppers identified credit-card security as their chief service issue, followed by quick and hassle-free merchandise returns and an unconditional-return policy. While security concerns remain paramount in the minds of consumers, many retailers don't seem to view this as a key issue. It's likely that consumers will become more comfortable using their credit cards online as time goes on, but at this point e-tailers should not underestimate the importance of these security concerns.

Applying the Conceptual Model to Service

Businesses that want to compete on service as their primary attribute, or even those that wish to simply bring their service component up to industry standards, must listen carefully to the voice of the consumer (see Figure 4.1).

FIGURE 4.1

Competing on Service

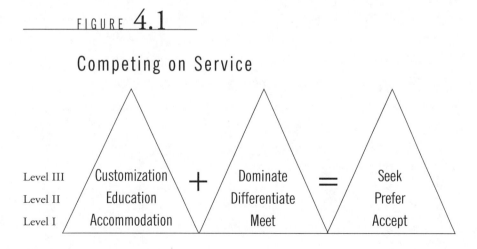

Level III	Customization	+	Dominate	=	Seek
Level II	Education		Differentiate		Prefer
Level I	Accommodation		Meet		Accept

The first level for service is *accommodation*—meeting consumers' fundamental expectations. For instance, customers expect that they should rarely have to wait in line or on the telephone for answers to their questions, and that they should be able to unconditionally return merchandise with which they are unhappy—for whatever reason—and that the returns should be quick and hassle-free. In the case of an e-commerce operator, consumers expect the website to use a natural-language service agent that is able to respond to nearly all questions, however obscure, without sending them along a dead-end path. In other words, *"If you accommodate me, then I'll accept you, and you will be a choice that I may make."* Catalog retailers such as L.L. Bean have set the standard in this regard. Stories abound of consumers who have returned items used for several months or years, hoping to get them repaired, only to have the company send them a new replacement, free of charge.

To be accommodated, consumers must feel as if they are respected and treated fairly by the company's personnel, and that the employees take seriously their discomfort or dissatisfaction with a purchase. Civility must be the hallmark of the business relationship. Companies that excel at accommodating consumers' wishes must focus on hiring and training salespeople and customer-service representatives who are committed to serving customers first and making sales quotas second. This has important ramifications for the reward-and-measurement program a company deploys. Service-centric companies avoid metrics that reward "churn and burn," opting instead for programs that focus on customer satisfaction. Remember, you get what you measure, so if you're providing your call-center workers a bonus based on the number of calls they handle per hour, don't be surprised if your company gets low service ratings from customers.

At Level II of service-oriented competition, consumers want *education:* They want information about the products and services. They expect their questions to be answered by knowledgeable staff members, people who are trained to speak intelligently about the products they sell and service. Employees must also speak in language the consumer can understand. At this level of competition, the consumer says to the company, in effect:

"Educate me and I will prefer you—all else being equal—to other companies that sell or provide similar products and services."

Consider the example of Geiger's Clothing and Sports, a small, family-run store in the Cleveland suburb of Lakewood, Ohio. The company faces numerous challenges in remaining relevant to consumers. The store is located downtown, not in a suburban mall, and it sells items that are commonly found in numerous retail formats, ranging from department stores, sporting-goods chains, and discounters to specialty stores and the Internet. It's clearly a product-focused company, specializing in sports and outdoor apparel for the active person. But it also has determined that a strong secondary focus on service can spell the difference between maintaining a solid customer base and losing sales to the Internet. To that end, the company hires salespeople who have specific areas of expertise so that they can help customers sort through the myriad styles and types of gear.

Bob, a Geiger's customer, told us a story about a visit to the store when he was looking for a high-performance parka. The young woman helping Bob turned out to be a ski instructor who knew a great deal about the performance attributes of the coats the company carries. She spent more than an hour educating Bob on the features and benefits of each coat, explaining which brand or style would be most appropriate for his needs. "It's hard to know which features are really important for what you want to do and which are just 'bells and whistles' that don't mean much in the way of performance," said Bob, who bought a $140 coat— and felt much more confident doing so as a result of the service he received.

At Level III, a business aiming for a 5 on the service attribute must offer the consumer individualized *customization* of the product or service. If that effort is successful, the consumer can say, *"If you continue to treat me as an individual, I will continue to seek you out as my company of choice for the products or services you carry."*

But what does customization really mean? Companies dominate on service by customizing or tailoring merchandise—for example, selling one item from a prepackaged set, placing special orders, cutting, trimming, or refashioning products to meet a customer's special needs. Customization and personalization take on particular significance in a business such as home building. "Consumers are looking for us to help them satisfy a vision," said Cathy Baum of Stanley Martin. "Everybody who is buying a house, whether it is their first or last home, has a vision of how they live and how they want to live, and they want the house they buy to satisfy that vision and to feel good to them."

Customization can be a tricky proposition, however. Consider the amount of seemingly customized and personalized direct mail you get from businesses like banks and airlines—mail that is addressed to you, but with your name misspelled. Such attempts at customized service reveal just how fragile a strategy this can be and demonstrate how easy it is for personalized service that's executed poorly to have a negative effect on a company's relationships with its customers.

One company that has experienced tremendous success because of its customization capabilities is St. Louis–based Build-A-Bear. This company, the brainchild of former May Department Stores executive Maxine Clark, is a classic example of a new spin on an old idea. It's debatable whether the world really needed another teddy-bear store. But each Build-A-Bear store offers customers the opportunity to create their very own personalized teddy bear—complete with a given name, birth certificate, and appropriate attire. Working with the store's staff, a customer chooses the desired "skin," has it stuffed to his or her specifications, and dresses it in the outfit of his or her choice. The finishing touch is a "Cub Condo" box in which to take the bear home.

Dell has set the standard for service in the high-tech area. Dell's website offers not only a selection of prepackaged computers that include the most popular features but also an option that allows consumers to choose from a menu of components and thus design the computer of their choice. At the end of the selection process, the Dell site presents a summary of the consumer's choices, totals the price, and allows the customer to keep the configuration on tap for later review and changes. An 800 number allows a consumer to contact the help desk at Dell to talk with a human being who can answer any questions. But the service doesn't end with the purchase. All Dell customers have access to live customer-service technicians around the clock, every day of the year, in the event they're faced with a problem that they can't solve on their own. What is the additional cost to the customer of such service? Not one penny.

Customization is something that many Internet companies mastered—so much so that what's par for personalization and customization online became significantly higher than in the physical world. The major Web portals or search engines such as Yahoo!, Excite, and Alta Vista offered visitors the ability to tailor the site's presentation and content to their own needs. Amazon.com pioneered and popularized the recommending of new books, music, and other items to customers upon their signing on, giving at least the appearance that "somebody knows me in there." And most online retailers allow customers to track the status of their orders on their own.

Technology such as the Internet will alter the service equation. As consumers become increasingly used to the level of customization that most online businesses offer, they are likely to make similar demands of physical-world operators. As that happens, will human-based service become less important? We think that depends on whether a business chooses to be at par, to differentiate, or to dominate on the service attribute. If a company is attempting to be a 3 (par) in service, it may make sense to use some technology-enabled solutions; but to be a 4 (differentiate) or a 5 (dominate), people will remain the key—as you'll see in the case studies that follow.

Case Study

How Superquinn Keeps Customers Coming Back

Superquinn isn't just an Irish supermarket chain. In the words of one blissed-out meat-department employee, it's a cult. Every employee, and most of the customers, are fervent cult members and Feargal Quinn, the company's founder and CEO, is Ireland's universally acknowledged and revered Pope of Customer Service. Quinn, the quintessential Irishman, with perpetually dancing eyes and more stories than an errant teenager, is a modern Irish institution. He served as the country's postmaster, turning the Irish Post Office into a profit-making entity, and currently serves in the Irish Senate.

Superquinn is a company conceived and executed in its founder's image. Everything inside Superquinn's stores exists to enhance the customer's service experience. Every detail—from the largest to the smallest—is almost obsessively customer-centric. Scissors are positioned near the broccoli display so shoppers can trim the hard stalks and pay only for what they will actually eat. A picture of each produce supplier hangs above the product they supply so consumers know who's really responsible for the food they're about to buy. All perishable products are fresh to a point that would drive most American supermarket managers mad. And Quinn is the head cheerleader of his own parade, regularly bagging groceries and moving from customer to employee and back in what seems like one long, dizzying, uninterrupted conversation focused on delivering ever-increasingly improved levels of service.

A visit to a Superquinn store is a life-altering experience, not in the metaphysical or theological sense but, rather, in how one views the way a retail operation—grocery or otherwise—should be run. The seventeen-store chain in and around Dublin competes first and foremost on the attribute of service, backed up by some of the freshest and highest-quality products around.

Feargal Quinn opened the first Superquinn in 1960 as a small grocery shop in Dundalk, a town north of Dublin. Quinn's father—also a grocer—instilled in him early in life that the key to building a good business was to satisfy your customers so completely that they always returned. Quinn took the advice to heart and has built Superquinn into one of the most successful and respected retail companies in the world. Today, Superquinn employs more than 4,000 people, commands a 20 percent share of the Dublin grocery market, and has racked up an impressive list of industry awards. But most important to Quinn is the fact that Superquinn's customers wouldn't dream of shopping anyplace else.

Service and More Service: The Boomerang Principle

SUPERQUINN'S FORMULA FOR SUCCESS

PRIMARY ATTRIBUTE: SERVICE

- Posts a greeter at the door to welcome people, help them get a cart, offer coffee, or fetch a wheelchair.
- Pays close attention to packaging of products to ensure that quality is not being sacrificed for low cost.
- Promotes visibility of store managers in the store instead of in their offices.
- Offers food sampling throughout the store.
- Provides umbrella and carryout service to customers' cars.
- Posts signs around the store explaining the nutritional content of fruits and vegetables to help customers make more informed choices.
- Positions a customer-service counter near the entrance of every store to help customers with questions or complaints.
- Will stock special items—even those carried only by a competitor—for customers, to eliminate the need for them to make special trips for one or two items.
- Employs aisle monitors in charge of specific areas of the store to whom customers can go with questions.
- Trains fishmongers and butchers in culinary skills so they can help recommend cuts and preparation ideas to customers.
- Operates a child-care center, staffed by trained professionals, where customers can leave their children to play while they shop.
- Uses its loyalty program not just to collect data but also to create new services.
- Has formed a joint venture with a respected bank to provide financial services in its stores.

Superquinn's success can be traced to "The Boomerang Principle," which Quinn describes in his book *Crowning the Customer: How to Become Customer Driven* as a simple philosophy of doing everything to keep customers coming back—which often means looking past a short-term expense to long-term customer loyalty. Indeed, Quinn and his management team offer numerous examples of programs or services that, from an immediate bottom-line standpoint, might not have made sense to adopt, but that have generated thousands of dollars of additional business in the long run. Store staffing is one example. Quinn staffs the stores with more than 300 employees even though they could run with 200. The additional employees focus on customer service. There's even a concierge, who can recommend restaurants and organize parties. These services may not contribute to the bottom-line profit, but they set the company apart from other supermarkets.

How does Superquinn do it? How does it embody the essence of Consumer Relevancy? In three ways:

1. **Do the simple things right.** As mentioned earlier in this chapter, many companies offer all kinds of value-added services yet forget about the simple things that customers really appreciate. A large measure of Superquinn's success can be traced to the fact that the company *never* forgets the little things. For example, all of its stores have a greeter posted at the store entrance whose job it is to not only make a good first impression but also to help customers get situated in the store so they can go about their business. The Superquinn greeter looks after shopping carts, offers a cup of coffee or soup to shoppers, helps a mother seat her children in the cart, or fetches a wheelchair for a disabled shopper. The greeter is also responsible for recognizing new customers and explaining what they will find as they make their way around the store.

   Packaging of products is a big deal at Superquinn as well. For example, the company introduced a special type of air- and water-tight insulated bag for fish and meats. The bags not only help seal in the freshness of the products (they maintain a chill for an hour longer than plastic bags), but they also prevent the products' smells from intruding on other items in the shopping cart. And they eliminate customers' need to repackage the products for refrigerator or freezer storage. "The bags are more expensive, certainly," noted Cormac Tobin, a business manager at Superquinn. "But it's a better service for our customers. They value it, and it's a real point of difference for us."

Another small, but noticeable, difference at Superquinn is the constant presence of the store managers and supervisors on the floor. Early on, Feargal Quinn made it a policy that all managers do their work on the shop floor. Managers can frequently be found doing their paperwork at empty registers, on a box of wine, on a shelf—all in the name of remaining accessible to customers and employees.

Also on the list of little things that count for a lot is an umbrella service for unprepared shoppers who get caught in a sudden downpour, package carryout to customers' cars, and a delivery service to consumers' homes. There's also a variety of in-store food sampling—from the fresh-made pancakes in the bakery section to the myriad domestic and imported cheeses.

Is that bag of potatoes too heavy to lift? No problem. Simply put the special laminated tag in your cart indicating which potatoes you want, and the bag will be brought to you as you pass through the checkout lane. Are you unsure of which fruits and vegetables are best for specific dietary requirements? Just look for the dozens of signs and brochures around the produce department that spell out vitamin content and other nutritional information for every item carried. Are you tired after an hour of shopping? Don't worry. There's a chair at the checkout lane (and a complimentary glass of champagne if you wish).

2. **Go the extra mile.** Superquinn also does a lot of big things right. One of these is the customer-service counter. While many retailers hide their "complaint department" on the top floor or way back in the store (right next to the restrooms), Superquinn places its service

counter right at the entrance of the store. In doing so, it subtly but powerfully communicates the idea that the company values service and that it takes customer input and complaints seriously. These counters are staffed by one or two employees who are responsible for dealing with a variety of questions, issues, and problems, and also for answering the store telephones. In most cases, the customer-service counter representatives can resolve any issue on the spot as they see fit (only in rare cases will they get the store manager involved). This helps defuse any problems quickly and gets the customers back on their way. The customer-service employees will often phone a customer in a few days to ensure that everything has been resolved to the customer's satisfaction.

Another example of going the extra mile is Superquinn's willingness to stock special items for specific customers—even if only a competitor carries that item. Niall Brougham, manager of the Balinteer store in Dublin's southern suburbs, says this service is just good business. "We recognize that we can't carry everything for everybody in the store—it's just not possible," he told us. "However, we do have a spot in the storeroom where we keep special items for customers who have requested them. For example, there's one woman who really prefers a certain brand of juice that's carried only by our competitor Tesco down the street. This customer would do all of her shopping with us, and drive to Tesco just for the juice. So what we do now is go down to Tesco ourselves and buy that juice, bring it back to our store, and keep it here for her. That not only saves her an extra trip, but it also keeps her out of a competitor's store."

Superquinn pays close attention to the types of people it hires and how those people are positioned in the stores. For example, every aisle in the store has an "aisle monitor," whose job is to make sure that the aisle is properly stocked, clean, and free of obstacles. Each aisle has a sign posted with the aisle monitor's name and photograph so that customers know whom to ask for help. In addition, trained cheese and wine specialists can guide customers through a sampling and purchase and tell shoppers anything they need to know about a specific vintage or cheese. And all Superquinn butchers and fishmongers are trained in culinary skills as well as the art of sausage-making or filleting, so they can help recommend cuts and preparation ideas to customers.

Sometimes, going the extra mile means, literally, *going the extra mile.* A case in point involved Jerry Twomey, a project manager with Superquinn who used to manage one of the company's stores. "One time, something got out of hand with a customer while I was away," he recalled. "When I returned, I was made aware of it, and I immediately jumped in my car and drove out to the customer's house to apologize for our error and see if there was anything we could do to make up for it. I ended up spending two hours there, talking about all sorts of things. I think we spent only fifteen minutes discussing the problem; the rest of the time we talked about the weather, their children. Sure, we resolved the problem, and they appreciated it. But we also made them feel that we really cared about them and, in the process, learned a lot about what was important to them."

3. **Exceed customers' expectations.** While there are many points of difference between Superquinn and its competitors, some programs are clearly light-years ahead of anything most other retailers are doing for their customers. One such program is the company's child-care service. Every Superquinn store is equipped with a playhouse area—staffed by trained child-care specialists—where customers can leave their children to play, free of charge, while they shop. The program, the brainchild of Superquinn Customer and Human Resource Adviser Margaret Jones, was started twenty-five years ago and has grown to be one of the principal draws for mothers. "We truly believe that our child-care centers remove the burden of grocery shopping for our customers with kids," Jones said. "The kids actually look forward to 'going shopping,' and the mothers can shop without hassles and without the worry about what their kids are doing."

Interestingly, Jones pointed out, there has been a tremendous unexpected benefit to the program. "Because we don't have pre-school in Ireland, Superquinn has become, in effect, schools that help children learn and land in the community," she said. "I can't tell you how many times we've gotten comments from schools in the area that say they can tell within six months that a Superquinn store has opened nearby because of the difference in the entry class to junior school. The children are completely socialized, they understand the rules, they know how to share and generally how to play together."

The child-care centers are not cheap. According to Jones, Superquinn invests $1 million a year in the program. But, she noted, the program more than pays for itself in the goodwill and loyalty it engenders. "Yes, they're expensive, and they don't take in any money on their own, but they're an example of what you do because it feels right," she said. "We've had lots of women in our customer panels tell us that they came to us initially for the playhouse, and they're still shopping here even though their kids are sixteen. And we know that a lot of people drive past our competitors to shop with us just because of the playhouse."

Superquinn has also reaped major benefits from its SuperClub customer-loyalty program. Ireland's first such program in the retail industry, SuperClub is managed by SuperClub Target Marketing (which is wholly owned by Superquinn) and includes more than twenty partner companies. Customers enrolled in SuperClub accumulate points based on various interactions with partner companies—most often, buying specific products or services. Customers can then cash in their points to buy gifts from the SuperClub catalog or receive discounts for purchases at partner companies.

In and of itself, the program may not seem special. Many companies offer customer-loyalty programs. What makes SuperClub unusual is how Superquinn uses the program to create services valued by customers (which helps explain why 80 percent of the company's customers use their SuperClub cards). For instance, the company's famous "goof points" program rewards customers with additional SuperClub points for finding and pointing out problems in the stores—such as a wobbly shopping cart, an out-of-date product, a depleted supply of plastic produce bags, etc. The idea is sheer genius: It turns the company's entire customer base into troubleshooters, it infuses an element of fun into the shopping experience, and it keeps the store's employees on their toes.

The SuperClub program also makes it possible for Superquinn to understand its customer base more fully. First, the card clearly identifies customers as members of a particular household, which gives Superquinn the ability to garner information not only on specific transactions but also on the purchases of entire households over the course of time. Furthermore, when a customer presents his or her SuperClub card at checkout, the cashier—by swiping the card into the point-of-sale system—can display some very useful information on the POS screen. On the cashier's side of the screen, for example, the customer's name appears, which enables the cashier to appropriately address the customer. On the customer's screen, a running tally of SuperClub points is displayed, thus giving instant feedback on where he or she stands.

"Many companies make the mistake of making loyalty the game," said Tobin. "Loyalty isn't the game. It's the result of a well-played game."

A third program that is gaining in popularity is Tusa Bank, the joint venture between Superquinn and Trustee Savings Bank. Tusa not only offers customers the convenience of doing their banking while grocery shopping but also enables consumers to enjoy in a financial institution all of the high-service qualities that Superquinn embodies. "The challenge with Tusa was really to design a bank that is on the customers' side," noted Jerry Twomey, who was Superquinn's point person in the joint venture. Added Tobin: "Tusa is really a good point of difference for us. Customers will enjoy a nice interaction, good service, personal attention, longer hours, and SuperClub points as well." And with Tusa tied into customers'

SuperClub cards, the service and cross-marketing possibilities for Superquinn are endless.

Bringing Quality Products to Market

SUPERQUINN'S FORMULA FOR SUCCESS

SECONDARY ATTRIBUTE: PRODUCT

- Has an in-store bakery that produces fresh bread every four hours.
- Offers a high-quality salad bar and home meal-replacement items for time-pressed customers.
- Insists on twice-daily deliveries of produce, meat, and seafood to guarantee freshness.
- Works with a select group of suppliers on an exclusive basis to ensure product quality and innovation.
- Offers its own private-label program of products that meet even higher standards for quality and freshness.
- Cuts most seafood and meat to order to further promote the freshness notion.

For Feargal Quinn and his team, the most important thing next to service is having consistently good products unlike those you can get anywhere else in the country. Or, as Twomey said, "Of course we want to completely wow customers with our service. But if the food's not fresh, of excellent quality, why would they come back?"

Indeed, Superquinn has made a name for itself on the basis of its innovative approaches to sourcing, handling, and merchandising grocery products—whether it's produce, meat, seafood, or baked goods.

1. **A baker's dozen.** Immediately upon entering a Superquinn store, shoppers are treated to the smell of freshly baked breads. And it's not

just a marketing gimmick. With six to ten bakers working the ovens in each store, Superquinn lays claim to being the largest bakery in Ireland (the stores of the company's competitors are all served by a central bakery, according to Niall Brougham). Because of the company's policy to never sell bread that's more than four hours old, customers can be sure that the loaf they're buying is fresh.

2. **Salad days.** Although common in many North American grocery stores, the fresh salad bar is a concept in its infancy in Irish supermarkets. Each Superquinn store has a beautiful display of vegetables and salad items that are replenished throughout the day. A salad-bar "manager" is responsible for ensuring the quality and presentation of the salad bar. Brougham explained that a store policy currently in place helps the salad-bar manager keep the products looking good while keeping the managers of the fruit and vegetable displays elsewhere in the store on their toes. "In my store, Carl is responsible for quality control of the salad bar," he said. "When Carl thinks something needs to be upgraded on his bar, he's free to scout out the fruit and vegetable displays for an item that may not meet our standards for selling to customers, but would be fine for a salad. If he finds such a piece, he's free to take it from the display. Of course, this will affect the margins of the guy in charge of the fruit and veg display, so it encourages him to only put out the best."

Complementing the salad bar is Superquinn's successful "home meal-replacement" (HMR) program, which offers customers a variety of high-quality prepared foods ready to be taken home, warmed up, and eaten by hungry, time-pressed consumers. Again, although HMR has taken hold in many U.S. supermarkets, it's still a novelty in Ireland. But, judging from the positive response to Superquinn's HMR offerings, that's likely to change soon.

3. **Freshness and safety count.** Superquinn insists on twice-daily deliveries—at 7 A.M. and in the early afternoon—of all its fruits, vegetables, meats, and fish. To encourage the practice, each store

sports only a very small cooling room—no more than a few hundred square feet. When a delivery arrives, employees must discard product that is either on the shelves or in the cases—a policy that would seem wasteful. But, according to Tobin, Superquinn stores have been able to master the forecasting necessary to make such a practice work. "Our waste on fruits and vegetables is between 1 percent and 3 percent," he explained. "And while no one is happy about throwing products away, we encourage our colleagues to have some waste. Because if they don't, they're understocking. To make sure that we're in that range, we have a really tight infrastructure with our suppliers, good communications, so that we can adjust the forecast easily if we have to."

To further demonstrate product freshness to customers, Superquinn posts signs above each produce display that indicate exactly when each batch was picked. In the meat and fish sections, the staff avoids pre-cutting large quantities of product in favor of cutting to order. "Customers want to see their meat or fish being cut just for them," Tobin said. "It really helps drive home the idea of freshness for them."

Meat safety is always a concern, but it has become particularly important in recent years following the mad cow disease scare in Britain. To reassure customers that its meats have been properly handled, the temperature of each display is checked, recorded, and posted every fifteen minutes. And to reassure shoppers that the meat is safe, Superquinn maintains 100 percent DNA traceability of every piece of meat it sells. In other words, if a customer has a problem with a chop or steak, the store can trace the cut back to the exact animal from which it was taken. "Certainly, this is retrospective," noted Tobin. "But it does reassure customers, because they feel confident that we would never take any chances with our meat, given all these safety checks."

For customers seeking the highest standards of food quality, Superquinn offers the private label "Superquinn Select." Products bearing the Select label are subject to strict standards relating to food safety, taste, tenderness, freshness, animal welfare, and "Irishness" (which is particularly important to a small country whose industries rely upon strong support of residents for survival).

4. **Innovative products.** Superquinn is roundly recognized for its innovation in bringing new products to the tables of the Irish people. One of the best-known items is its sausage. The Irish are "mad about sausage," said Tobin. With only eleven stores in Dublin, Superquinn controls about 32 percent of the city's sausage market (about 15 percent countrywide). Unfortunately for foreigners, the sausages can be bought only in Ireland, as Superquinn has no intention of selling them anywhere but in its stores. "People come from all over for our sausages—it's one of the big things that get people in the stores," Tobin said. "If we sold them elsewhere, we couldn't control the quality, and we wouldn't be getting people into our stores." That's not to say that foreign visitors haven't tried to bring them home. According to Tobin, Americans routinely try to smuggle them back into the States—mostly to no avail. "The customs guys at JFK [Airport] love our sausages," he said, laughing.

Tobin pointed out that the ingredients—and the fact that the sausage is made fresh every day in the store—set Superquinn's sausage apart. Most sausages have about 30 percent meat, with the rest made up of cereal fillers. Superquinn sausages are 65 percent meat and 35 percent fillers. This, combined with the Superquinn proprietary seasoning, gives the company a true destination product.

Perhaps the only other food that the Irish eat more of than sausage is potatoes. Tobin pointed out that the Irish are extremely demanding when it comes to potatoes, and that Superquinn had a tough time getting potatoes that pleased its customers. So the company decided to develop its own potato that would exhibit all the characteristics that customers wanted. "We worked with a company in Germany to develop the seeds, and then partnered with a farm here in Ireland to grow the potatoes," said Brougham. "It's our best-selling potato—it's superb. And none of our competitors would ever put themselves through that trouble just over a potato."

The potato story is reflective of a larger philosophy at Superquinn that governs its relationships with suppliers. To ensure product freshness, safety, quality, and innovation, Superquinn works with a select group of suppliers—the company calls them "partners"—on an exclusive basis. "We're going to do business with the most innovative beef supplier, the one with the best hygiene and DNA traceability," said Tobin. "The best seafood supplier. The best produce supplier. And our relationship will be exclusive in Ireland, so that although our suppliers can work with anyone outside the country, here they work only with us."

What makes these arrangements work, said Tobin, is the fact that there is complete pricing transparency throughout each relationship—a rarity in the grocery industry. "They know how much we make on an item, we know how much they make, and we work as a team," he explained. "Our partners are free to go around the store and make comments to me—negative or positive—and I will make comments to them. We want to work with partners who will help us drive business for both of us."

Empowerment Is the Key to Great Service

A few minutes spent with any Superquinn employee—"colleagues" in company parlance—are enough to convince anyone that these people love their jobs, and that this enthusiasm transfers to how the employees treat each other and customers. The root of that enthusiasm is the empowerment that all employees feel to do what they think is right—and that empowerment starts at the top.

Jerry Twomey recalled several instances in which he helped out colleagues reporting to him as a store manager—not because there was a policy on how to do it, but because he felt that the company supported him in his decisions. One day, he discovered that a colleague's husband had been out of work for two months, and that the couple were having trouble making their rent payment. So he cut a check for that month's rent from the company checkbook and helped organize two job interviews for her husband. The following week, the woman's husband was working. "That is something that I feel we as a company have to do for our colleagues," Twomey said. "If they feel that they are wanted and look forward to coming to work, they are going to make my job so much easier."

But empowerment doesn't mean that employees have free rein. "The difficulty in our model is determining how you can empower people and still let everyone know that they can't do something that is against the culture of the company," explained Feargal Quinn. "So we try to always communicate to our colleagues that they are allowed to do what they think is right as long as their actions add to our services. For instance, if you think something is good but can be better, great. But you can't take a particular sign down because you don't like the color—that's not adding to the service."

In the end, service can mean many things to many people. For Twomey, service—from a customer point of view—is pretty simple. "I think our customers define service this way," he said. "They can come in and get everything they want to get, and can be looked after in the process. They're made to feel a part of the company, and they come out happy. If a customer comes out of our store frustrated, we haven't delivered our service."

From our point of view, Superquinn represents a Consumer Relevancy paradox. The company clearly dominates on service, but its product differentiation is so great that one could claim it has also achieved a 5 in product. And since Quinn is so monomaniacally dedicated to serving customers in every way possible, his company is aggressive on price (though not a price leader), seeks to create an intimate bond with its customers, and rates highly even on access. Can't shop because your spouse has called and informed you she is bringing an important client home? No problem. The Superquinn team will be happy to special-deliver your groceries to you. In fact, Superquinn managers are given incentives depending on how well they manage their business to certain households. As for access, if you want anything in a Superquinn, the tenets of the cult of service dictate that someone will stop whatever he's doing (unless, of course, he's already assisting a customer) to either help you find it or actually get it for you.

The company does overextend a bit in terms of creating an experience for shoppers, suggesting to us that it may be leaving a few gross margin points on the table. Earlier in this book, we said Superquinn practiced unconscious Relevancy. It is simply one of the finest companies we've seen. No company is perfect, however, and if Superquinn were to try to expand dramatically, it would have to either sacrifice some of its slavish devotion to customers or really put pressure on its bottom line.

Case Study

Tremor: Whole Lot of Shakin' Goin' On

Claudia Kotchka carries two business cards, an appropriate gesture for someone whose life and passions span two unique cultures, each—perhaps ironically—contained within the solid, tradition-bound walls of Procter & Gamble. Her "Procter" card reads "Claudia Kotchka, Vice President, eBusiness Ventures, Procter & Gamble." Her second card reads "Claudia Kotchka, CEO and Chief Barrier Buster, Tremor." Between the two cards lies the story beneath this case study, a story not about how a manufacturer can use Consumer Relevancy to sell a product but, rather, about how a manufacturer sells when Relevancy *is* the product. "The whole business-card thing was interesting," Kotchka told us. "They came around and asked me what I wanted on my business cards, and I said, 'CEO, Tremor,' and they said, 'No, how about something else?' So, I said, 'Okay, how about Chief Barrier Buster?' and they said, 'Well, no.' So, we settled on Vice President, eBusiness, and I got a Tremor business card too." That spirit of understanding the importance of working both inside and outside the P&G system has served Kotchka well and helps at least partially explain how she moved Tremor from idea to project to product in less than a year.

Tremor is a unique venture for Procter & Gamble. For one thing, it's an almost pure service offering—that is, the product is a service. For another, Tremor actually encourages the solicitation of business from direct P&G competitors. The Tremor team's organizational model has no parallel inside Procter, and if all that's not enough, Tremor violates the Holiest of Holy P&G principles—it recruits members from the outside of an organization that, until now, has always promoted from within rather than recruit specialists from the outside.

Even as you read this, Tremor is very much a work in progress, and the ultimate design and manifestation on the Internet is almost certain to change based on consumer leanings. In fact, based on continual customer feedback, the Tremor site will be changing constantly. So, before we explain its business model, let's look back at its brief history. "It started when I was in fem care [feminine care] at P&G," Kotchka explained. "One of our most important target audiences was teenage girls, and so we were always trying to find ways to connect with teenage girls and to offer them things that were new and different. And we knew it was important to try to get their input."

That input, however, proved elusive. "We just couldn't find anyplace on the Internet to get it," Kotchka remembered. "So we thought, maybe we should start a place [website] for teenage girls. Teenagers in particular are a difficult group to reach, and from the beginning we understood that it was important to have a two-way conversation rather than 'shouting' at teenage girls. We actually were thinking about starting an e-commerce site, but we realized pretty quickly it wouldn't represent a good business proposition for the company. Not enough teenage girls have credit cards of their own or spend a lot of money online."

Kotchka knew she had the beginning of a great idea and used Procter's traditional process model to help it germinate. "At P&G we're always thinking about what it is the consumer really wants and using those insights to put more definition around the product idea," she said. "So we started talking to teenage boys and girls. We found out they felt lots of things were missing on the Internet, like the chance to be really heard and access to opportunity. When we asked about existing teen sites, we heard things like: 'A lot of the sites designed for teenagers assume we're stupid'; 'They act like all we care about is the latest teen celebrity'; 'We'd like to be able to talk to other teens—people our own age'; 'We'd like a chance to be heard by adults'; and 'We don't get respect.'"

Kotchka and her coconspirators created an Internet hierarchy of teenage needs and decided that there was a white-space opportunity. Teens have many needs, a variety of which could be met by the Internet but weren't. "What we found was that there weren't any sites that teens felt were at the next level—operating a site where teens could get personalized information, had the opportunity not just to speak but to be heard, and go to get access to opportunity—the doors open, if you will," Kotchka said. "Our issue was whether the Web could help them or if a company could help them. We knew there was a big white-space opportunity there, one that fit nicely P&G's core mission of improving the lives of the consumer. We have a visual metaphor for our brand—your first set of car keys—because to a teenager those keys mean they're independent, they can spend time with their friends, and there's a real sense of responsibility."

There's no question that Tremor began as a website idea, but Kotchka is quick to point out that it's not just another dot-com. "We want to be a brand teens trust online *and* offline," she said. "And outside the United States, the Internet isn't as important as cell phones and those kinds of things. As a marketer, you want to be a brand that stands for something to consumers, a brand they can trust in a variety of mediums."

That said, Tremor's original incarnation was as a Web-based presence. The problem, of course, was how to build a site that didn't suffer from the faults of other teen-oriented sites. "We instinctively knew the best thing to do was to have teens develop this site, not us," Kotchka said. "We certainly aren't cool, so we decided to recruit teen 'MVPs'—teens who are early adopters, thought leaders, mobile, very social, connected, online, and very passionate about something."

The landscape of cyberspace is so littered with dazzling business prospectuses and abandoned PowerPoint presentations genteelly begging for venture capital that it's easy to believe that the road to digital hell is paved with good ideas. Kotchka got the idea that eventually became Tremor in January 2000. She went to her boss in the feminine-care business, only to be told there was no funding available. She then took it to A. G. Lafley, currently Procter's president and CEO but then the head of the company's Health and Beauty Care division. Lafley (who was largely responsible for the company's Reflect.com consumer-direct beauty site) was sympathetic but, like Kotchka's direct boss, didn't have any funding.

That left only one place in the P&G pantheon to turn—then-chairman, president, and CEO Durk Jager. "It was A. G.'s idea," Kotchka explained. "He said, 'I don't have any money; go see Durk.' So I did. I said, 'I want to get venture capital for this idea,' and he said, 'No, *I* want to be your venture capitalist.' So he sent me away, and when I came back with my plan, he asked me a question, a really great question: 'Are you set up for success?' he asked. 'If you stay in one of our business units, you'll run into all of our corporate problems, and I should know because I'm the biggest bureaucrat, but I'd be interested in testing a new culture in P&G.' "

Tremor is the result of that experiment in "new culture." "Like any dot-com, we've got our pot of money and our burn-rate calculations," Kotchka said. "And unlike other P&G entities, we have an entirely different compensation system. You get a bonus if you hit milestones, and if you don't hit them you don't, and the whole team gets bonuses—it's all or nothing, which is very different from the traditional P&G model that recognizes and rewards individual excellence. We have our own profit center, funded by the CEO. We have separate office space. All Durk insisted on when he agreed to fund us was that we adhere to two rules: We must follow the company's purpose, values, and principles; and second, we have to be funded internally. That's it. We've hired from the outside. We don't have functions. We have key staffers who live in San Francisco and Los Angeles. You'd think, given our setup, it would be easy to break the rules, but we still have to get people paid, and that means we have to have the right function codes, and our people don't have specific functions, so it's sometimes very hard to get some things done."

Jager's predictions about the problem of being an entrepreneur trapped inside a labyrinthine bureaucracy proved uncannily accurate. The CEO left the company following a dramatic downturn in market capitalization, but the good news for Kotchka and Tremor was that he was succeeded by Lafley, who was a believer. "So we put together a plan and a team and asked ourselves, 'What is it going to take to pull this off?' We built an answer using good, solid P&G strategy work—looking at where we could play, how we could win, and in general challenging ourselves to think about whether or not we had a business that would 'work' in P&G terms,"

Kotchka said. "That's where we came up to the B2B side model. We knew we were marketers who needed something like Tremor, so it was logical to assume it might also be useful to other marketers. We're a B2B marketing-service model, and that's just very different from anything else that P&G has ever done. We're used to selling products here."

Tremor was conceived before business-to-consumer dot-coms began to fall from the NASDAQ stratosphere, losing both their allure and market capitalization in the process. "We actually did all this before the B2Cs crashed," Kotchka said. "But I had taken a hard look at them, and their business models didn't make any sense. Most of them were selling advertising, and we were a huge buyer of that advertising, so we knew they weren't working all that well as advertising vehicles. I mean, here you had all these companies getting all this venture capital, and they had no plans for profitability. It was all so anti-P&G, because we believe that as a company you've always got to be in it for the consumer, and if you're not, whatever you're doing isn't going to work. So we tested the notion of a B2B model with Cover Girl, which is the one big teenage brand we have. We leveraged personal connections in other businesses to float the idea and got an extremely enthusiastic response. Finally, we told ourselves, 'Hey, this looks like it will fly. Let's see if we can put all the pieces together.'"

Those pieces can be roughly grouped into three buckets: the consumer offering, the business model, and future directions. Kotchka began by explaining the consumer offering: "Our mission is to empower teens. But you can't tell teens you're going to empower them, because they don't get it and they don't like it. So you tell them you're offering them an opportunity to speak out and be heard and have doors opened," she said. "Of course, you also have to connect them to other teens and have some relevant content—those are the minimums to play. One of the things our ad agency came up with to describe all this is captured in the phrase 'Type Louder!' And teens understand what that means. When you log on to the site, you hit our home page, which is basically like the front cover of a magazine, with headline stories you can personalize. Once you're on the home page, you might type in that you're interested in, say, salsa dancing in the Midwest, or safe sex, or relationships, politics—all kinds of topics—and you'll be taken to all types of sites that relate to your interest, sites that are actually put together by a teenager who's passionate and knowledgeable about the area. You can go to that site and become a member, and if you do, you get access to the site's bulletin boards and chats. Naturally, you don't have to be a member. Let's say you're a high school soccer player. You might go to a site featuring an online chat with a college coach explaining what it takes to play at the college level. Or you might go to another site where one of our authors has reviewed a concert or interviewed the band, and what you're reading is what a teen thought, not what some adult thought. And there's a product-and-service model that might let you test a new lipstick by clicking on and receiving a free sample before the product gets to market."

Kotchka said Tremor's goal is to recruit 8,000 domestic "MVPs"—teens who are mobile, visible, and passionate—into the site's corps of participants. "Being an MVP doesn't necessarily mean being the captain of the cheerleading squad—it means being thought of as a leader by your peers," she explained. "That's one of the comments we received from our initial research. Teens believe everybody thinks they're all the same, when the truth is, we've got a really diverse set of teens with really diverse sets of interests." The Tremor team and a marketing service went to places where teens hang out, like malls, in the top twenty-five U.S. cities. Potential participants were screened and then interviewed. The Tremor value proposition and opportunities are explained to those who pass through the selection process. Those who accept the offer are signed up, unless they're under eighteen, in which case a parental waiver is required. "The only glitch is that they have to have access to the Internet, and we prefer home access," Kotchka explained. "Other than that, they just have to be willing and be early adopters and thought leaders."

For P&G, the Tremor business model is a bit out of the box. "Our charge was to 'go forth and find revenue,' " Kotchka joked. "A. G. [Lafley] asked us if we thought we needed to be a separate company in order to sell to competitors, which he felt very strongly we should do. I guess one way of looking at the 'good news' is that when you look at where teens are spending their money, you find they're spending most of it in categories such as music, in which P&G doesn't currently play. So I don't have to really worry about our ability to sell our services to P&G's traditional competition to make this work. And, in terms of the B2B offering, the credibility of P&G proves immensely helpful even when you're marketing to our traditional competitors."

The model is simple. Let's say Unilever calls Tremor and says it wants to launch a new hair-care product. Kotchka and her team can do a variety of things to help Unilever design the product. "We know which teens are hair-involved and which aren't," she explained, "so we can get them feedback on the whole product idea and concept. Then there are things we can do for them from a marketing perspective. We'll find advocates for them or help them develop advocates who will recommend the product to friends. The first phase is involvement. If any teen helps design a product and/or provides feedback, they become almost automatic advocates. The second phase is that they go out and tell their friends. So the whole idea is to get them involved, let them sample, and find out who likes it. We give them incentives, from fun ways to tell their friends about the product through samples and e-mails to getting them to write about the product on their sites. The only thing is, we can't ask them to say nice things if they don't like the product. The teens like this because they like accessing products before they're in the marketplace. You could say we provide early market seeding."

What they get, she pointed out, are a lot of opportunities, such as trying products first and interviewing the people developing a product. "These kids are so smart. The first question they inevitably ask during an interview is, 'How do you make your money?' So we tell them," said Kotchka. "They tend to be very skeptical of marketing in general. If you are a shampoo manufacturer and you try to tell teenagers your product is neat and cool, they go, 'Yeah. Right.' We let teens say what they want to say. If they say a product sucks, then it sucks." One of the items beta-tested by Tremor was a food product that teens in fact did think "sucked." Even though the feedback was negative, the Tremor team made sure the product reviewers received a letter from the manufacturer whose item they trashed. "The letter said, 'Thanks for your input—here's what we're doing based on what you told us,' " Kotchka said. "In our model, they always hear from us."

Tremor's revenue stream comes not from the teens but from the companies that use the site's services. Kotchka explains that there is a wide range of pricing, although there are two basic revenue models. "For established companies, the pricing is all over the map, depending on, say, whether the company wants access to soccer girls or all teens," she said. "We track the cost of [purchasing commercial marketing] trial and awareness efforts, and we're less than those kinds of things. Then we also look at things like barter in selected cases—what a company has to offer that might be right for us. In the case of smaller companies, where they might have no money but a great idea or great product or service, we might offer to do the entire marketing campaign or handle distribution or something else for a stake in the company. In general, every pricing program is designed to meet the unique needs of a company, and, believe me, all those needs are very, very different."

Even though Tremor is barely off the drawing board, Kotchka and her team are already looking down the road. "This is Phase One of our model," she explained. "We're looking at what other kinds of things we could offer and provide to other companies and P&G. For instance, a lot of cool, neat products don't come from big companies, so maybe through Tremor P&G could help with things like distribution in exchange for taking a stake in a company or sharing in the revenue stream. The next thing we want to do— and do very quickly—is go global. We just have to prove our model first. As a teen, I want to know what's going on in Tokyo or London. I want to be able to talk to other teens on specific topics. Certainly one of the first things to do is to get an Internet site up in the top fifteen global Internet teen markets. But we also want to very quickly move past the Internet as well."

She noted that wireless applications are bigger outside the United States, particularly in Japan and Scandinavia. "We need to look at how teens are using technology, especially those technologies that eventually will get here, so we can speed up the technology transfer," said Kotchka. "There's great learning to be had about how technology moves across platforms. We really have to make sure we're on the leading edge of technology and that we're using what teens use to communicate with—not what we think they should use or what we are comfortable using. That's why we're not just a dot-com. We're using several different technologies in addition to the Internet." Beyond this, Kotchka believes the Tremor model—but perhaps not Tremor itself—could be extended to other age groups.

Authenticity is a key part of the R&D of marketing Tremor's brand of Relevancy. "The culture here is different," Kotchka explained. "Everyone here has the same size desk. Everything is open. We get this great funky furniture really cheap if we let the manufacturer use our space in their ads. We have teenage interns whose job is to hang with us. We're having teenagers decorate our whole space. Our general motto is 'Whatever it takes': We define the work and then match the work to people's experience and skill sets. We just move people around, and to work here you have to be totally flexible. Everybody on the team reports either to me or to Terry Pardue, our Chief Reality Officer. You can't come here if you want to build big hierarchies. One of the things we wanted to eliminate was the command-and-control model. We just don't have that. We've got this naive idea about flat hierarchies. We started with a group of seven, and now we're thirty-five. In the beginning, the right hand didn't know what the left hand was doing, so we had to put processes in place, not hierarchies. But we had to let people know who has decision rights. We've got a chart that says who makes decisions on what, and everybody makes decisions. Our 800-line folks [the Consumer Service group] are on our floor right next to us, which is very different for P&G. They're great. They let us know as soon as something's really right or wrong, which is easy because they're here, not five states away. Everybody here feels empowered, which at Tremor means that people know you've got work to do and you have to get it done, and if you can't, you've got to get help. We don't have politics, which is just the biggest waste of time and energy in almost any company. That said, I wish we were even more externally focused than we are."

Kotchka emphasized that everyone on the team is outside talking to teenagers. "They're the consumer; they're in charge," she said. "We try very hard to do that, but we're still not spending the amount of time doing it that we should."

Tremor is scheduled to launch in mid 2001. Given that, it's a challenge to say where Tremor will eventually end up on the Relevancy matrix. While it clearly intends to dominate on service, it's too soon to identify the attribute on which the site will eventually differentiate itself, because it has no direct competitors—yet. But what excites us about Tremor is that at the heart of its value proposition lies *our* value proposition: Listen to consumers—on their own terms—get ahead of the rest of the pack, and the market should reward you.

SELF-DIAGNOSTIC: SERVICE

- Are you willing to truly customize your product or service offering to match the needs of an individual customer?
- If you're differentiating on service, are your customers educated or informed as a result of having done business with you?
- Does every potential customer entering your business feel that you genuinely care about them, or do you herd them through like sheep?
- Do you routinely talk to your customers, trying to discover what they define as average, good, and superior service?
- Have you approached your competition as a consumer—flown their airline, purchased insurance from them, bought a seat at their stadium? How did their service levels feel to you as a person—not as their competitor?

CHAPTER 5

I Still Haven't Found
What I'm Looking For

Access, Physical and Psychological

IN IRELAND, WE RAN across the "Lock Hards" of Dublin, "business-people" identified by their unique and distinctive headgear who have taken access marketing to a whole new level. The Lock Hards patrol Dublin's busy commercial districts, unsolicitously directing harried motorists into tight parking places. "Lock 'er hard, now," they yell at drivers who try to squeeze cars into spaces more appropriate for unicycles. Once an exhausted motorist has succeeded in wrestling his vehicle into the temporary safe harbor of the curb, the Lock Hards approach him. "Sure it'll be safe here, then?" they ask, the very picture of solicitousness. "I could keep my eye on it, although a man's time ought to be worth something to him. Still, you know, the old neighborhood's not what it once was." The Lock Hards have incorporated both dynamics of the access attribute—the physical (where a car can or should be parked) and the psychological (the threat that you might not be able to drive your car upon your return)—into one common market offering.

Consumer businesses could learn something from the Lock Hards. For decades, companies have defined access by the age-old real-estate adage of "location, location, location." And, in fact, access used to be all about real estate. This explains why there's a Golden Arches on every corner from Chicago to the Champs-Élysées and from Louisville to London. It's why there is a gas station on every corner and ATMs in every kind of retail setting. It explains the promiscuous parade of coffee bars, ice cream stores, and nail parlors. It also explains why every mall or public retail space from Nashville to Nice has the same set of stores—The Body Shop, Foot Locker, the Gap, and The Limited—in all their various and sundry mercantile manifestations. More recently, the gas-station/convenience-store industry modified the formula, moving into neighborhoods and central-city locations, and banks dropped branches in high-traffic areas in neighborhoods and suburbs around the country. And companies such as Starbucks, Dunkin' Donuts, CVS, and Walgreens have excelled at monopolizing space in key office buildings, strip malls, thoroughfares, and other "consumer intercept" locations, holding tightly to the belief that location is everything.

However, a new definition of access is starting to win over today's consumers, a definition that has a lot more to do with psychological access—the perception of being able to easily and successfully navigate the physical plant of a business, whether you're talking about a supermarket, bank branch, or auto dealership, and find what you're looking for—than it does with the size of a parking lot or whether you get there by making a right-hand turn.

Now, we're not suggesting that consumers want to be inconvenienced. After all, access is like the ante in a poker game. If you're not accessible, you're not in the game—you're not in business. But access today is clearly a multidimensional attribute, full of nuances that extend far beyond real estate. Location no longer is everything; it's simply one component in the mosaic of differentiation. We believe there are two primary reasons for this change. First, we are largely a mobile society—ready, willing, and able to travel some distance to get what we want. Second, the Internet allows us to reach nearly anything, anywhere, at any time.

Today access has less to do with location than with giving consumers the ability to interact with a company where or when they want with minimum interference or hassle. In the banking business, for instance, access is no longer just about building branch offices; today it's also about establishing a network of easily accessible ATMs. For a retailer, access is about providing shopability—or a mental map—for customers. It's about ease and convenience. It's about shoppers finding what they want and personalizing that store to their individual needs.

This new and emergent class of access is being driven by such developments as the resurgence of mail order, the popularity of QVC and the Home Shopping Network, and the steady rise of Internet shopping. Among the most mainstream of the new access-dominant businesses is Amazon.com. The company's website is easy to locate and navigate and includes myriad value-added services, demonstrating that the new definition of access encompasses more than just shopping. Amazon doesn't simply provide access to books or CDs; it provides access to community, through such services as book reviews by other consumers.

In the physical world, Dollar General, while dominating on price, also has successfully captured this new notion of access by focusing on ease of internal navigation in its almost 5,000 stores. "We need to be quick in and quick out," said Bob Carpenter, the company's chief administrative officer. "Our stores have to be about 6,500 to 7,500 square feet, and the reason we want that size is because when you walk in the store, you need to be able to stand in the door and see every part of the store—nothing to block you, so that you can see what you want and get it and come out. That means that I can't have any counters that go above eye level. In a small store, if the counters go above eye level it feels very crowded to a customer. They can't see what they want, and they have to go around and search everywhere and try to find it."

Understanding that access is about shoppers finding what they're looking for, Dollar General has established a consistent "map" for all of its stores. "We put nonperishable food items immediately on the left when you walk in," said Carpenter. "Those are items that people pick up quickly, and they usually come in to grab one of those. And when they do, they also generally want to grab some detergent or some housecleaning chemical or paper towels, so we put those on the back wall. And then you might need to pick up deodorant and toothpaste, so we put those on the right side up toward the front, so that then you've got to walk past some of our basic soft lines in order to get the toothpaste on the way to the door. Now, if you really just wanted to get the two main things, you could get them easily at the front—that would be the nonperishable food on the left and the toothpaste on the right. The point is that you can walk into any one of the stores, and everything will be in exactly the same place, so that you know where they are and you can see it the second you walk in."

With a very different type of model, Amway also has made access a point of differentiation. Consumers can buy almost anything they need—insurance, autos, appliances, furniture, food, and other packaged goods—and have it delivered without ever leaving their homes. And it's all done with a model that is based on a consumer-to-consumer, neighbor-to-neighbor community.

Known for face-to-face encounters with potential customers, Amway distributors come from the ranks of ordinary citizens looking for ways to increase their monthly incomes and find new careers. The company has built its reputation as a convenient, easily accessible retail source for household detergents, cleansers, and personal-care items. Along with other home-delivery retailers, Amway has helped define the attribute of access for millions of Americans, as well as consumers in other parts of the world.

And the company is expanding its model of access with its new Internet site, called Quixtar. Established in 1999, Quixtar is both an online shopping arena and a place to recruit new distributors. Consumers can buy the traditional home and health-care products—soaps, detergents, vitamin-powered drinks, and water-treatment items. But the new site also offers a range of electronics, jewelry, and personal items—more than 10,000 products from over 1,500 companies.[1] A customer can purchase a Sharp television/VCR combo, a Seiko watch, or hundreds of other products without ever knowing that the site is a branch of the Amway Co. According to Ken McDonald, the Amway executive heading up the e-commerce venture, the Internet site seeks to distinguish itself by offering a wide range of non-Amway products. "We're convinced," he said, "we can make more money . . . by building two businesses that are different than just by tweaking one business."[2]

The sense of community these businesses create is a form of psychological access, in contrast to the physical access of an actual building, website, or interior store layout. This psychological access is often tightly linked to the attribute of experience. In this sense, access serves as a portal—an open door, figurative in some instances, literal in others—to the consumer experience that is tied to a particular business. Consider a city block with four bars across the street from one another, each attracting a completely different crowd. The physical access is the same for all four, but the psychological access is very different.

Starbucks also serves as an example. The coffee chain's ubiquitous units are placed in high-traffic locations, and therefore are accessible in a physical sense. However, the psychological accessibility associated with an individual unit has as much to do with the company's success as does ubiquity. In one neighborhood, the Starbucks shop might have a sleek, upscale feel, appropriate for that area's consumers. In another, oversized couches and funky lighting might better fit the community. Such an approach transcends physical access. Consumers enter not so much for the cup of coffee but because they're looking for access to a community of people like themselves.

During the course of our research for this book, we began to notice examples of this in our own experience. On a visit to Los Angeles, Fred was struck by how different the crowds were as one moved down the block from Rande Gerber's Skybar, with its sophisticated and hip California crowd, to a bleeding-edge bar full of the tattooed, branded, ritually scarified, and pierced set, and on to a Starbucks where PIBs (people in black) mumbled earnestly into their cell phones. Fred, the epitome of Midwestern chic despite his own fashionable Manhattan address, noted that all of the establishments operating on one of L.A.'s hottest strips used access as a way of creating a sense of affiliation, which in turn was leveraged into community building, which was then leveraged into a commercial model.

Back in New York, recalling his experience in the L.A. Starbucks, Fred complained that the PIBs didn't seem particularly interested in a customer who didn't know a latte from a chai, let alone a grande from a venti. Could it be that he was right? Was Starbucks really trying to chase out business if it didn't come swathed in black? We decided to put it to a test, a little participant anthropology done in the name of Relevancy.

Fred's office sits next door to a Starbucks in midtown Manhattan. You have to pass by one of New York's thousands of street vendors selling coffee for a dollar or less to get to the Starbucks, where you can get the same size coffee for almost $4. Waiting until the morning rush was over, we entered the Starbucks—Fred dressed in his Midwestern best and Ryan bearded and clothed head to toe in black. The clerk watched us enter and must have noticed us talking to each other, since we were the only customers in the store. "I'd like a coffee," Fred said. The clerk rolled his eyes and, with a sigh as palpable as the wind off a Jamaican Blue Mountain top, asked, "What kind of coffee?" "You know," Fred said, "a regular coffee." "You want a Colombian supremo?" the clerk asked. "Sure, I guess so," Fred responded. "What size do you want?" the clerk asked, by now avoiding any eye contact. "A large," Fred said. "Grande?" the clerk suggested. "Is that a large?" Fred asked. With a look of disgust, the clerk spit out, "We have four sizes: short, tall, grande, and venti." Fred, now completely confused, offered, "How large is tall?" This prompted a snort from the clerk as he grabbed and displayed a tall cup. "That's pretty small for a tall" was Fred's reaction. "Can I have the biggest one?" "Venti?" the clerk asked. "If that's a large!" Fred retorted, feeling his Detroit upbringing rising in his throat. Thankfully, Ryan intervened, and the process was mercifully completed.

The clerk turned to Ryan, smiled and, with a look that said, "Sorry you're encumbered by a philistine," asked, "What can I get for you, sir?" "I'd like a grande misto," Ryan replied. "Certainly, sir," the clerk said, producing a perfect café au lait. "See you again," he said, pointedly ignoring Fred. On the way out, Fred asked, "So what's a misto? It's not on the menu." "It's a café au lait, and the Starbucks menu is a little like the prices at Tiffany—if you have to ask, it's not for you," Ryan responded.

Fred pondered the point for a moment, walked over to a trash container, and dumped his venti Colombian supremo. "What's up, brother?" he asked, approaching a street vendor. "Doin' good," the vendor replied. "Whatcha need?" "How 'bout a large coffee, my man?" Fred answered.

"Hey, no problem," the vendor said, taking his dollar. "That feels better," Fred said, and it did.

The search for a certain comfort level, community affiliation, and sense of connection is crucial for consumers in today's world, where people rush through their lives, where they have numerous acquaintances but few friends, and where Internet chat rooms sometimes serve as the only relief from an otherwise disconnected existence. What's the lesson for consumer businesses? There is a pot of gold for the retailer or service provider that can create a sense of connectivity and community—that is, psychological access—as a means of differentiation.

The concept of access as a portal extends to other attributes as well. The insurance maverick Progressive Corp.'s accessibility is the starting point for the service that it provides. Access begins at the scene of an accident when a claims adjuster pulls up in a white SUV bearing the Progressive logo. Damage assessment is done on the spot, followed by the company's Immediate Response claims service. Access—both physical and psychological—acting as a portal to service.

The potential power of converging access and price spurred the establishment of Priceline.com and its Internet-based, name-your-own-price formula. While the notion of haggling over price is as old as commerce itself, it has rarely been a scalable model in the modern world of business-to-consumer transactions, with the possible exception of auto purchases. Clearly, Priceline sought to dominate on price, yet even from the beginning its business model depended on accessibility provided by the Internet. The fact that Priceline's initial success in areas such as food and gasoline purchasing didn't continue doesn't negate the potential of how Internet access can be leveraged by price operators. In fact, it can be argued that the Internet adds an entirely new meaning to the term *access*.

"All of society is reengineering the information layer of what it is that we do," said Jay Walker, founder of Priceline.com.[3] "Inasmuch as things are information, they are going to change. What brand you want to buy is information; what price you want to pay is information; what substitutions you might be willing to take is information; what store you want to go to is information; what you're buying this week is information. All these information components were always frozen in a very specific configuration, which is: Store advertises products; consumer looks at ad; consumer makes decisions; consumer writes decisions down; consumer goes to store; consumer tries to execute decisions. We said, Guess what, that information architecture is probably not the winning architecture in an age where information can be processed in new and different ways. We set about saying what the information architecture would really look like in a world in which new architecture not only could be created but also could be designed very specifically to deliver value to all players in the market. So that's what we did—we designed a new information architecture."

Of course, as with any of the consumer-value attributes, there are exceptions to the rule of access. In fact, there are some consumer businesses, such as Strand Book Store and Filene's Basement, which have succeeded in part by hindering easy access. Sometimes, it seems, the thrill is in the hunt.

Strand Book Store, at the corner of Broadway and Twelfth Street in New York's Greenwich Village, is renowned for its vast inventory of new and used books, hundreds of thousands of them stacked on shelves that rise to the ceiling. There is a semblance of order—books are arranged by subject, then by author—but the sheer scale makes finding a particular book a daunting experience. And for those customers without acrophobia, the store provides ladders for reaching the tops of the stacks.

The Strand has successfully made browsing and its quirky layout essential elements of its identity, and the store appeals to thousands of tourists and loyal locals. But such an operation is unique and rarely if ever scalable.

Need proof? Consider Filene's Basement. Housed in the basement of the landmark Filene's department store in downtown Boston, the original Filene's Basement served as a clearinghouse for merchandise and was a pioneer of off-price retailing. It was a bargain-hunter's paradise, where one could score a past-season name-brand suit for half the original price. Part of the store's "charm" was its chaos. Items—mostly clothing—were packed on shelves and in bins wherever there was room, and shoppers would squeeze through the narrow pathways, vying with each other for a particularly valuable item. Pricing seemed simple: Items went on sale at a given percentage depending on how long they had been on the shelf. In practice, however, the process was anything but simple. Customers would dig through a pile of clothes, look for a date on the tag, then check the discount list to determine the actual sale price. If an item had been on the shelf for a week, say, it was 25 percent off; two to three weeks, 50 percent off; more than three weeks, 75 percent off. Consumers would come dressed for the occasion, knowing they would have to try on clothing in the aisle, as there were no fitting rooms.

The format worked for years; Filene's Basement even became a tourist destination. Seeking to replicate the formula elsewhere, Filene's began opening discount stores in select cities around the country. In a leveraged buyout, company management took the Filene's Basement unit public and opened more stores. But the uniqueness of the original outlet was missing in the new stores, and, after several years of expansion and mounting losses, Filene's Basement Corp. filed for bankruptcy protection. In February 2000, Filene's was purchased by Value City Department Stores.

Other companies, like Coors beer and Krispy Kreme doughnuts, created a sense of exclusivity through their inaccessibility. Like the Strand or Filene's Basement, these businesses turned lack of access into a point of competitive differentiation. However, again, the model is rarely scalable, or, once it is expanded, the mystique associated with its former inaccessibility is lost.

There are also cases where apparent access is, in fact, no access at all. Take automated telephone menus, which were designed to simplify the customer-service process but often succeed only in frustrating consumers by limiting their access to a live human being.

Companies pursuing the myth of excellence are often tempted to think of access in traditional, highly one-dimensional terms, opening as many physical distribution points as possible. Years ago, the management of 7-Eleven took this path, with the result that shuttered 7-Elevens became a routine feature of the urban landscape across the United States. The manufacturing equivalent of this folly would be to open plants wherever any significant customer was located, rather than as pieces of an integrated supply chain. There are exceptions, of course. In industries like commercial paper, mill location can be a critical element of total strategy. But for most businesses this simply isn't true.

Applying the Conceptual Model to Access

It's clear, then, that physical access alone will not be a viable strategy going forward for businesses that choose to dominate or differentiate on access. To succeed, they must take the concept of access to a far higher level. When our conceptual model (Figure 5.1) for Consumer Relevancy is applied to access, here's what happens:

FIGURE 5.1

Competing on Access

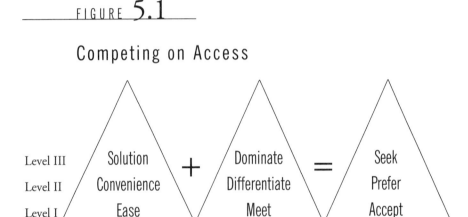

	Solution		Dominate		Seek
Level III	Solution		Dominate		Seek
Level II	Convenience	+	Differentiate	=	Prefer
Level I	Ease		Meet		Accept

At the basic threshold of competing on access (Level I), consumers are saying, "Make it *easy* for me to find what I need, and to get in and out of your store or location in a hurry." At the level of consumer preference (Level II), consumers are telling businesses to make the experience *convenient* for them. At the highest level, in which they actively seek a company (Level III), consumers define access not only in terms of ease and convenience but also in terms of whether that business provides *solutions* to their lifestyle problems or offers that psychological sense of connectivity and community. For instance, some consumer-direct companies such as Hallmark and Blue Mountain will remind customers about birthdays and anniversaries by sending an e-mail a few days in advance. The companies can then deliver a card or a floral bouquet in time for the special day, thus providing consumers with an easy solution.

Our consumer research helps clarify how this conceptual model of access applies in the real world. For one thing, location placed very low on the list of responses among those related to access, shattering the long-established notion that location is everything. The elements of access that mattered most to consumers exist inside the four walls of a building or inside the computer screen, rather than in the ease of getting there. Brick-and-mortar businesses hoping to compete on access should focus on four key areas: facility cleanliness, price visibility, convenient hours, and facility organization and layout. Two similar factors were considered important for online businesses: clearly stated charges such as shipping (the virtual equivalent of price visibility) and the ability to quickly find what you're looking for (organization and layout). A third key factor in the wired world was the ability to rely on the company when consumers were in a bind and needed something quickly or unexpectedly.

1. **Cleanliness.** First and foremost, consumers focus on a facility's physical appearance: Is it well-maintained and free of trash, clutter, and obstacles such as unpacked boxes, portable shelving, racks of merchandise or literature, ladders, buckets, and items that have fallen off the shelf? Do customers have to go out of their way to find or retrieve an item (such as film, which is often stocked behind the customer-service desk at supermarkets and drugstores)? Accessibility applies to both the physical and the psychological space—particularly in the case of grocery stores and drug and convenience stores, where consumers pointed to a clean, well-maintained store as the aspect of access that they considered most important.

2. **Price visibility.** The second factor in the access equation is clear and visible prices. Consumers want the prices clearly marked on the bin, the shelf, or the item itself, so that when they arrive at the checkout counter they don't have to wait for a price check. Many people say they feel embarrassed in these situations, as customers waiting in line behind them grow increasingly irritated. While grocery stores have implemented unit pricing—a helpful service to those consumers

who comparison-shop—the majority of shoppers don't understand its function or are confused by the numbers.

Clear, visible prices are particularly important to online shoppers. Consumers repeatedly told us they wanted to see all charges—especially shipping and handling fees—stated up front, not hidden in the small print at the end of an order. Successful Internet retailers like Amazon.com state such charges clearly, taking some of the anxiety out of the ordering experience. Consumers configuring a new computer at Dell Computer's website receive an updated price for the total package clearly marked and stated both as a onetime price and as a monthly charge for a business lease.

3. **Convenient hours.** Today, businesses from convenience stores to restaurants operate on the "always-open" model—twenty-four hours a day, seven days a week. Yet, a 24/7 strategy is not the best solution for every company. Considerations such as product offerings, consumer demographics, and physical location must be taken into account. For businesses that serve the very young or very old, for instance, such a strategy is likely to be fruitless, because those target consumers rarely venture out of their houses after dinner.

Of course, in the case of the Internet, a business is open throughout the day and night, ready to take an order, begin a delivery process, and compete with physical outlets for sales to certain consumers. In some instances, a company with both a physical store and a website may discover that the two ventures are competing for the *same* consumer. In others, the two can exist and even profit side by side, as appears to be the case with Amway and its Internet site, Quixtar.

In the end, it is important that companies focus on operating hours that are convenient for their target consumers, not hours that simply keep facilities open on the off chance that someone might come in at any time. Clearly, the return on investment (ROI) of the latter is questionable at best.

4. **Organization and layout.** To succeed on access, businesses must make it possible for customers to find exactly what they're looking for,

even on a first visit. One of the biggest gripes among the consumers we spoke with is the difficulty they encounter finding their way around a facility. Ekow, a thirty-two-year-old university administrator, summed up most consumers' feelings: "So many places I go, stuff is just randomly thrown up, and you really have to dig for what you're looking for. A lot of times, there are no signs telling you where things are, and the aisles are so small that two people can't even pass in them."

One key point of contention related to access today is the size of a facility, particularly in the case of discount and grocery stores. Many of these retailers continue to expand the size of their outlets in the belief that consumers want more of everything in one place. Grocery retailer Winn-Dixie, for instance, which operates nearly 1,200 stores in the Southeast, increased the average square footage per store to almost 44,000 square feet in 1999, up from 36,000 square feet in 1995. In 1999, while closing or remodeling smaller stores, the company built or acquired an additional seventy-nine stores averaging 51,000 square feet.[4] The average supermarket operated by Pittsburgh-based Giant Eagle tops out at nearly 100,000 square feet.[5] And Meijer, the mass merchant/supermarket superstore chain headquartered in Grand Rapids, Michigan, builds stores comprising more than 200,000 square feet of selling space.

So, is bigger better? Not really, according to consumers. The shoppers we spoke with are looking for less imposing structures that are easier to navigate. While they like the *idea* of one-stop shopping, the reality is not particularly appealing. "Stores are getting so large that there's no personal relationship between the customer and the store," noted Osomo, a twenty-five-year-old state government policy analyst. Tony, thirty-six, a university administrator, agreed: "We have these huge supermarkets that have every service you can imagine. But they're so impersonal, the crowds are overbearing, and the lines are so long. If you're there just to get a gallon of milk, you're in trouble. I tend to avoid them because I don't want to have to fight for a parking spot and stand in line for fifteen minutes."

Sometimes consumer concerns blend with corporate convenience. The building of smaller formats allows companies to gain strategic advantage while addressing the latent consumer desire for more easily accessible retail spaces. Wal-Mart, for example, while continuing to build more of its large supercenters, is also rolling out a number of Neighborhood Market stores, which typically are 50 percent smaller than the company's traditional units.[6] Similarly, The Home Depot, whose average store is approximately 130,000 square feet and carries between 40,000 and 50,000 products, is test-marketing its 39,000-square-foot Villager's Hardware format.[7]

Tops Markets, the Buffalo, New York–based division of Dutch grocery giant Royal Ahold N.V., is dramatically downsizing its future stores, citing the need to "shorten the amount of time tired consumers must spend shopping for groceries," according to Brad Bacon, a company executive. The new formats will average 55,000 square feet—down from the 65,000 to 90,000 square feet the company's traditional stores comprise. In addition, the new Tops format will have wider, shorter aisles to promote "quicker access to check-out lines anywhere in the supermarket," said Bacon. Conversely, Giant Eagle continues to add more footage and services "to extend the time customers spend in the store."[8] We're betting on the Tops strategy.

Winning on Access

The key to reaching the level at which consumers seek out your business lies in consistently delivering better than your competitors on one of the five value attributes. Companies that choose access as their primary focus must first make it easy for consumers to find what they need and to get in and out in a hurry. The same holds true for online shopping. No one wants to waste time "leafing" through Web pages in search of an item.

For a company to dominate on this attribute, however, it must move beyond a basic level of accessibility and make its operation increasingly convenient for consumers. That can include something as simple as having an adequate number of checkouts open during the busiest hours. After all, why should a supermarket's best customers—those whose baskets are overflowing—have to wait to check out while shoppers with just a few items are able to move quickly through the express lanes?

While the definition of access today has shifted to internal navigation, location is still critical if you want to dominate on access in certain businesses, including hotels, restaurants, and airlines. Unfortunately, a great location usually comes at a steep price. Take, for example, the hotel business. Anyone who's tried to book a room in New York's Times Square, Miami Beach, or the central business district of any major city has encountered some degree of sticker shock. So why can't somebody build a decent hotel near everything at a price that's affordable?

Well, somebody has: Jurys Doyle Hotel Group in Ireland. The company's highly successful Jurys Inns prove that it is, indeed, possible to have both a good location and an attractive price.

Jurys Doyle launched Jurys Inns in 1993 in Ireland, with the opening of Jurys Christchurch Inn (Dublin) and Jurys Galway Inn. While most hotels typically charged a wide range of rates—depending on the type of customer, how many people were staying in a room, and what amenities the hotel offered—Jurys Inns came on the scene as a three-star property with a fixed price and limited amenities (for example, no porterage or room service). At the same time, the company was committed to being in the heart of the key cities it serves. Today, its nine Jurys Inn properties are located in Dublin, Belfast, Galway, Cork, and Limerick (Ireland's largest cities); and in London, Edinburgh, Belfast, and Manchester in the United Kingdom.

Edward Stephenson, general manager of the Jurys Christchurch Inn in Dublin, explains how the company was able to secure its prime locations without breaking the bank. "To encourage reinvestment in the cities, the government introduced an urban-renewal scheme, which provided incentives and capital allowances to companies that built in the city," he told us. "So we had a great opportunity to put hotels into key city-center locations. The places we built in are now prime locations in the heart of the city center. The renewal scheme and capital allowances have been very successful in transforming these areas, and now we're in some of the best spots in the country. This really has been the key to our success."

The two sites that Jurys Inns occupy in Dublin would be the envy of any hotel operator: The Christchurch location is within walking distance of Dublin's popular Temple Bar entertainment district and Grafton Street shopping area; the Custom House site is adjacent to the Irish Financial Services Center (IFSC) and a five-minute walk from many large office buildings. Jurys Christchurch Inn has achieved some staggering results: Stephenson said that his property had an occupancy rate of 97.7 percent for 1999, with 100 percent occupancy from May through October, the height of tourist season. Jurys Custom House Inn, which also does a brisk year-round trade, serves both business travelers who need quick and easy access to the IFSC and leisure travelers seeking a key city-center location.

For corporate customers, easy access also means getting in and out of the hotel itself in a timely manner, as Derek McDonagh noted. "The ease of access, the location, and the convenience are very important to our business customers," said McDonagh, deputy general manager of the Custom House Inn. "They have to be able to check in quickly, eat breakfast quickly, and be on their way quickly, so they can get on with their business. We can't have them waiting behind a tour group of fifty people."

Jurys caters to a psychological aspect of access as well. Customers know there are no secret charges to be avoided—that what they've bargained for is what they get. The customer offering is clear and transparent.

The company can do all this while maintaining reasonable prices. Depending on the property, a clean, well-equipped room can be had for between $60 and $85 a night—a bargain by any big-city standard. To keep its prices low, Jurys eschews the services that the full-service hotels offer. "This is what our customers want," said Jennifer Lee, group human-resources manager. "They don't want to pay a higher price for a desk of porters when they can carry their bags to the room themselves, or pay for a room-service facility that they may not use."

The company also ensures a high degree of standardization and consistency in its operations (all the rooms are identical, whether you're in Belfast, Cork, or Manchester), to make employee training and physical maintenance easier and to ensure brand consistency in the consumer's mind. "Our inns concept is very simple for customers—one price, that's what you pay, no hidden charges," said Stephenson. To maintain its access/affordable-price model, the company must guard against "amenity creep." "We don't need more amenities," Stephenson explained. "We need to keep things at this level, make sure it's well-maintained, and keep the three-star rating. We do, however, listen to our customers and to our staff, and we respond to their changing requirements."

The notion of access isn't important just in the business-to-consumer market. It works equally well or even better in the business-to-business space, as evidenced by companies as large as Dell and as (relatively) small as Circles.

Case Study

Circles: Where Access *Is* the Product

CIRCLES: SELLING SOLUTIONS 24/7

PRIMARY ATTRIBUTE: ACCESS

- Offers total travel, entertainment, and lifestyle solutions to customers.
- Allows customers to extend solutions to their customers.
- Rounds out employee recruitment, hiring, and retention package.
- Helps customers achieve functional work/life balance.

SECONDARY ATTRIBUTE: SERVICE

- Customers can count on Circles delivering service to their clients effectively 100 percent of the time.
- Ability to consistently make customers "look good" to their clients.
- Ability to reduce stress and strain on key employees.
- Ability to create employee peace of mind about domestic crises.

You could think of Circles as a mother's dream come true, if, of course, you're talking about Janet Kraus's mother (more on that in a moment). At Circles, access is not only the most important product—it's also the only product. Cofounded in Boston in 1997 by CEO Kraus and Chief Growth Officer Kathy Sherbrooke, who met while studying at the Stanford Graduate School of Business, Circles defines itself as "an innovative personal services provider that reliably completes simple, complex and unique tasks by integrating leading-edge technology and proprietary knowledge with high touch assistance." We'd define it as a business-to-business cyber-concierge service that will find for its clients' employees or customers anything they want—from a reliable dog-walker in Des Moines to a rare Ashkenazi dictionary.

The company offers services to about seventy-five corporations and, through them, more than 300,000 people. Circles will find you a restaurant or spa; plan a party; buy, sell, or rent a car; plan a vacation or arrange for a passport; shop for you; organize your money matters; buy, sell, or rent a condo, apartment, or house, as well as find somebody to clean it; and generally do any kind of shopping you could conceivably want done. You can't access Circles' services as an individual consumer, but you can if you're an employee or customer of one of the client companies, which include Razorfish, Cap Gemini Ernst & Young, American Semiconductor, First Data, Hyperion, Millennium Pharmaceutical, and Natural Microsystems Inc. Circles is venture-backed by TL Ventures, Trident Capital, and GE Capital.

Contracting with a personal-services company is becoming an increasingly popular perk for corporate employers interested in strategic employee acquisitions or retentions. And, in a commercial environment in which U.S. corporations, on average, lose half their employees in five years, a growing number of companies believe they should tie into a personal-services company as an effective way to build employee loyalty.

In a sense, the idea behind Circles first surfaced in Kraus's mind when she was twelve years old. "My mother entered the paid workforce when I was twelve and my brother was two," Kraus told us. "She had her child care covered, and she had everything as programmed as possible, but at the same time there were a million and one things she would look at and say, 'I would pay to have someone do these things if I could find someone who could think and do it.' And I remember I used to say to her, 'You could pay *me*,' but, of course, I was just twelve. But it stuck in my mind. That's what people want—a solution that covers a broad array of things, nothing specific. This week I might want someone to cook my meals, and next week I might say, 'Oh, my gosh! My trip to Florida got messed up, and I need somebody to fix it.' It's really what my mother was asking for—having smart people on call to do what's required."

At Stanford, Kraus and Sherbrooke studied under Jim Collins, author of *Built to Last: Successful Habits of Visionary Companies.* "He was trying to distill the essence of what distinguishes great companies from good companies," Kraus said. "And it didn't come down to mission, it didn't come down to vision, and it didn't come down to objectives. What it did come down to were values—and values described broadly—the question of 'What is it you value; what's at the core of what you're doing?' "

It was also at Stanford that Kraus and Sherbrooke decided they were going to form a company together. The only problem was that they had no idea what kind of business they wanted to be in. "We got in a car and drove across the country for five days," Kraus recalled. "And for five days, we talked about what kind of company we wanted to build and what were the values we wanted to build into our company. We looked at doggie day-care centers and wellness centers with massage therapy, but it really wasn't about a specific business at all. It was about what kind of company it should be and what needs were out there in the community that we could address."

Eventually, the Circles cofounders quit their jobs and devoted themselves in earnest to the project. "When we started, we had two rules," Kraus said. "Work started every day at 8:30, regardless of the fact that there was nothing to do. The second rule was that I had to wear my shoes to work, which actually meant I had to walk from my bedroom to my extra bedroom fully dressed." The name "Circles" was agreed on before Kraus and Sherbrooke knew what the company was going to do. "Think of the names of some great companies," Kraus explained, "names like Sony, Apple, and Disney. They are all words people find generally likable, even if they don't know why. They are names that can be filled with all sorts of subtle messages. 'Circles' seemed to fit our values philosophy: The world works in circles; it's hard to break a circle; there are circles of power—it's a powerful symbol. And since we didn't have a business, the name didn't have to stack up to anything."

So with the name chosen and the two work rules firmly established, all that remained was to decide what kind of business Circles was going to be. "We began by basically doing all sorts of consumer research, secondary research, looking at things like Yankelovich data, trying to identify the trends we thought we had the strengths and ability to address," Kraus said. "What hit us were issues like time stress, the issue of work-life balance, and how to use technology to deliver services. So we looked seriously at our original ideas like doggie day care and massage/wellness centers. We studied Streamline and Peapod [two different Internet-based food-centric home-delivery services]. We loved the service. I wanted to be a customer, but we had no interest in running that kind of business. We were looking for something that took less hands-on capability and was more scalable."

Kraus and Sherbrooke conducted consumer focus groups and asked people what they wanted and needed most. "Overwhelmingly what we heard was 'I need help with my "to do" list.' When we asked them what was on that list, we heard so many people say so many different things that at first we were stumped," said Kraus. "We told ourselves that we couldn't possibly do all these different things. We also realized it would be hard to get individual consumers to pay us to do what we'd have to do to provide all these services. Then we realized there were other possible 'customers'—big companies that might want to provide a variety of services to employees and/or clients. So we shaped our possible offering list from everything to a set of things. Not too surprisingly, 80 percent of the requests fall into the same categories: getting tickets to shows, arranging limos, selecting gifts, locating a dog walker, picking a house cleaner. But there's also stuff that's pretty unusual. We were once asked to find a three-and-a-half-inch-wide staircase for a dollhouse; we had to find an Ashkenazi dictionary that had been printed only in Argentina; and once we had to have a chain saw delivered to a hotel when a Cap Gemini Ernst & Young consultant built his trade-show exhibit in his hotel room and then couldn't get it out the door. We were also once asked to find a suit that a client had seen in a magazine three years ago. He knew it had been an Armani suit, but he had no idea what magazine he had seen it in. We found the magazine, but that suit was no longer made. We were also once asked to find glass slippers for somebody's daughter's birthday."

Paradoxically perhaps for a company whose product is access, part of Circles' strategy is to deliberately limit access to its offerings, thereby making access to it more valuable. "Since you aren't able to get this as a consumer, when you see it as an offer from a company you have a relationship with, it triggers that old notion of something that's somehow even more special," Kraus said. Circles' clients offer services to employees and/or customers. In most cases, companies fully subsidize the Circles cost ($30 to $100 per employee or customer, depending on what range of services is contracted for by the client company, plus a $10 to $40 additional hourly charge per actual use). Kraus noted that some clients choose to offer Circles' services free for a while and then sign up customers on a subscription basis. The actual cost per person also varies by the degree of personalization requested. Having anyone at Circles service a request is one cost; a personal assistant costs more; and a personal assistant permanently assigned to specific people costs even more.

Kraus believes that it isn't a problem for a Boston-based company (all Circles' 250 employees, including 150 highly trained personal assistants, work from a central office) to service accounts on a national basis. "The question is 'What is local?'" she said. "Is Wellesley, a suburb of Boston, really local to Boston? Not really. We have to use the same sort of references to service Wellesley we would have to use to service Louisville, Kentucky. Also we're currently exploring—through our relationship with a hotel chain—ways of tying into physical concierges all over the world."

There are other players operating in Circles' commercial space. LesConcierges Inc. and Two Places at One Time, for example, compete in the corporate concierge area. Circles differentiates itself from its competitors in several ways. True, companies such as Abilizer (formerly Employee Portal Perks at Work), Motivano (formerly Perks for You), and Xylo (formerly Employeesavings) all offer high-tech portal sites. However, Kraus insists that Circles' site is the only one committed to a strategy that combines high-tech (providing personal assistants with a sophisticated Internet infrastructure that taps into the best websites more accurately than generic search engines) and high-touch (employing highly trained, service-focused assistants).

There are other strategic and tactical competitive differences as well. Circles is an almost full-service concierge. The service range is deliberately fixed but still covers a staggering range and depth of categories. Where Two Places at One Time's value proposition is driven by the placement of a physical concierge on location, Circles' offering is Web-based and driven by a database. Circles also allows clients to know the name of its service-providing partners, while other services tend to keep their partners shadowed in the background.

Kraus also believes that Circles' basic vision of customer needs helps it differentiate its offering. "People have a psychographic profile that differs on different days," she said. "Some days you want to do things yourself; other days it's, 'Forget it, I just want to get rid of this thing and let somebody else do it.' We become the short cut. Service providers can't buy their way onto our portal. We're not doing the eyeballs thing. We're doing the partners thing. We are building a channel of access to the best of the best. One of our core competencies as a company is finding, accepting, sorting, and creating relationships with the 'best.' I like to think of ourselves as a short cut to your answer."

In terms of its business strategy as it applies to the Consumer Relevancy model, Circles attempts to dominate on access; differentiate on service; and stay "in range," says Kraus, on price, product, and experience. A number of concierge companies offer similar "products," and Circles is not the cheapest digital concierge, nor are its offerings universalized to the point of marginalizing profit or return on investment. In terms of the experience attribute, it's in the nature of the concierge business to respect all customers, and Circles isn't claiming that it's the only service that can, for example, walk your dog. "At the end of the day, you could say we're a relationship marketing company," Kraus said. "It's all about *you*—learning about who you really are and how we can become more relevant to you."

SELF-DIAGNOSTIC: ACCESS

- If you're involved in either the business-to-business or business-to-consumer worlds, are you offering your customers a real solution to their needs, say, arranging extra shipments or "shopping" the competition for a last-minute purchase?
- If you think you're differentiated on access, ask yourself exactly how convenient it is to do business with you. For example, if you're a manufacturer, do you do electronic data interchange? Do you encourage electronic funds transfer, facilitate order processing, or customize terms?
- If you're in a customer-facing business, how easy is it for your customers to find the goods or services they are looking for? Do you facilitate their ability to access their choices or just try to "lead" their purchasing patterns?
- If you have a website, do you respond to customer communications in real time or only once a day?
- If you want to dominate on access, are you willing to go to the customer if need be, or do you insist they somehow come to you?

CHAPTER 6

Why "Good" Is
Good Enough

Choice and the Issue of *Product* Bandwidth

YEARS AGO, WE WERE invited to a dinner hosted by August Busch III, chairman and CEO of the Anheuser-Busch Co. The dinner was held at The White House, arguably at the time the finest restaurant in Anaheim, California. One entered the event by walking down an artificially created aisle that terminated at the feet of the host. "Bud or Bud Light?" Busch asked each guest in turn. If the answer was "Bud, please," Busch nodded to a barman to his left. If the answer was "Bud Light, please," the nod went to the barman on his right. "Good evening, Bud or Bud Light?" the genial Busch asked us when we had made our way to the front of the reception line. "Would you happen to have an O'Doul's?" we asked. "Get this man an O'Doul's," Busch commanded an unwary waiter. "We don't carry that—is Sharp's okay?" the poor waiter asked. (For the uninitiated, Sharp's is produced by Miller Brewing.) Not an award-winning display of service, but that's another story.

The point here—especially for manufacturers—is that what you think of your products doesn't necessarily translate directly into how those products are treated in the market. The White House thought it had an effective range of non-alcoholic beers, but the range didn't match the minimum expectations of America's most powerful brewer. On the other hand, August Busch was justifiably proud of the O'Doul's brand, but that pride didn't seem to matter much to the poor waiter, who, we're pretty sure, quickly learned the error of his ways.

The majority of consumers who don't have their names on a product have grown up in a culture where it's assumed that "Coke" or "Pepsi" really means whatever cola the establishment serves, and where non-alcoholic beers and a whole range of other products from facial tissues (Kleenex) to copiers (Xerox) are treated as generics rather than brands. In the same way that we were misguided about how consumers view price, we thought we understood what they wanted out of product. Naturally, we assumed everyone would want "the best" (recognizing that "best" is relative, subjective, and personal)—or at the very least something approximating the highest quality. After all, companies spend hundreds of millions of dollars every year advertising that their brands are "new," "improved," or "13.7 percent better" since reformulation. These claims center around the idea that what consumers want are products differentiated by their efficacy or features. What consumers told us is that they don't care about efficacy claims they can't verify in their kitchens or laundry rooms or performance claims that can be tested only in a wind tunnel or on the Autobahn.

Differentiating on product only succeeds by inspiring consumers with true product innovation, real white-space differentiation. This can happen at multiple levels of product and consumer sophistication and at various price points. Let's contrast a customer at Gander Mountain, a Midwestern sporting-goods company, with one at REI. Both customers are looking for "outdoor" equipment. The Gander Mountain shopper may be looking for a range of tents that are "good enough" to withstand a gentle summer rainstorm at a Wisconsin campsite, while the REI shopper may be looking for a tent "good enough" to withstand a storm in the Himalayas. The Gander Mountain customer may be inspired by the choices he or she sees to take their family camping, while the REI shopper may be inspired to dream of summiting K2 or Mount Everest. The same is true of someone shopping at The Home Depot versus someone wandering through Domain, a high-end home-furnishings retailer. Both may be looking for inspiration for their homes. In the case of the former, that inspiration may come in the form of a limited selection of screen doors; for the latter, it might mean a velvet sofa. Once again, what's important in all these examples is that the retailers are product-dominant; that dominance is based on offering a tight range of products, any of which will "work" for the consumer, and that, at the highest level, will inspire a customer.

As we've already stated, today's consumer is time-starved and stressed. The majority will gladly trade off a little quality that they often can't even perceive or verify to gain some time and reduce the hassle of their daily lives. The real product-related opportunity revolves around redirecting a significant portion of all those R&D, advertising, and marketing dollars away from incremental and unclear quality claims to developing true breakthrough products that have clear, unique consumer benefits. And until that happens, the majority of consumers won't care enough about these claims to pay a significant brand tariff. The message for both manufacturers and providers is clear; for the majority of consumers, "unless your product inspires me, I am immune to your performance claims." This helps explain the rise of private-label products as well as why so many shoppers switch when their favorite brand is out of stock.

This brand blurring has created new market opportunities. Witness Priceline.com, whose entire business model, whether for airline tickets or hotel rooms, is based on brand flexibility—the idea that consumers are not as loyal as manufacturers might like them to be when faced with the prospect of significant savings. "What Priceline does is say we can collect demand from consumers prior to the specification decision, before the customer specifies, and we can find out at what price the customer is willing to trade off the right to specify in return for savings," said Jay Walker, founder of Priceline. "For many people, it's like they've won something. In many ways, they have. They've traded off a little bit of their brand flexibility in return for savings, and they are the winner."[1]

While Priceline's model arguably proved successful for airline tickets, the company stumbled when, seduced by the myth of excellence, it attempted to extend its business model to a wider range of product categories such as groceries and gasoline. In the case of airline tickets, Priceline acted as a matchmaker between the corporate need to fill vacant airplane seats and the consumer desire for discounted airfares. But in the case of grocery products, the formula backfired. Priceline correctly guessed that, within reason, consumers would accept a range of good choices over the "best" choice in their favorite grocery categories. And it also correctly predicted that offering consumers a discount on products they were already going to buy would prove popular with shoppers. But here's where the problems started: To offer the Priceline discount, participating grocery retailers had to run the risk of creating the appearance they were artificially inflating their everyday prices, thus violating the principle of fair and honest pricing (see Chapter 3). In addition, with neither retailers nor manufacturers willing to permanently underwrite the discounts, the business profit model was fatally flawed. Lessons learned: Even relevant offerings need to make money, and business models need to work for every link in the value chain.

While discounting prices—especially on items that are routinely purchased—can be an effective method of temporarily stimulating sales, it's also clear that there is a distinct and viable market, both in the physical and the online world, for those consumers who want the best regardless of price. Great franchises like BMW, The Sharper Image, and the Ritz-Carlton have been built serving this market, and they prosper by inspiring their customers with greatness and charging a premium for it. We're not saying that you can't sell a Lexus to a small, if significant and profitable, market segment who see their cars as their reward for hard work or a public manifestation of their success. What we are saying is that in the mass market you'll still sell more Hondas.

One significant caveat at this point: Today, online consumers differ significantly from their peers in the physical space. Brands matter in cyberspace, where, it seems, only the best is acceptable. Nearly 80 percent of online shoppers said they want top-quality products, and close to 60 percent are concerned with online merchants' ability to maintain adequate inventory of their merchandise. There is a significant difference in the way consumers treat service-based and product-based Internet providers. They're willing to accept Web-based service brands such as Charles Schwab in their own right (albeit with concerns about credit-card security) but when it comes to the product these services (such as Amazon or Priceline) offer, they want only the best products, quality they can verify offline. Perhaps because cyberspace is still new territory for so many consumers, they are afraid to enter the murky world of reverse logistics, making known brands function as implicit warranties. This is illustrated by one of the few real missteps Wal-Mart has made in the past few years. When the company initially launched its website, it didn't allow shoppers the option of returning Internet-sourced goods to physical Wal-Mart stores. The resulting consumer fallout was at least partially responsible for causing Wal-Mart to rethink, and eventually relaunch, its online offering.

But let's go back offline for a moment. Consider the top two product-related responses from shoppers of physical stores to our original survey. Asked to rank a series of product preferences, consumers told us: "Retailer provides consistently good merchandise quality" was far and away more important to consumers than "Retailer offers top-quality products throughout the store."

A number of our direct interviews said they were unlikely to spend the extra money on top-of-the-line or branded products if they perceive that a less expensive—and, often, less well known—item is likely to be "good enough." That wasn't always the case. "It pays to go first-class" is a slogan that dominated during the 1950s, when lower-end products did not engender a feeling of confidence among consumers. But today most consumers told us that they're just looking for goods and services that are functional and do the job.

What's more, consumers have been so conditioned by out-of-stocks that they regularly trade off one item for another, making the offering of a range of good choices more important than the offering of only one best choice. Encouraging consumers to trade off is, in fact, a tried-and-true advertising technique. It's been used for years by mass merchandisers and appliance and furniture retailers, which will advertise an outstanding deal, knowing they'll have only a few units per store. Somewhere in the ad, you'll find tiny print that reads "While supplies last" or "Quantities limited." The companies know that the deal will get consumers into the store and that many of those customers will trade off to another brand or item if the deal item is no longer available. While the topic of out-of-stocks ranked behind quality among online shoppers, it's still a critical issue for businesses attempting to dominate on product. Our research made it clear that being out of stock in the consumer-direct world is a particularly egregious error and is usually a deal breaker. In the physical world, switching to a different color or style when faced with an out-of-stock item often beats getting in the car and driving to another retailer. However, online shoppers indicated they were more likely to switch to another retailer's website when faced with an out-of-stock.

The Essential Elements of Product: Quality, Depth, and Breadth

As with most of the attributes, product has a multitude of dimensions. Chief among them are quality, depth, and breadth. Companies that choose to compete on the basis of product (which we use to refer to services as well as tangible items) must determine the most appropriate mix of these three elements.

At a basic level, a company must set the quality bar for its products: Will we always offer the most innovative products that are made to exacting specifications (and, consequently, are very expensive)? Will we go for items that are of lower quality but are more affordable to a larger pool of consumers? Will we shoot for somewhere in the middle? Companies must select a product "quality range" that spans some segment of the "good, better, best" spectrum (Figure 6.1). At the high end ("best") are businesses such as BMW and Tiffany; at the low end ("good") are companies like Payless Shoe Source and Ames. Of course, a product's quality must be consistent with its price tag and represents the trade-off point at which consumers will opt for savings. Payless sells a staggering number of shoes because the price point matches consumers' expectations for the product. Consumers know they won't get the highest-quality shoes, but they will get a reasonably fashionable product for $11 or so a pair.

Our research also pointed to a certain emotional-commitment range associated with product quality—a range that runs from disposability on

FIGURE 6.1

Product Quality Range

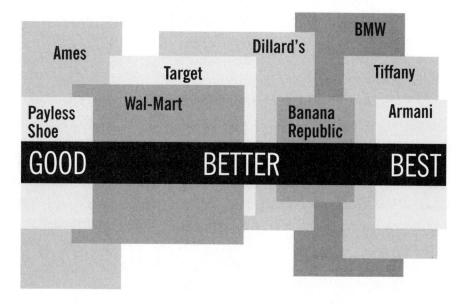

the one end to attachment on the other. Of course, the emotional commitment associated with a certain type of product varies depending on the individual. At the disposable end are products to which a consumer has little or no emotional attachment. For some, that may be cars, leading them to buy low-priced but reliable used cars; for others it may be the $11 pair of Payless shoes that they wear several times and throw away. You might call it the Bic lighter approach to products. At the other end of the spectrum are products that consumers feel strongly about and to which they feel a bond or an emotional attachment. Consumers who have an emotional commitment to cars will shop carefully and spend a considerable amount of money on a car that they'll likely wash by hand every weekend.

The notion of the instavidual that we developed in Chapter 1 became particularly critical when we talked to consumers about the product attribute. Most noted that product quality and what qualifies as good enough will vary depending upon the moment of need. If a consumer needs something fixed fast, the all-purpose wrench sold at 7-Eleven may be good enough at that particular moment. But if he's looking for a set of tools that will last over time, he's more likely to turn to Sears' Craftsman brand. Which leads to another important product distinction that emerged during our research: In the realm of "good" product, the manufacturer is the consumer's trustmark, and a shopper will search for that specific brand; in the realm of "good enough," the retailer is the trustmark, and any brand carried by that store will suffice.

Breadth and depth are also key aspects of the product attribute. Companies choosing to compete on product must decide whether they will consistently have the deepest selection of products in the category they serve, such as Toys R Us and Staples, or the broadest assortment of items for their market, like Target or The Home Depot. General Motors' Chevrolet division, for example, has chosen to compete on product breadth, offering virtually every type of vehicle possible, from sports cars (Corvette) and low-priced coupes (Cavalier) to family sedans (Malibu), pickup trucks (S-10), and sport-utility vehicles (Blazer). Ferrari, on the other hand, competes only on the tip of the high end of the premium sports-car market.

Minneapolis-based Best Buy has opted for a depth approach to product and has staked its reputation on being the country's preeminent consumer-electronics retailer. Going from the brink of extinction in 1996 to $10 billion in annual sales in 1999, Best Buy turned its fortunes around by positioning itself with a depth of product selection in the electronics category. According to Richard Schulze, the company's founder, chairman, and CEO, Best Buy has pinned its hopes for future growth on serving "technophiles and early adopters—people who have a high level of interest in adult toys, new emerging technological products."

But it's not just the product focus that sets Best Buy apart. The company's attention to its secondary attribute, experience, gives it a powerful one-two punch. Because the retailer's salespeople are on salary rather than commission, there is no high-pressure sales situation. "Best Buy's whole approach is that customers need to see, learn, and understand a product," said Schulze. "They need to feel comfortable asking for information without being pressured to buy anything."

Ultimately, we believe that, thanks to the growth of online businesses, product depth will become an increasingly more difficult strategy on which to dominate in the physical world. Let's take books. There is simply no way on earth that the biggest Borders physical store can stock one-tenth of what an online bookseller can carry. In the virtual world, then, product depth may actually increase, as it becomes the key differentiating strategy for many businesses.

Extending the Product Attribute

Beyond the three key elements of the product attribute, there are additional nuances that emerged from our research. One important consideration for product-dominant businesses is the notion of product extension. How far can they take their brand or product? That question has become particularly crucial today as companies attempt to migrate from the physical world into the online realm. A strong argument can be made that a business must be consistent with its brand promise if it is going to successfully transfer from the physical to virtual space. However, the execution of that promise may vary. Consider the case of outdoor-lifestyle retailer Eddie Bauer, a successful product-dominant company that understands the essence of Consumer Relevancy. According to Janice Gaub, the company's vice president for brand marketing, Eddie Bauer is a brand ". . . embodying values very much in sync with what [our] consumers want."

An unswerving commitment to its product lies at the core of the company's operating philosophy. The Eddie Bauer brand is universally recognized for its quality and value to consumers: a good fit, high-quality materials, and hassle-free service. "There's a physical comfort in wearing these clothes, but there's also a large emotional component," said Gaub. "Instead of cutting-edge fashions, Eddie Bauer describes a lifestyle for people who want to be authentic, make their own choices, and aspire to a higher quality of life without appearing presumptuous."

This philosophy extends to the company's many product extensions and licensing agreements, from home furnishings and eyeglasses to the Eddie Bauer Edition Ford Explorer. "Our customers are not people who sit around and let life pass them by," Gaub noted. "They're very active and like to do things. We have picked very strategic partners that have the same identification and convey the same type of lifestyle—which really helps reinforce our positioning." A cynic might note that there really aren't that many Eddie Bauer Explorers at the foot of K2 and that some of those hiking shorts shore up waistlines whose closest encounter with the wilderness was the sixth hole at Pebble Beach, but that isn't the point. Eddie Bauer markets as much to people's self-image as to their reality, and its efforts are, more often than not, right on target. The approach is so powerful that it works regardless of channel, although a different secondary attribute is used in each of the three primary channels the company sells through.

- **Physical stores (secondary attribute: service).** Since its acquisition by Spiegel Inc. in 1988, which itself is controlled by the German catalog retailer Otto Versand, Eddie Bauer has expanded the number of stores to more than 500 in fifty states, as well as various joint ventures in Japan, Germany, the United Kingdom, and Canada.

- **Catalogs (secondary attribute: access).** Well before becoming a fixture in malls, Eddie Bauer landed in the homes of millions of consumers via its catalogs. Today, that tradition continues, as the company mails more than 120 million catalogs a year, which carry products from flannel shirts to bedsheets.

- **Internet (secondary attribute: experience).** Since the fall of 1998, the division has worked on developing a popular website, eddiebauer.com, which offers visitors not only a full range of products and options but also an easy-to-navigate Internet experience that keeps people coming back. Among the innovations is a virtual dressing room, which gives consumers the opportunity to test various combinations of clothing, simply by clicking and dragging images with a mouse.

The website further cements the company's product play. "Because of the Eddie Bauer brand recognition, consumers put a lot of trust in the product—and that removes a huge obstacle to their willingness to make a purchase on the Web," said Gaub. If that purchase turns out to be the wrong size, color, or style, the consumer can return it by mail or in person, no matter which channel was used to make the purchase. Such versatility is possible only where the corporate culture supports it, both by training personnel and integrating the company's logistics systems across all three channels in order to handle such requests.

As with all the attributes, there is plenty of interplay between product and other attributes. Arguably, that interplay may be even more important with product, as it is difficult to sustain a pure product point of difference given the ubiquity of distribution today. When consumers can buy the same product virtually everywhere, a company has little ability to leverage product alone. The connection between product and price, of course, is particularly strong. In fact, consumers we spoke with rarely talked about product without talking about price. This connection helps explain the success of off-price retailers such as T.J. Maxx and Marshalls.

There's also an affinity between product and service that's particularly pronounced among specialty companies and high-end retailers that focus on product depth. These types of businesses are expected to provide a higher-quality, better-educated staff that can answer specific questions from shoppers. A consumer buying a $5,000 Sub-Zero refrigerator, for example, wants to know more than just that the fridge will keep things colder than the standard-issue GE model. The notion that the service level must be consistent with the product offering holds true at the other end of the spectrum as well. High-end service from a lower-end product retailer confuses the message to consumers and is expensive to execute.

Applying the Conceptual Model to Product

So, how do you execute a consumer-relevant product-dominant strategy? Consumers' first demand is for *credibility* in a company's products—the threshold or Level I in our model (Figure 6.2). Businesses must offer

FIGURE 6.2

Competing on Product

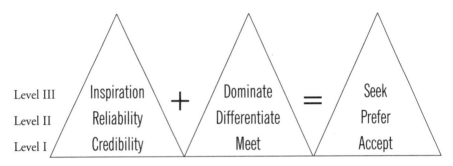

Level III	Inspiration		Dominate	Seek
Level II	Reliability	+	Differentiate =	Prefer
Level I	Credibility		Meet	Accept

product that meets basic expectations and a minimum utility threshold. In other words, even a cheap wrench should still be able to loosen a rusted nut.

Now, how do you move to Level II? At the second level, consumers demand *reliability*—that is, consistently good merchandise and a low out-of-stock condition. At this point, consumers will begin to prefer you as a provider of those goods or services. How do you achieve reliability? Whether it's a $50 Swatch watch, a $500 stockpot, or a $5,000 sofa, the product must do what it purports to do. FedEx touts its reliability with the message that the company is the choice "When it absolutely, positively has to be there overnight." Allstate Insurance does the same with its "You're in good hands" policy. Maytag, with its commercials depicting a bored repairman with nothing to do, created one of the most famous reliability promises of all time. The perception of reliability is a principal result of successful branding and the expectation that such brands will always perform consistently.

Reliability also extends to the company that sells the product. Consumers expect their goods-and-services providers to be in stock on the items they carry—regardless of the season, holiday, or location. A common complaint among the consumers we interviewed was that companies advertise a certain product, only to underestimate the response to the promotion. Such situations, if they happen often enough, will drive shoppers elsewhere.

Businesses that achieve Level III of the product pyramid provide not only credibility and reliability but also *inspiration*. Such companies carry products that are unique, unusual, or hard to find—items that cause the consumer to aspire to a higher level of lifestyle. Consumers will seek out such providers because they have become a lifestyle choice. Companies like Williams-Sonoma, Tiffany, Rolex, Brookstone, The Sharper Image, and Ferragamo provide this level of inspiration.

But inspiration is not confined to high-end businesses. The Home Depot uses its footprint and buying power to offer everything a consumer might need to turn that weed-filled expanse of scrub brush into an immaculately manicured garden, or the musty old basement into the ultimate entertainment room. At this level of competition, product-oriented businesses can depend on loyal customers to keep coming back year after year.

Ikea International A/S, the mid-priced Swedish furniture retailer, has also achieved the level of inspiration with its bold and stylish designs that are accessible at price points well within reach of most consumers. Playing off the inspiration theme, Ikea invites consumers to "Imagine the Possibilities," while the home-furnishings section of a recent catalog was subtitled "Ideas and inspiration for every room in your home."

Even at the lower end of the price spectrum, product-focused consumer businesses are able to inspire their customers. Among discount retailers, Target Stores does this better than anyone. Through strong advertising and marketing and unusual alliances, the company has built a reputation for quality products at a reasonable price. For instance, Target has formed an exclusive relationship with Michael Graves, an award-winning architect, to design hip, Target-only products ranging from watches, clocks, and cookware to frames, home accessories, and small appliances. With these and other low-priced yet stylish items, Target communicates the notion that "discount" doesn't have to mean "average" or "boring." In the process, it has won the intense loyalty of legions of consumers who look to the company to help them stay on the cutting edge of fashion without draining their bank accounts.

Clearly, companies that want to compete on the product attribute must first understand their target consumers' product quality and price thresholds, as well as the importance that potential customers place on brands. But regardless of where on the quality and price spectrum you are operating, dominance in the product realm is defined by your ability to challenge your customers' imagination and help them paint a picture of a lifestyle in which your products play a starring role.

Case Study

Record Time: Playing to the Tune of Relevancy

Record Time's story isn't just a simple uplifting tale of how a nice Midwestern boy found true happiness played out against a rock 'n' roll beat. We didn't go to Roseville, Michigan, to find proof that youthful passion can survive into your forties (although that in itself is a comforting thought). We went there for two distinct reasons: First, Record Time is a great example of how what we call "unconscious relevancy" can be leveraged into a value proposition; and, second, because it also demonstrates that Relevancy isn't just a "big company" strategy.

We believed Consumer Relevancy worked in businesses of all sizes, and we found proof in the story of Mike Himes, a music lover who has followed popular music down the road from what's now "classic rock" to techno and beyond. Along the way, he built a modest but profitable business. But most of all, he beat the odds, and he did it by understanding what some of the biggest retailers in America don't—you have to do business with customers on their own terms, not your version of their terms. It seemed to us that too many business books offer good advice, provided you are a Cisco, Ikea, Microsoft, Nokia, or Sony. But what do business books say about more modest businesses? If we were right about the role and function of the five attributes, shouldn't we be able to demonstrate their impact in every business, regardless of size? At Record Time we found a homegrown version of Relevancy acting as a commercial juju protecting the business against deep-pocketed national competitors and the onslaught of technologies that threaten to disintermediate an entire retail channel and maybe even the entertainment conglomerates that feed it. Most important, the company's Relevancy model has helped Record Time build an operating system for staying even with "the kids."

RECORD TIME: BECOMING THE PRODUCT

PRIMARY ATTRIBUTE: PRODUCT

- Inspires customers by bringing them cutting-edge artists, particularly in the indie rock, techno, and dance music genres not available at other music retailers.
- Hires salespeople who are themselves deeply involved with music either as artists, DJs, or just devoted fans.
- Doesn't carry much depth in certain areas (say, classical and country) that are unpopular with target market.
- Has a separate "Dance Room" where customers can listen to product and "hang out" with other aficionados to get ideas about what trend-setters are listening to.
- Encourages live in-store performances by local artists.
- Has sponsored certain artists by, in effect, becoming multiple-label music distributor.

SECONDARY ATTRIBUTE: SERVICE

- Key staff members are always on hand to suggestively sell customers or give detailed explanations about artists, labels, or musical styles.
- Regular customers are often advised about the availability of favorite artists or new genre offerings.
- All new releases for the week are posted in a prime in-store location.

"Last night I actually watched C-Span for the first time," said Mike Himes, somewhat puzzled by his own admission. It was July 12, 2000, and the occasion triggering Himes's newfound concern with the affairs of state was the broadcast of the Senate Judiciary Committee hearings on digital music. It had indeed been, as Hunter S. Thompson might have said, a day full of great weirdness. Viewers were stopped by the image of songwriter and Utah Sen. Orrin Hatch (yes, he's penned more than 200 tunes, including an immortal tribute to Muhammad Ali titled "The Difference Makes a Difference") grooving to Metallica in the privacy of his own office.

But Himes's interest transcended the natural human fascination with the bizarre. As founder, sole proprietor, and one-man R&D department of Record Time, Michigan's largest-volume independent music store, Himes was worried that Napster, MP3, or another Internet-based player might succeed in their efforts to give the planet, or at least its wired population, the technology to mass-reproduce music, essentially for free. The convergence of that technology with his target market's natural sociopolitical inclinations could force him out of business, something that strong regional competitors like Harmony House and national chains from Best Buy to Borders and e-tailers from Amazon.com to CDNow have so far failed to accomplish. "They [younger customers] hate 'The Man,' " Himes told us. "And anything that seems like it hurts 'The Man' is seen as sort of cool." Himes himself walks a daily tightrope of hipness that separates being "The Man," as in, "Dude, you're the man," from being "The Man" as in "Ain't nothing like beating The Man at his own thing." Staying on the right side of that line is a full-time job.

Being Relevant is tough enough, but staying Relevant as a product-dominant business in the face of a perpetual whirlwind of changing post-adolescent trends and styles is quite another. Add to that the problem of running a business that caters equally to African-American urban youth fueled with dreams of being the next big-house, dance, techno, or hip-hop artist and disaffected blue-collar suburban white kids, searching for the latest indie bands or Goth and heavy-metal music, and you begin to understand the difficulty of crafting a Relevant offering. And all this has to be accomplished without the tricks available to big retailers—no advertising agency, no marketing department, no gigantic promotional tie-ins to major entertainment corporations. Himes's version of Consumer Relevancy is built the hard way: one customer at a time.

"The first time a kid comes in here and starts talking about a kind of music I can't understand, I'll know I'm too old for this business," he said.

"The other day, I realized I have a woman working here who wasn't even born when we opened our first store. That kind of thing could start to make you feel old if you thought about it too long." But there isn't too much danger of that happening. Music seems to be the one thing that Himes thinks about all the time.

The road to Relevancy-based entrepreneurship began modestly enough. "I had originally worked from Christmas of 1979 until May of 1981 at Musicland in Ann Arbor [Michigan]," Himes recalled. "I started as part-time Christmas help and worked myself up first to assistant manager, and then I got my own store [to manage]. It's then that I realized that everything at Musicland was so structured and corporate that all my ideas and energy couldn't be used. I was still young, so I went to Peaches." At Peaches Entertainment Corp., Himes met Mike Luzo, a store manager, who eventually became his partner. When Peaches shuttered its Michigan operation, Himes and Luzo picked up some "almost free" fixtures from their former employer and opened a 1,200-square-foot store in East Detroit (now Eastpointe, Michigan). "We used 700 square feet to sell, and a back wall we moved back as we grew. We finally got rid of the wall," Himes told us. "And a couple of years into it, I bought out my partner, who was never involved because he had a family, which meant he had to work a day job, where I was single and had no commitments. Six years later, we moved to a 4,800-square-foot spot on the corner of Gratiot and 10 Mile [a major suburban intersection], and six years after that, we moved down Gratiot to our current location."

In 1996 a second unit was opened, in upscale, suburban Rochester, which was eventually relocated in 1999 to the trendier if decidedly more proletarian suburb of Ferndale. But the flagship store is what still sets the tone for the company. It's where Eminem came in his "real" Marshall Mathers III, pre–Slim Shady days, and Kid Rock before he "made it." And it's where legions of techno musicians, ravers, and house DJs hang out, all believing that Record Time is "their" store.

Himes didn't take any money out of the operation for almost three years. "I always put more and more back in," he said. "If you special-ordered something I'd drive the next morning to a distributor in Detroit, pick it up, then rush back and call you to tell you we had gotten it in. I did whatever I could do to win over customers, and eventually it caught on. Of course, a lot of it was timing. The time we grew the fastest—sales doubling every year for five years in a row—was when CDs first gained mass acceptance. We had a huge 'vinyl' crowd coming in to buy CDs. They were bringing in piles of used records and taking CDs, and we'd double our money on the used records. Sales snowballed, and during 1985–86 until 1990–91 they were straight off the charts."

Later on, Himes developed a mission statement. "My mission was basically to make people happy, to give them a product at a price they'd pay so they'd come back," he said. "I have a little trouble saying this, because it's best to stay humble, but in those days it was just the combination of my personality and music knowledge that began to win people over. People come here because they want music, and I'm here because I know about music. I want to make sure there's an environment that they have a good time coming to, someplace they can escape the day-to-day stress. Music is an outlet. It's fun, or at least it's supposed to be fun. We all have busy lives. People don't come here to hear our problems; they come here because it's nice, bright, it's a busy place where something's going on all the time and where people either know what you're talking about or can find it for you on a computer, in a book, or somewhere, and get you on your way."

Competition has always been tough in the retail music business, but it isn't Best Buy or the Boys from Bentonville that trouble Himes the most— it's technology. "If you look at the worst-case scenario, record companies *could* just eventually skip the record stores, and artists *could* skip the record companies if they wanted to. David Bowie's doing that right now," he said. "Our biggest challenge is to get the people who work for us excited and to have the proper mix of people working here so that someone knows at least a little about rap, hip-hop, alternative rock 'n' roll, and electronic music. You try to find people in those scenes to help you. It's hard to find people who have a passion for music who also have the personality to work retail, especially with what we can afford to pay them.

"There's so much music out there right now and so many different kinds of music. We have to carry over five decades of music, from the rock 'n' roll of the 1950s right through to the more futuristic stuff. Someone will come in and want something from one of those eras, and you've got to have somebody selling who knows that we carry it, where it is, and what they're talking about. That's why I still make myself active on the sales floor and do a lot of the buying. I have to work harder than anyone else. Over the years, I've learned more imaginative management skills than 'follow the leader,' but that's still the one that seems to work the best."

Most of Himes's customers are between fifteen and thirty. "The ones who buy the most are seventeen to twenty-five," he said. "Part of why we've done well is because we've been around for a while, and we've kept customers who are now making money. They have disposable incomes, and now the record companies are catering to them by remastering the 'hair bands' and staging eighties reunion tours for bands like Poison, Warrant, and L.A. Guns the same way they've rereleased the Beatles' *Yellow Submarine* for the boomers."

And there's the issue of psychodemographics. "We're a blue-collar store in a sense," Himes said. "Blue-collar customers—from the middle class on down—party more. They spend proportionately more on music. They live more from paycheck to paycheck, and they're not as tight with their money. They're more apt to blow it. There just seems to be more passion for music in a blue-collar area."

As his business grew, Himes found it more important to spend more time on the floor. The biggest threat to his business, he believes, is if he were to wake up one day prosperous and decide he could finally afford to relax and delegate the customer-contact work to a subordinate. "There are a lot of people in this business who have been bigger than us and are gone," he said. "The reason? The people who ran them lost interest in what they were doing or got a touch of the King Midas problem. I'm at the point where I could look back and say to myself, 'I've got a huge store now and a second store that's coming along, so I think I'll go golfing all the time.' But my passion and commitment is still to the music and the customer. I'd still rather be on the floor helping a customer than in an office. In this business, you can't keep up with what's going on unless you're out on the battlefield. I still buy the trendiest stuff in the store. I'm here for the music, and I love people too, so I guess I'm in the right business."

Of course, catering to everyone means holding large amounts of certain types of inventory that doesn't turn quickly. "My philosophy is to try to make as many people happy as possible, offer special services—we can get almost anything in a week, unless it's an obscure import, and that seems to keep most people coming back," said Himes. "But we also try to not be so drastic, wild, or underground that an older person might feel awkward. You know, they come in here, and all of a sudden they notice everyone here is way younger than they are, so they run to Borders, which is like a retirement home for music buyers."

Despite his passions and philosophy, Himes delegates certain purchase decisions in areas like "aggressive rock" to employees who feel strongly about the genre. "You need feelers out there, either people on the front line who live that music, communicate with people who are buying that music, and report back to you, or people who are the buyers themselves or distributors who specialize in certain forms of music," he said. "You have to give them a budget and let them go." Himes's employees reflect the customer base and range in age from seventeen to forty-three; about 75 percent of them are men.

A good deal of Record Time's business over the years has centered around the sale of used tapes and albums and, more recently, used CDs. But offering cheap copies of *Led Zeppelin II* does not an empire make. So in what may be described as the ultimate Relevancy play, Record Time actually became several record labels at one point in its history, helping to save a whole genre of music in the process. "About 1985 or 1986, three or four guys from Detroit pretty much started a new kind of electronic dance music, which was a little more 'electronic' than house music, which became known as techno," said Himes. "The sound started catching on, and while they all had independent releases in America, they ended up being more accepted in England and Europe. They started traveling over there and got big record deals and became household names. We got involved first because I was always progressive and into new stuff, but at the time, I was mostly into hip-hop—anything that was scratchy and noisy I bought, and then these other techno bands started coming out, and I started getting into that sound."

At the time, Record Time was a distant third even in the suburban Detroit independent music-store circuit, trailing such competitors as Car City Records, Harper Woods (still the place for classical, jazz, and vinyl collectors), and Sam's Jams in Ferndale, then the state's largest independent music seller. But techno, and its devoted audience, were about to leapfrog Himes to the front of the pack, even if it meant he picked up a few enemies in the process.

"People always came to us second or third with what they had to sell," he said. "So I started to see a pattern in what they [the competitors] bought. They'd never buy dance music or abrasive alternative. So I said, 'Hey, I like this music, and I know I can't go head-to-head with those big guys.' I started to carry more and more of the product they wouldn't and developed a niche. We had one row of dance. Then we brought in a band, and then it was two bands. Then we moved to our second store, and it became a whole room inside that store with its own stereo system, and we became the first stop for local musicians. They'd bring in their stuff and drop it off because we were the only store on this side of the Atlantic that gave them the time of day. We started selling a lot of it, and then the other DJs started coming in to shop. We never advertised much, but the DJs had exposure to tons of people. Things just spread, and before you knew it, we were the biggest dance store and used store on top of it."

In the process, Himes got to know the bands and DJs. "At the time, there were only two other distributors in America that were buying their stuff, and they were shipping it all overseas," he said. "So I started a distributorship that didn't ship much overseas, just to the American market— small college stores at places like Oberlin and others. I even went to the New Music Seminar in New York and handed out flyers to other stores just to advertise and get product out there. But you don't make much wholesaling even when you sell a ton of product. We were making only a 20 percent markup, and in the last couple of years the store was basically subsidizing the distribution, and we realized the labels really didn't need us anymore. There were only five or six labels when we started, and now there are fifty or sixty out of Detroit alone. When we got going, we were actually several labels too, just to keep everything going. But it all made a name for us internationally, because we started exporting, which was really the only way to make money with techno at the time. You could maybe sell 100 total copies of a record in America, where one European account might buy the same record 300 units at a time."

While Himes always sold his dance and techno music lower than anyone else, some of the artists and DJs he essentially underwrote thought he had sold them out. But wounds heal, and today dance music accounts for 25 percent of the company's gross sales.

Dance and techno put Record Time on the map, but how does Himes make sure it doesn't get blown off, especially by price players like Best Buy and Media Play? "I think price might have been bigger two or three years ago than it is now," Himes said. "We've weathered a big storm; 30 percent to 40 percent of the independent record stores closed over the last three years because of Best Buy, Media Play, and Circuit City and the onslaught of prices at cost or below. Price was a big deal, because people were saying, 'If I'm buying three CDs and I can get them for $5 less at Best Buy, that's lunch.' Then those stores started carrying less music, and today price isn't as much an issue. People still look for price, and since we've become established, they look to us as having a competitive fair price. Of course, there are still some who shop to save a penny here or there. We match all advertised prices, and, believe it or not, we've got customers who don't even bring in the ads because they know the price is below our costs and they don't want to hurt us, so they'll buy that [advertised item] from, say, Best Buy and then come here to do the rest of their shopping."

Himes has also made some economic trade-offs in pursuit of Relevant product. He only reluctantly put listening stations in Record Time's stores. Music labels underwrite the stations, and Himes could have had them earlier, but he didn't want to be forced to agree to the kind of product that went in them. He retains total control of which CDs are featured at the stations. Again, it's hard to be "The Man" when you have to take money from "The Man."

Staying true to his customers and the product they love continues to be the key to Himes's Relevancy strategy, and so far it's working. Former customers Kid Rock and Eminem have come back to support Record Time, and Kid Rock's platinum album is displayed in a shadow box in the main store. Why have they continued to support Himes? "Well, Eminem shopped here when he was a kid, and we took care of him," Himes said. "And when you take care of people, they just keep coming back. The same thing's true of Kid Rock, who did appearances in the store before he made it. People remember they might have seen him here first, and they tell everybody else about their experience."

Himes's strong identification with the customer molds his business philosophy. Asked about his corporate culture, he told us, "I ask myself if this is a store I'd want to shop at. Are these prices I'd pay to have what I want? Is it what I think of as a nice atmosphere? These are the rules I've lived by since day one," Himes said. "If you can't say that you'd shop in your store yourself, you shouldn't be in business. You're not doing it right. I'm not a textbook business guy. I'm not even hands-on with the financials; my wife does that and then gives me the stuff I can understand. I'm just driven by the music and the customer, and I leave the other stuff to people who do it better. My part is being out there talking music."

SELF DIAGNOSTIC: PRODUCT

- If you're a manufacturer, do your customers really stock your products because consumers see them as inspirational, or do they carry them just to fill out their inventory?
- How often are you out of stock on items your best customers want?
- If you're a retailer or reseller, are all the items you offer really credible, i.e., does each offering pull its own weight in the minds of consumers?
- Do your products or services allow your customers to think of themselves in new and exciting ways?
- Do you carry items your customers don't want—even at the expense of items they do want or would find inspirational—because of some arbitrary business practice, or in order to capitalize on the availability of promotional or marketing funding?

CHAPTER 7

Do You Really Get Me?

The *Experience* Factor

THERE'S MANY A SLIP between intent and the register. We were visiting a retailer in St. Louis who was justifiably proud of his company's commitment to the city's older neighborhoods and African-American community. Dressed in typical corporate uniforms (suits and ties), we walked through the retailer's central-city unit. The store was immaculate. The product mix had been tastefully adjusted to reflect the real buying patterns of the neighborhood, but with the same attention to quality, cleanliness, and attractive merchandising that we had seen in the company's suburban units. Pricing appeared to be in line with the chain's general pricing policies, and many of the store's employees lived close to their jobs.

What we saw frankly impressed us, but we soon learned it was because we weren't looking at the store through the eyes of the consumer. Our next stop was at one of the chain's older, suburban units. The store wasn't half as attractive as the store we had just visited. The fixtures were older and somehow dingier. As we wandered through the aisles, an older African-American customer stopped us (guessing by our appearance that we were executives of the company). We learned that he actually lived just blocks away from the central-city store we had just seen but drove twenty-five miles to shop at this unit. "Why don't you shop at the other store?" we asked. "It seems much nicer." "Racism," the man replied. "Racism?" we asked. "Sure," he said. "Didn't you see that big sign explaining all of the pieces of ID you need to get a check cashed there? You don't see a sign like that here, do you? It tells me they don't trust black people, and that's what I call racism."

The truth, of course, is that while we no doubt had looked at the sign, we hadn't in fact *seen* it the same way the customer had. The next day, at a meeting with the company's executives, we started to relate the story. "One of your customers thought you discriminated against African-Americans in that store because . . . ," we started to explain. "Probably because of the check-cashing sign," one of the executives said, essentially finishing our sentence. "It's a problem, all right." Opening up a beautiful store might have succeeded in showing community members that the company cared about them, but that single check-cashing sign screamed out that they weren't trusted and therefore were not respected, a serious issue for anyone trying to trade on the attribute of experience.

A serious issue, but one that's generally missed, for the simple reason that many businesses often make the mistake of equating experience with entertainment—and entertainment alone. Entertainment can augment an already solid offer and contribute to the consumer's experience, as in the case of Southwest Airlines or grocery retailer Stew Leonard's, but it isn't a substitute for a solid offer. When entertainment is the only thing standing between a customer and an essentially inferior product or service, consumers can be counted on to tire of an offering, at least once the initial novelty wears off. Think about "eatertainment" phenoms such as Fashion Café, Planet Hollywood, All-Star Café, and the Hard Rock Café. In fact, the eatertainment industry as a whole has encountered a fairly rocky path for just this reason.

Our research led us to the conclusion that substituting entertainment for a solid business value proposition—just like high/low pricing—is not a winning strategy. But doesn't everybody want to have fun? Of course they do, and guess what? They can entertain themselves better than you can entertain them. With options like mountain biking through war zones, base jumping off skyscrapers, ocean kayaking, and a multitude of high-altitude extreme activities from which to choose, not to mention 100 channels on cable TV, the Internet, movies, cultural and sporting events, and much, much more, consumers just don't need that parking-lot petting zoo or a magician in the supermarket. Subscribers to the myth of excellence are as prone to gratuitously add entertainment to the offering as they are to promiscuously—and unnecessarily—discount prices, overlooking the fact that what experience-oriented customers really want is a sense of intimacy, not dancing bears in the soft-goods aisles.

While many business operators like to think of today's consumers as time-starved whirlwinds grateful that companies combine juggling demonstrations with picking up the dry cleaning, the truth is that today's instavidual consumers are really consummate time editors, constantly deciding what activities to edit in and out of their daily lives. You want time-starved? Talk to farmers.

There was a time when, in fact, consumers did look to retailers and other businesses to provide entertainment—a time when they didn't have the litany of leisure options available to them today. We can all point to examples from our past. Ryan remembered how his mother used to demonstrate sheet music in stores. She would play the piano and sing while customers gathered around to listen. The entertainment aspect was clearly a vital part of the experience for shoppers. Time wasn't at such a premium then, but entertainment was. Today most of us don't have that degree of gentility—or time—in our lives; we are unlikely to stand and listen to someone sing for fifteen minutes in a music store. Instead, we'll buy our CD and get out the door, or order it from Amazon or CDNow, or download it directly off the Internet from MP3.com.

It's clear, then, that entertainment alone will not keep consumers coming back. The coarsening of American society in the past twenty years, the general declining civility level and increasing feeling of isolation—a sort of social devolution—have made it more important for consumers to get respect from the companies with which they do business. Why? Because they're not getting it anyplace else. The need for respect—to be treated like a human being—shouted so loudly at us as we reviewed the research that it's hard to believe all companies don't market it along with their more traditional goods. Nearly three-quarters of consumers in our survey said that courteous and respectful employees were "most important" to their shopping relationship, and 66 percent said that having a company treat them as a valued customer was a critical component of their commercial interactions.

Over the past few years, news headlines have repeatedly told the tale of consumers enraged about the poor treatment and lack of respect they have received at the hands of businesses:

- "Why Everyone Is So Short-Tempered" (*USA Today*—7/18/00)
- "Passenger Dies in Air Rage Terror" (*The Mirror*—9/19/00)
- "Privacy Concerns Cool Holiday Spirit" (*Infoworld*—12/5/00)

Increasingly, consumers are venting that rage, whether it's aimed at airlines, retailers or other businesses, with verbal—and, occasionally, physical—assaults against employees. Take the case of Miranda Smith, a twenty-one-year-old suburban Detroit resident who was arrested for assaulting a clerk in a Hudson's department store, apparently after being dissatisfied with the service she received. And stories of airline passengers exploding in fits of air rage abound. Other angry consumers have taken their gripes to the Internet, with websites such as sucks.com providing a forum to blast offending businesses.

Of course, the need for respect works both ways. The cashier, the airline-gate agent, or other employee on the front line who becomes the target of a customer's rage is likely to respond in kind. Consider this diatribe, titled "The Helliday Season," posted on the Web by a Minnesota student and retail employee: "Then there are the customers. 'This bottle is in the wrong slot!' screams an aging woman with platinum blond hair and Sears Weatherbeater eyeliner. 'I wasted seven minutes to walk back here and check on it myself, and it's in the wrong slot. You have to give it to me for that price. You're making my daughter late. I don't have time for this.' Okay. But you do have time to scream at me for twenty minutes? I didn't put the bottle there. You know who did? A customer. Yes, a whiny, screamy, navy-blue-slacks-and-chartreuse-blouse-with-magenta-buttons customer. Not me. I have enough of my own things to worry about, lady . . . keeping the diapers full that YOU pull out and mess up; cleaning up broken bottles of perfume that YOU dropped and left . . . picking up the circle rack of sweatpants that YOUR drooling three-year-old knocked over. . . . I can only do so much. Kiss my f---ing ass. I don't say that, of course. You know how it is . . . if the customer says the blue jacket is green, well, it's green, right? Customers are NEVER WRONG!"

How's that for evidence of the breakdown in civility, human values, and communication in today's world? While the growing mutual disrespect that has developed in recent years between consumers and businesses represents a significant change in society, it also offers an opportunity for companies that can create a culture of respect. Those that do will be able to provide an experience that transcends the exchange of money for goods or services. In this sense, experience is all about the feeling a consumer has when he or she visits or shops a business—a feeling that goes far beyond simple entertainment.

Howard Schultz, CEO of Starbucks, understands the importance of this form of experience. He knows that the hundreds of thousands of consumers who stop in a Starbucks shop every day are buying more than just a cup of coffee. "Coffee has been at the center of conversation for hundreds of years," said Schultz.[1] "We are trying to create a 'third place' for our customers . . . a place between home and work where people can come to get their own personal time out . . . have a sense of gathering. . . . Starbucks has become an extension of people's front porches. There's a level of trust in what we stand for, a sense of reliability. . . . The reason that our customers come back is the quality of the experience."

In much the same way that there are two kinds of access—physical and psychological—our research indicates that there are also two types of experience: the external experience, that is, the entertainment factor, whether it's a piano player in the store or a chef demonstrating how to make shish kebab; and the internal experience, which is tied to the feeling a consumer has about doing business with a particular company—a far more personalized sense of experience. Here's how a consumer might make the distinction: "It's not the experience associated with the store that counts as much as my experience of myself in the store. How do I feel when I'm in the store? Am I treated with courtesy and respect? Am I treated as a valued customer? Are my concerns handled in a positive manner?"

Is it possible to provide both the external and internal experience? Sure. Stanley Marcus, for instance, ran Neiman Marcus as if it were a theatrical production, yet he also understood the value of providing a personal experience for consumers. Take the story he liked to tell about the time he created a "million-dollar parfait" for a particular customer. Marcus started with an expensive champagne glass, lined it with silk scarves, and added layers of diamonds, emeralds, and rubies. The finished creation resembled an ice cream parfait, sporting a price tag of a cool $1 million. Marcus turned the entertainment aspect—or external experience—of the transaction into a sort of private theater—or internal experience—for that individual shopper.

Connecticut-based Stew Leonard's also succeeds in combining the external and internal aspects of experience. The company's stores are replete with animatronics, sampling stations, and a boatload of other bells and whistles. But the entertainment factor is backed up with friendly, courteous, knowledgeable, and respectful employees, who supply the internal element of the experience equation.

The bottom line for businesses? Companies that put all their resources into entertainment—or the external experience—and forget to treat customers with respect are leaving money on the table. The yearning for respect among consumers is so great that of the five value attributes as they're defined today, experience may offer the greatest hidden treasure trove for consumer businesses.

Experience is perhaps the most difficult attribute to accurately define. Like the attribute of service, it is largely subjective, representing in effect the consumer's response to all of the attributes. People new to Consumer Relevancy often have a difficult time distinguishing between service and experience. After all, your "experience" of a commercial transaction is largely formed by your perception of the service you received in the course of that transaction.

So, where does service stop and experience start? Think of it this way: In addition to a customer's subjective analysis of a transaction, service has objective, tangible aspects that can be measured. We like to say that the bottom line of service is how you feel about a business as a result of having done a transaction, while experience is how you feel about yourself as the result of a transaction. If a business accommodates and educates its customers and customizes its offering, consumers will generally walk away with a positive service impression. Experience, by contrast, is far more internalized and infinitely more difficult to quantify, because it is dependent on my perception of whether or not I've been treated with respect, that a business *really* cared about me, and that a business displayed a sufficient level of intimacy to make me feel special but not so much that I feel invaded or compromised.

Richard Schulze, founder, chairman, and CEO of consumer-electronics retailer Best Buy, explains how his company translated this notion of experience into action. "We seized on connecting with consumers by providing them what they really wanted, which more than anything else was a fun, engaging shopping experience that was totally without pressure or intimidation," Schulze said. "One of the first wins we had with that strategy was our ability to attract female consumers, who historically had been talked down to by commission salespeople who used intimidation and took control of the transactions so aggressively that a lot of the women who were shopping opted to go to Wal-Mart, Target, Sam's, or someplace else. They'd buy whatever it was they happened to have on the shelf and say that, you know, this is good enough, rather than endure the kind of strategies that were used. Well, our strategy, which was so much more friendly, really locked on to the female marketplace. At one point, as much as 48 percent of our customer base was female versus 52 percent male. Contrast that with a more traditional consumer-electronics store that we competed with, where it was 75 percent/25 percent male/female. So we won with the American female consumer by giving them a shopping experience that was much more closely aligned to ones they were experienced with."

Clearly, the key factor for a company attempting to dominate on experience rests heavily on the interaction between customers and employees. Consumers we spoke with identified the following items as the most critical aspects of experience:

- The company's employees are courteous and respectful.
- Consumers are treated as valued customers.

- The company's staff responds to customer concerns in a positive manner.
- Salespeople promote a positive image about the products or services the company sells.
- Employees dress to reflect/complement the atmosphere of the company.
- The interior visual appearance (e.g., décor, signage, layout) of the company's bank branch, store, or showroom is pleasing to the eye.
- Music or videos that enhance the customer's experience are played in the facility.

The environmental factors—signage, music, employee dress—help set the stage for the consumer. These elements create the first impression of the company, and provide some indication of the personality of the store or business and the type of experience consumers might expect from that company. For example, Williams-Sonoma, the kitchen-supplies retailer, understands the role environmental factors can play in creating a strong first impression. There's always something brewing in the store for consumers to sample—an interesting tea, a new coffee blend, a mulled spiced cider at Christmas. The aromas are powerful draws to the store. Similarly, the loud, pounding music in a Hot Topic store, a favorite among Generation Y shoppers, is appropriate for the target market and sends a message to its customers that "this place is for you."

But while environmental factors create the first impression, the treatment that consumers receive from employees provides the *lasting* impression. Tara, a thirty-nine-year-old cosmetologist, echoes the sentiments of many consumers. "I'm sick of store clerks judging customers by the way they look," she fumed. "You could have a guy who looks like a bum off the street and not know he's a multimillionaire. Why do employees have to be so judgmental and rude?"

Conversely, a good experience can be just as memorable—and potentially profitable for the company. In fact, our research made it clear that in today's society a positive experience with a company has come to be viewed as the exception rather than the rule. "When I go into a store and the employees are pleasant and helpful and smile a lot, it's a great experience," noted one consumer. "I remember being in stores like this and thinking, 'Wow, that owner must really be on the ball.' "

This is true for Internet businesses as well as for those in the physical world. Most consumers we interviewed said that being treated as a valued customer is the most important element of creating a positive experience in consumer-direct dealings. Many also noted that the visual merchandising of a company's products on its website or in its catalog defines their experience with that firm. And even in the wired world, consumers want to be able to make contact with real people. Retailers such as REI have learned to do more with their websites than simply reproduce the company catalog. REI's site gives consumers an opportunity to ask questions of the staff, check the competition's prices, and contact other consumers who can vouch for a pair of hiking shoes or recommend a particular mountain trail in West Virginia.

As companies rush to establish an online presence or play catch-up, they may run the risk of confusing customers about the brand experience. Barnes & Noble has worked hard to create a pleasant environment in their physical stores, complete with coffee bars and armchairs. Their Internet site developed a parallel strategy, offering consumers a place to read and respond to reviews written by their peers and make connections with other readers. But the website doesn't have to worry about the inventory problems faced by the physical stores. In terms of the book-buying experience, consumers in physical stores might be told they have to wait several weeks for the same book they could order online and receive in several days. Barnes & Noble is aggressively working to integrate its online and physical markets, but other companies are struggling to blend the virtual and physical experiences.

Unresolved, the conflict, or the perception of one, between a company's physical stores and its website has the potential to eventually destroy the sense of experience that a business is trying to develop. Companies must ensure that the experience delivered by their websites is the same as—or complementary to—what consumers would find in the physical environment, unless they are creating an entirely different company and brand on the Internet.

Applying the Conceptual Model to Experience

So what must businesses do to compete successfully on experience? Applying the conceptual model for Consumer Relevancy provides a picture of the implications for experience (Figure 7.1). At the threshold level (Level I), consumers say, "*Respect* me, or I will look to your competitors for the products and services I need." Consumers simply want to be treated as human beings. "Get pleasant, helpful employees," said one consumer. "Don't make customers feel like they're pressured to buy something," noted another. Simple, basic stuff—yet largely overlooked by most businesses, judging from our research.

FIGURE 7.1

Competing on Experience

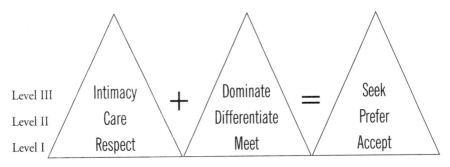

Level III	Intimacy	+	Dominate	=	Seek
Level II	Care		Differentiate		Prefer
Level I	Respect		Meet		Accept

At the second level—where consumers begin to prefer a company—the relationship between consumer and business deepens to include *care*. At this level, consumers are saying, "Show me you genuinely care about me and my needs, and I will prefer you to other companies in most situations." In addition to employees' attitudes, care also encompasses environmental factors such as signage, music, and employee dress. After all, if companies don't care about the image their employees and stores convey, how can they care about their customers? But any show of care has to be sincere, or consumers won't buy it. Consider one consumer's experience at an Ann Taylor store: "The young saleslady was eager to help me," she recalled. "She was with me from the beginning to the end of my shopping trip. She suggested things to me, made honest comments, and seemed to care about what I bought. I was more eager to spend, and I thought the whole experience was worth it."

The Ritz-Carlton Hotel Co. has a tangible approach to ensuring a high level of customer care. Hotel employees—from housekeeping staff to hotel management—each have a discretionary fund of $2,500 to handle any customer problem or complaint. One night we were sitting in the bar of the Ritz in Laguna Naples, Florida. An inebriated client—on his fourteenth screwdriver—began to lecture the cocktail waitress on the wonders of the ashtray being graced by the rather sodden presence of his Macanudo. "How much can I give you for this ashtray?" our client asked more or less coherently. "Nothing, sir," she said. "But I want it. I really want it. It's beautiful," the client insisted. "That ashtray isn't for sale, sir," she said politely but firmly. "But don't go anywhere—I'll be right back." Within ten minutes, she arrived back at our table with a small, tastefully gift-wrapped box. "Here you are, sir," she said. Our client unwrapped the box, and inside rested a presumably new and certainly clean version of the ashtray that our client was currently designing his next dream home around. "But you said I couldn't buy this ashtray," he said, somewhat confused. "Well, that's right," the waitress said. "I bought this one for you, and that one is dirty, after all."

Level III is the customer-affirming experience. Here, the consumer feels a close bond with the company, a degree of *intimacy,* interaction, and trust that leads to a long-term relationship. At this level, the consumer says, "I believe you have my best interests at heart, that you will tell me the truth because you respect me as a human being and care more about me and my satisfaction than you do about making a sale." Or, as Sandra, a twenty-three-year-old department-store buyer, put it, "It's really nice when the stores I normally go to know me personally."

That aspect is not lost on cybermerchants. Many of us have gotten personalized e-mails from Amazon with book or music recommendations. In contrast, how often does a similar type of communication occur in the physical world? Ryan points to his own experience with a brick-and-mortar retailer near his office that he's shopped in since it opened a number of years ago: "I've literally spent thousands of dollars at the store, but when I walk in, nobody says hello to me, nobody knows who I am, nobody says, 'It's nice to see you again.' When I log on to Amazon, it says, 'Hi, Ryan Mathews, here are some recommendations for you.' At least the software knows who I am." The challenge for Amazon's collaborative-filtering software, which recommends books and CDs based on past purchase patterns, is to satisfy the future needs of customers with eclectic buying habits who don't establish a clear pattern.

Certainly, e-tailers aren't the only businesses that understand the value of providing a positive experience. Transportation-services company BostonCoach, for example, has made it a clear point of distinction. You don't have to take many taxi rides from La Guardia Airport in New York to experience the true meaning of anxiety and abuse. But for an increasing number of travelers across the country, BostonCoach represents a more civilized (albeit expensive) alternative for getting from the airport to their destination. A wholly owned subsidiary of Fidelity Investments, BostonCoach seeks to wrap all the amenities of its offering—safety, convenience, dependability, comfort, and, above all, respect for the customer—into a single package that the company refers to as "The BostonCoach Experience."

When traveling via BostonCoach, customers are picked up by a courteous, professional driver. He addresses you by name, opens doors, handles your luggage, makes sure you're comfortable, and can probably tell you what happened on Wall Street that day—but only if you want him to. To top it off, BostonCoach will get you where you're going when you need to be there: The company has a 99 percent on-time performance record.

Companies that succeed in dominating on experience and maintaining a high level of respect for their customers stand to gain big. Yet the experience attribute is a difficult feature to scale. It may be company policy to respect, care about, and establish trust among customers, but getting the people who work on the front lines to act on such a policy is a tough task.

While there are many companies that operate at Level I, and some that have reached Level II, there is just a small group of businesses that truly dominate the competition on experience. Among these companies are Southwest Airlines, Midwest Express, Gourmet Garage, and Ireland's Campbell Bewley Group.

Case Study

Southwest Airlines and Midwest Express: Bringing Civility to the Air

Talk to just about anyone who flies on a regular basis, and you'll hear how bad air travel has become. And it's not just the lost luggage, delayed flights, cramped quarters, and inedible food that are at issue. It's the attitude and performance of airline employees that add fuel to an already explosive situation. The bottom line: Airlines could provide a much better experience if they just made respect for the customer a higher priority.

But how do you accomplish that? Ask the folks who run Southwest Airlines and Midwest Express, two of the biggest success stories in the industry. Despite Southwest's "no-frills" approach—no assigned seating, no meals or snacks, no preferential treatment—the traveling public has consistently ranked the airline as one of the best in the United States. In the public's mind, Southwest has become a company renowned for the consumer experience it provides.

Colleen Barrett, executive vice president for customers at Southwest, attributes this response to the high level of personal and respectful treatment the company's passengers receive. "Our basic business is short-haul, point to point," Barrett said. "Ninety percent of our business is really that of a commuter carrier. Because we offer low fares for such flights, we actually get to know many of our frequent fliers by name. And they know us. I can't tell you how many calls I get from customers along the lines of 'I haven't seen Sandra Smith at Gate 3 in San Antonio for the last two weeks. Is something wrong?' Similarly, I get calls from our flight crews who say, 'Colleen, John Jones has flown with us for the past seventeen years, and we just read in the newspaper that he's had a heart attack. Can the company send him some flowers?' These are just some examples of the degree of bonding that goes on between Southwest personnel and the consumers they serve."

How does Southwest create a culture in which such bonding is recognized and rewarded? There's no formula for it, said Barrett, other than "practicing the Golden Rule inside and out every day: Do unto others as you want them to do unto you."

Southwest selects new employees largely on the basis of their "attitude profile." New recruits are expected to show an interest in people, respect them, and be eager to respond to their needs. "We hire for attitude, not for skills," Barrett said, "because we believe we can teach the skills. The attitude—the desire to help people, to care for and about them, has to already be there in the new hire. This is not to say, of course, that we don't look at a pilot's skills. Southwest has extremely stringent flying requirements. But we've turned down some top guns even though they had letters of recommendation from U.S. senators, because we felt they didn't fit our attitude profile. We've interviewed as many as fifty people for one position—a ramp agent in New York. Why? Because we're looking for those few who are servant leaders, altruistic people with a sense of humor to boot."

Milwaukee-based Midwest Express has also risen above the fray by excelling on experience. Midwest started operations in the early 1980s as the corporate shuttle for employees of Kimberly-Clark Corp. because, according to Dan Sweeney, director of business performance at Midwest, "employees were experiencing such a high level of dissatisfaction flying on commercial carriers." Within two years, the airline went commercial.

Operating under the slogan "The best care in the air," Midwest has grown to a $400 million, 3,000-employee national airline offering premium-class service. "Our foundation is based on a number of key corporate values," said Sweeney. "For instance, we always focus on the customers and try to treat them as if they are guests in our own homes. We want to always strive for honesty and integrity and being responsive to customers' needs and expectations. And respect for the individual is critical. And we do so by hiring extremely customer-conscious, friendly, and caring people."

Unlike Southwest, whose experience tends toward the "fun and zany," Midwest creates an upscale and sophisticated environment on its flights, including the in-flight dining service. "We have color pictures of each meal we serve, so that everyone in the kitchen—many of whom don't speak English—knows exactly what the meals should look like on the plate," Sweeney said. "Then we have a very complex logistics process for transporting all of the meals—which are on china and linens—from the kitchen to the aircraft without tipping or spilling. And we spend a lot of time with all of our flight attendants to help them understand all the elements that make up the dining experience: the presentation of the meal, the offering of choices, the way you hold and pour wine and champagne, the timing and flow of the service."

While Southwest competes secondarily on price with its no-frills operation, Midwest's secondary attribute is product. The company's planes feature two-by-two, leather-covered seating for more legroom and "seatroom." All travelers get complimentary newspapers and are treated to baked-on-board chocolate chip cookies.

But in the end, Midwest pins its winning formula on its people. "When we hire people, we really want to understand their value systems to see if they match up with our values," said Sweeney. "We're looking for team players who actually care about people. Once we get new employees on board, we invest heavily in training them. Everyone goes through a two-day orientation process where we talk about our strategy and philosophy, and how we work together to make it happen. After this, they go into an eight- to ten-week technical training program to learn more specific things about their jobs—for instance, flight attendants learn the aircraft equipment, CPR, first aid, etc. But even during this, there's continual reinforcement of our strategy as it relates to caring for our customers."

According to Sweeney, the greatest challenge Midwest Express faces is avoiding complacency. "When you've achieved the position we have, it's natural for people to feel like, 'We've done it—we've arrived!' But, as you know, customer expectations are continually being redefined and changing. We need to make sure that we do the things we have to so that we always have the credible, consistent, and reliable experience—the clean plane, friendly and caring people, the terrific meal—that our customers expect every time they get on the airplane."

Case Study

Campbell Bewley Group: An Authentic Experience

Bewley's coffees and teas are more to Dublin than Peet's or Seattle's Best are to Seattle. In a very real sense, Bewley's and its flagship coffeehouse on Grafton Street *is* Dublin. Walking into Bewley's is like walking back into Dublin's, and Ireland's, history. You'll find the corner where a young James Joyce came to write not marked by a bronze memorial but occupied by another Dubliner, maybe an Irish senator and maybe a street sweeper. It doesn't matter. Stay in Dublin long enough to need a good cup of coffee or tea, or maybe a morning "fry" or a superior afternoon teacake, and you'll find your way to Bewley's. The company, its products, and its stores play such a pivotal role in Dublin's self-image that when Bewley's ran into trouble in the 1980s, there was a formal debate on the floor of the Dial, the Irish parliament, as to whether the government should purchase the ailing company. The argument was simple: How could Dublin exist without Bewley's?

It seems that every Irish man, woman, and child and even most tourists are familiar with Bewley's coffees and teas, and many—if not most—Dubliners have spent more than a few hours relaxing in one of the company's famous cafés sprinkled about the city. So what makes Bewley's so special?

"Without a doubt, the most valuable element of Bewley's is its authenticity," noted Donal O'Brien, Bewley's managing director of retail and franchising. "With Ireland being a very 'cool' place at the moment, an awful lot of people are trying to create Irish authenticity. We don't have to create it—we've had it since 1840. Our cafés are where people like James Joyce and other writers came and got their inspiration. That history is still firmly in the minds of the locals and, indeed, in the minds of visitors who come looking for that quintessential Irish experience."

Bewley's was founded in 1840 by Samuel Bewley and his son, Quakers who operated the company on the principles of the Society of Friends, to bring tea to the Irish people. In 1893, the company introduced coffee to Ireland and by 1927 was operating a number of cafés, bakeries, and even a chocolate factory. The cafés quickly developed a reputation as places where people could meet, converse, eat, and possibly be inspired to poetry and prose.

The company flourished until the early to mid-1980s, when it fell on hard times, at least partially the result of the family consistently insisting on putting Quaker philosophy ahead of commercial gain. Still run by the Bewley family, the business needed financial help, and needed it fast. Enter Patrick Campbell and his Campbell Catering Ltd., which purchased Bewley's and began to reinvigorate and expand the brand. Campbell, an accomplished artist, made his money in the foodservice business, beginning by catering oil rigs in the North Sea. When a strike on one of the rigs threatened the future of his fledgling company, Campbell personally ferried food to the rig in the middle of a storm, delivering provisions and saving his contract. Campbell had been giving serious thought to leaving the world of business and pursuing his painting on a full-time basis, but the opportunity to save Bewley's put those plans on the back burner. "I felt that by getting involved with the company, I would be giving back something in payment for all my success," said Campbell. "I felt I had no other choice."

Interestingly, Campbell took over the company only after receiving several guarantees. The first was that the Bewley family members involved in the business remain in the business. The second was that under no condition was product quality to be sacrificed to improve bottom-line performance. "I told Mr. Bewley [the company's then-chairman] that he would continue to manage the product and I'd manage the bankers," said Campbell.

Today, the renamed Campbell Bewley Group—with Patrick Campbell as its chairman—runs more than thirty outlets across Ireland, the United Kingdom, and the United States (under the Bewley's name and the Rebecca's Café chain, which the company purchased in 1998). Bewley's coffees and teas are also available for purchase via the Web.

The company's primary competitive attribute is experience, and it is clearly differentiated by strong product quality. The coffeehouses themselves are competitive on price, and the retail prices on some of the coffees and teas may be slightly higher than other competitors. Bewley's coffeehouses are essentially self-service, with customers selecting their own goods and moving to a pay station. The secondary mall locations resemble Starbucks' kiosks in an airport, limiting the opportunity for truly full service. In terms of access, Bewley's has a relatively limited number of shops and is more concerned that the retail products are sold by a certain type of retailer, such as Ireland's Superquinn supermarkets, rather than seeking out ubiquitous distribution.

The Bewley's Experience

BEWLEY'S FORMULA FOR SUCCESS

PRIMARY ATTRIBUTE: EXPERIENCE

- Maintains intense attention to detail in physical plant.
- Does not offer waiter service, to encourage people to relax and linger and go at their own pace.
- Trains café staff extensively.
- Categorizes all café staff by "grade levels."
- Posts signs and table cards around the café explaining to customers the attention and services they will receive in the cafés.
- Solicits feedback from customers.
- Ties employee and management rewards and incentives to customer feedback.

While Bewley's history and authenticity are the initial attractions for customers, there's more to the Bewley's brand than a strong link to the past. The company spends a considerable amount of time, effort, and money maintaining the experience so that customers keep coming back. This is especially important today, as Dublin's renaissance has sparked the opening of a string of new, American-style coffeehouses—"cappuccino alleys," as O'Brien calls them—that are making a strong push to attract the younger crowd. By focusing on five key factors, Bewley's is staying a step ahead of its competitors and positioning itself for growth, both domestically and abroad.

1. **Maintaining attention to detail.** The physical structure of each Bewley's café is one of the most important facets of the experience. The high ceilings, stained-glass windows, mahogany walls and woodwork, open coal fire, brass trim, and red upholstery are as much a part of the Bewley's experience as the coffee and tea. For that reason, the company won't scrimp on the physical plant. For example, Bewley's is in the midst of revamping and modernizing all of its Dublin cafés while maintaining their distinctive character and details. The recent makeover of the flagship café on Dublin's chic Grafton Street cost $5 million. "We could have done it for less, and probably gotten away with it," said O'Brien. "But it would have removed some of the value of the brand."

2. **Prohibiting waiter service.** In a break from traditional practice at most food and beverage establishments, Bewley's operates without a waitstaff. The reason, O'Brien said, is to support the notion that it's okay for customers to take their time when visiting. With no one continually asking them if they need anything, customers feel more comfortable just "hanging out"—which likely plays a big role in the fact that more than 60 percent of customers come alone. Similarly, O'Brien said, women—who represent 45 percent of the cafés' business—are attracted by the atmosphere because they find it a safe place to enjoy a sandwich or coffee by themselves or to wait for a

friend. "There's still a feeling here in Ireland that women would not enter a public house on their own and sit there to meet somebody," O'Brien explained. "But in our cafés, women know they can relax there without being hit on by anyone or without being really conspicuous."

3. **Staff training.** Bricks and mortar only go so far in creating the Bewley's experience; employees play a major role as well. Café employees are categorized by one of five levels: white (initial trainee), blue, silver, gold, and diamond (shift leader). Table tents explain the code to customers. An employee must complete a series of training seminars and gain a certain amount of experience on the floor to move from one level to the next. Each move up comes with an increase in responsibilities and pay. Name tags are colored to reflect an employee's level—which, according to O'Brien, not only gives employees motivation to aspire to higher levels (and rewards those who have reached the top) but also helps customers understand the capabilities and authority of a particular employee.

Staff training at Bewley's is driven by the concept of multitasking. This has become especially important as the pool of available labor in Dublin has virtually dried up in recent years. "Instead of hiring three or four people to do a bunch of different jobs, we try to train one person to do all of them—and then pay them a lot more money," said O'Brien.

4. **Communicating to customers.** Bewley's customers are treated to an array of subtle—and not so subtle—hints of what they can expect at a Bewley's café. For instance, there's a sign at the entrance of every café that says customers can expect the staff to be friendly and helpful toward them, that the café will be clean and pleasant, and that the staff will address any problem efficiently. The message is reinforced with similar signs on tables and

counters that "give the customer the sense that, hey, these guys really want to make this nice for me," O'Brien explained. "It's a feel-good factor."

In addition, customers are alerted a week in advance to any changes that might be taking place—something that's especially important since Bewley's has a large number of regular customers. Managers also explain any changes and solicit customer reactions. The tactic is effective not only because customers appreciate the courtesy but also because their reactions to a proposed change provide a sense of whether an idea is likely to be a winner or a loser.

5. **The feedback loop.** Bewley's management believes that the only way to keep giving people what they want is to listen to customers and do what they say. The company solicits input via comment cards in all of its cafés. These cards ask for customers' thoughts on how things can be improved and encourage patrons to provide praise when appropriate. "Most comment cards can be very negative," said O'Brien. "They only encourage people to tell you when something's wrong. We thought it would be beneficial to our staff if we gave people a way to say, 'You know, I really love this' or 'Mary treated us so well on our visit.' "

The feedback from the comment cards is taken seriously by store staff and company management. A café employee praised by name is immediately rewarded by the store manager—with, say, two tickets to the cinema. For store managers, the feedback can mean the difference between a good and bad monthly evaluation. "If there's a sudden increase in comment cards in either direction, it's noted, and it affects the manager's overall scoring and evaluation," O'Brien explained. "If your comments are overly negative, it's going to make your evaluation go down, which will affect your bonus. But if the comments are very positive, you will get a better evaluation and a bigger bonus. That's the reason for giving customers a way to relate positive experiences as well as problems."

Uncompromising Product Quality

BEWLEY'S FORMULA FOR SUCCESS

SECONDARY ATTRIBUTE: PRODUCT

- Builds personal relationships between the coffee and tea buyer and the farmers/brokers around the world.
- Strictly controls the roasting and blending of the beans and tea leaves.
- Maintains an extensive tracking system to ensure consistency of blends.
- Provides café staff and corporate customers with comprehensive training on how to properly brew and serve coffee and tea.
- Rents, services, and maintains a variety of coffee machines to ensure that corporate customers are using the correct equipment.
- Conducts refresher training of café staff every three months.

Executives point out that the Bewley's experience would be nothing without the company's famous coffees and teas. Bewley's' reputation for great tea and coffee is the foundation upon which the business was built, and it's what sets Bewley's apart from its competitors. In fact, this reputation was the key factor in Bewley's favor when Campbell Catering purchased the firm in 1986. "When we bought Bewley's, it was hemorrhaging money very badly. It was about to go out of business," said Chairman Patrick Campbell. "There was very little value left in the business other than its reputation. But it was a great legacy that we knew we could build on and help bring back to life."

The quality of Bewley's coffees and teas begins in the fields of Africa, the Far East, and Central and South America, where the beans and leaves are grown. Paul O'Toole, Bewley's resident "buyer and blender," maintains strong relationships with his suppliers to ensure that he gets the highest-quality product. He visits the growers and the brokers around the world every few years to maintain a personal connection, and works closely with

Patrick Bewley, the great-grandson of the company's founder, who handles much of the responsibility for coffee buying.

All of the coffee beans and tea leaves arrive at the company's new facilities in suburban Dublin, where they are roasted and blended under controlled conditions. O'Toole maintains a detailed system for tracking the various coffee and tea blends from month to month to ensure consistency. "The Irish are the biggest tea drinkers in the world," he pointed out. "They don't always realize how good the quality of the tea they're drinking is, but they certainly know when that quality is compromised—even just a little bit."

A crucial element of the coffee-roasting process is the fact that the system is fully integrated and sealed. Such an arrangement is vital, O'Toole noted, because it helps trap the aromas of the beans as they are roasted, ensuring a higher flavor content. This process extends to the bags in which the coffee beans are packed. Rather than vacuum-packing their beans, Bewley's has designed a special package that enables the beans to remain surrounded by their aroma. "When you vacuum-pack, you're sucking all the air out of the bags, and with that, you're removing a lot of the flavor of the beans," O'Toole explained.

To ensure that the coffees and teas receive the same care once they leave the roasting-and-packing facility, Bewley's provides an array of services and guidelines for its corporate customers and cafés. For example, O'Toole and his staff maintain a training room in the headquarters facility in which café employees and customers are schooled in the basics of brewing and serving coffee and tea. The company also provides rental, maintenance, and refurbishment of coffee machines for its corporate customers.

For café employees, the training never ends. Each employee is trained every three months on the correct way to brew and serve coffee and tea—not as simple a procedure as you might think. To make a cappuccino, for instance, employees are schooled in exactly how to warm the coffee, the depth at which the frother must be in the cup to froth the milk to get a proper head, and the angle at which the cup is held when the coffee is poured. And tea should never be poured into a cup unless the cup is scalded first. ("Otherwise, the infusion isn't correct," explained O'Brien.)

"We are in the business of repeat customers," O'Brien said. "Therefore, we must make sure that every cup of coffee or tea is absolutely the best it can be. If you have eighty bags of tea, they represent eighty potential ways to satisfy customers or make them mad. If you have three hundred cups of coffee in a pot, and that pot wasn't made up to our standards, you'll have three hundred unhappy customers. So we can't, at any stage of the process, interfere with the core basic ingredients of the products, because our customers have come to expect a certain level of performance from Bewley's. If there's one thing our employees know, it's Don't mess with the tea or coffee."

The People Challenge

Although the café experience and superior product quality are the two most visible reasons for Bewley's success, the company's culture and people are equally vital, said Campbell. "Picking good people is the most important thing we do," he noted. "If we as managers pick good people, show them what we want done, and then don't meddle with them while they get on with it, we're going to be successful."

For instance, we were amazed at the passion Paul O'Toole brought to his job. He taught us how to slurp coffee and tea and spent half a day attempting to educate our proletarian palates on the subtle distinctions among blends of teas. After hours of slurping and spitting, we were convinced that there may not be anyone in the world who cares more about tea than O'Toole.

Later that afternoon, we sat with Patrick Campbell and told him about the crash course in tasting we'd received from O'Toole. "In America we'd take a guy like that and make him a media star," we told Campbell. "He'd be the perfect pitchman." "That he would be," Campbell laughed, "except for one small problem: Paul hates to talk to groups. Put six strangers in a room with him, and he'll mesmerize them with talk of tea. Put him in front of a room full of people where he can't build that one-on-one sense of intimacy, and he's much less comfortable." So, we asked, did that mean that O'Toole wouldn't rise higher in the organization? "Depends on what you mean," said Campbell. "He's compensated as though he were climbing the corporate ladder, because he's the best there is at what he does. On the other hand, I'm not going to force him to take any job where he won't be comfortable and where the company won't get the full benefit of his skills. It wouldn't be fair to him, it wouldn't be fair to us, and, in the end, it wouldn't be fair to the customers who place their faith in our products because Paul O'Toole is so vigilantly watching over the quality." We were impressed—a management model that really did seem to work *for* people.

Picking—and keeping—good people, however, is an ongoing challenge, especially as Ireland's labor market continues to tighten. Bewley's motivates and rewards its employees by offering shares in the company to those who reach their two-year anniversary. Management also hands out various awards in recognition of jobs well done. The efforts seem to be working. Campbell noted that Bewley's turnover is lower than that of most companies in its industry, and pointed to the fact that many employees have risen through the ranks. "We have a number of people who started out with us washing pots and are now running branches," he said.

In fact, one long-timer working in the company's Grafton Street café has become the most famous person at Bewley's, noted Campbell, and typifies what it means to excel in experience-based retailing. "She's been with us for fifty years—she's part of the institution, and also an institution in her own right," he said. "But do you know why she's so famous? It's because she always says hello or good morning, and she always says goodbye and thank you. It's simple stuff, really. But if we could get all our employees to do that, think how people would be talking."

Case Study

Gourmet Garage: The Rock 'n' Roll Supermarket

Gourmet Garage has carved out a special niche in the New York food world with its knack for discovering and promoting unusual food items. The retailer has created a unique environment as the self-described "rock 'n' roll supermarket" with stores that provide both the external and internal elements of experience.

The stores are high-energy and inviting: Tight aisles lead shoppers past the extensive gourmet cheese section, through the large produce area, to the prepared-foods counter. The accompanying soundtrack picked by the staff, which segues from classic Jimmy Cliff reggae to vintage John Mellencamp, is loud but appropriate. The stores' physical plants are as interesting as the products they carry. The facility on Sixty-fourth Street on the Upper East Side is a converted parking garage in the ground floor of a co-op; the flagship store in Soho is housed in an 1870s storefront with original tin ceilings and high windows; the Ninety-sixth Street site is shoe-horned into a neighborhood-defining thirty-story tower; and the Seventh Avenue store in the heart of Greenwich Village takes up an entire block in a Bauhaus-inspired 1930s-style edifice.

Complementing the physical plant and the unusual product mix is the staff. Smiles and helpful inquiries abound. In turn, the stores' customers—a diverse group ranging from thirtysomething professionals and New York University students in the Lower Manhattan stores to older, higher-income shoppers in the Sixty-fourth Street location—appear to be having fun as well.

An emphasis on reasonable prices also helps set Gourmet Garage apart from many other specialty food retailers. The company distinguishes itself as an experience-based retailer that competes on the secondary attribute of price.

The Gourmet Garage Experience

GOURMET GARAGE'S FORMULA
FOR SUCCESS

PRIMARY ATTRIBUTE: EXPERIENCE

- Passion for the business among the company leadership.
- In-store events and promotions that enhance the company's "fun, funky, and sophisticated" image.
- Rock 'n' roll soundtrack for each store.
- Unique, offbeat physical plants and storefronts.
- Interesting visual merchandising of specialty food products.
- "Diamond-in-the-rough," friendly and engaging employees.

The emphasis on experience and price is an unusual combination that has given Gourmet Garage a true competitive edge and enabled the company to post some impressive numbers. Started in 1992 in a warehouse on Wooster Street in Soho, Gourmet Garage has grown to four locations in Manhattan that generate an estimated $35 million in annual revenue. Not bad for a nine-year-old company, with no external financing, that is the brainchild of three men with widely divergent backgrounds and job experiences: Andrew Arons, chief executive officer; John Gottfried, president; and Ned Visser, chief operating officer. Arons is one of the pioneers of the specialty gourmet-food business in the United States: He started Flying Foods International in the early 1980s and eventually sold it to Kraft Foods. Gottfried is a former banker turned food editor who served as the food and wine critic for the *Village Voice* and penned occasional columns for *The New York Times, Food & Wine,* and *Travel and Leisure.* And Visser, who is trained in architecture, is a former manager of Maxwell's Plum, a famous New York bar. What brought them together? "We're foodies, not grocers," said Gottfried. "We came to this because of our passion for food. It's like someone who loves dance."

That type of passion is the single most important quality a company that competes on experience must have if it is to succeed. "When we started out, we were something really special," Arons said. "We were a destination location because we looked great against our competition such as Dean & DeLuca, which we thought were very, very overpriced at the time. We had beautiful products at great prices. Unfortunately, we really served as a spark to those merchants that had been in the business for twenty or thirty years. So we have to operate in a very organic environment in which we are willing to change and constantly innovate."

All three founders are in the stores every day, talking to customers, in an effort to continue to clearly define what separates Gourmet Garage from its competitors and to maintain its relevance to shoppers. Arons likens the exercise to a musician jamming with other musicians: "When you're playing the guitar, you have to listen to what's entering your ears and make sure that what goes out through your fingers is relevant to what's coming in."

The passion of the founders is one thing, but having that passion rub off on employees is another. Arons admits that finding the right people is difficult due to the combination of the tight New York labor market and the wages that Gourmet Garage must pay to remain competitive. "We look for people we call 'diamonds in the rough,' " he said. "These are inner-city people who have some very important qualities but who just need the right situation for them to come through. We look for the intelligence in their eyes, their smiles, a sense of humor—things that would enable them to function well as a top executive in a corporation were it not for the fact that they didn't have the opportunities that others have had. If they have these raw characteristics, we can train them and have some amazing results."

One such success story is Martin Nunez, a store manager, who was initially a produce stocker making $6.50 an hour. Now, according to Arons, he's a "hotshot store manager who just lives for the place." Nunez, who often comes into the store on his day off—"just to make sure things are right"—now earns enough to provide a comfortable living for his family and put away money to send his children to college.

Gourmet Garage's efforts to create a strong store experience are paying off in the form of positive dynamics between employees and customers. "Because our business is very residential-oriented, we have the same people coming into the same stores all the time," said Gottfried. "As a result, the cashiers have their own favorite customers, and vice versa, and shoppers will line up for their favorite checkout person. It's amazing. But because you have the same people coming in, you have to reinvent the store every day to keep the experience fresh."

At this point, Gourmet Garage's employee-training program comprises a standard employee-training package from the Food Marketing Institute, a Washington, D.C.–based industry trade association; an employee handbook; and a walk around the store. However, Arons said that he hopes someday to open "Garage University" to bring a more formal and comprehensive approach to employee initiation.

The company also strongly relies on promotional activities to help reinforce the store experience. A key belief at Gourmet Garage is "A dollar spent on public relations is worth $1,000 of advertising." So communications with journalists is fundamental to creating the company's continuing image as a pioneer and source of information on new foods. The company's

PR activities are built around a series of in-store events that extend the "fun, funky, and sophisticated" image that the company projects and support Gourmet Garage's strong identification with the professional chefs who comprise a significant portion of the customer base. For instance, in conjunction with the local National Public Radio affiliate each year, Gottfried arranges a weeklong series of in-store cooking appearances by celebrity chefs, many of whom are nationally known.

"It's very important that we create an environment where customers feel they are getting something of value and are being cared for," Gottfried said. "It's not a one-way relationship. In the case of the chefs' series, yes, it's great PR, but it also is educational for our customers. They learn from the pros how to shop and cook like a chef, and oh, by the way, we've got the food and ingredients that the chefs use."

The Budget Gourmet

GOURMET GARAGE'S FORMULA FOR SUCCESS

SECONDARY ATTRIBUTE: PRICE

- Special relationship with Metro Agri, a wholesale food business owned by two of the owners of Gourmet Garage.
- Active and successful private-label program.
- Centralized kitchen that helps serve as a value-added clearinghouse for products that may not sell in the stores.
- "Warehouse" look of the stores.
- Focus on promotion through low-cost public relations instead of big-budget advertising campaigns.

While Gourmet Garage's primary emphasis is on crafting the rock 'n' roll experience, there is a strong secondary focus on price. The company makes a concerted effort to offer innovative, high-quality items at affordable prices. The strategy is not without its challenges. For instance, the company's size tends to limit its purchasing clout with vendors. So how does a four-store specialty food retailer compete on price against larger outlets such as A&P's Food Emporium and Fairway, whose economies of scale and mass-market appeal give them greater buying power?

Arons, Gottfried, and Visser cite a number of factors that help them maintain their price points. The first is the unique relationship that Gourmet Garage has with its primary supplier, Metropolitan Agribusiness. Metro Agri is a wholesaler of meats, cheeses, produce, and ingredients to 200 New York restaurants. What makes the relationship special is the fact that Gottfried and Arons also own Metro Agri, giving Gourmet Garage affordable access to the products that many of the city's chefs use. In fact, Gourmet Garage is a direct outgrowth of Metro Agri. "John had founded Metro Agri and had a very successful wholesale business going," Arons recalled. "I approached him with the idea that we should open a retail outlet that was sort of a 'Costco meets Dean & DeLuca.' He bought into it, so we opened the doors to the public in November 1992, and 2,000 people showed up the first day. Since then, we have focused primarily on the retail side but still kept the wholesale business running as well. Wholesale is fun, but retail is COD, which means cash flow is much better."

Metro Agri is not Gourmet Garage's sole supplier. Other vendors compete with Metro Agri for the business, and each store is free to order from other vendors if a better deal is found. "If Metro Agri's price is equal to or better than another vendor's, then that's who they go with, but if the price or quality or reliability is better at another supplier, the store buys from them," said Gottfried. In the case of produce, 80 percent of the company's fruits and vegetables are bought and delivered directly from farms in California, which helps ensure quality and eliminates the middleman.

Another facet of Gourmet Garage's business that helps keep costs down is the private-label program, which is marketed under the distinctive Gourmet Garage logo. Private-label items comprise approximately 20 percent of Gourmet Garage's product mix but 50 percent of total sales, which translates into a solid profit. The company is vigilant about quality because of the important role that private label plays in its operation and the need to maintain the strong equity in the Gourmet Garage brand. Gottfried likes to think of Gourmet Garage as the "buying agent" for its customers, helping them find quality products at affordable prices. "We try to represent our customers when we look for items," Gottfried said. "We've pared down 60,000 potential SKUs to somewhere around 5,000. We preselect products for customers, and do the legwork for them. But we preselect with the best, not the mass market."

Gourmet Garage's centralized kitchen also contributes to the company's low-cost structure. The 5,000-square-foot facility, which operates sixteen hours a day and produces 3,000 to 4,000 prepared meals daily, is worth several million dollars a year in revenue. Its operation in the basement of one of the stores translates into low overhead, and its ability to serve as a value-added clearinghouse for items that may not sell in the stores helps turn what would otherwise be waste into profitable products. "Fruits and vegetables have to be ripe, but if they are too ripe—less than a day's worth of shelf life—they won't survive delivery to the home," Gottfried said.

The look and feel of Gourmet Garage's stores—essentially a warehouse-type model, featuring cut-cases and industrial fixtures and plumbing—does double duty in the company's strategy. The utilitarian design and decor contributes to the in-store experience and is less expensive than a high-end presentation. Arons believes that the stores' "complete lack of pretentiousness" is a huge strength. "Our format really reads as honesty for shoppers," he said. "People know that they're not paying for polished brass fixtures or fancy Italian marble, and they know they're not getting ripped off by our prices."

Finally, because of the focus on lower prices, Gourmet Garage doesn't run big-budget advertising campaigns. Instead, the company focuses on public relations. Gottfried notes that such a strategy is far less expensive and more effective than advertising, and capitalizes on his media relationships. The company's PR efforts result in continual mentions in food columns and articles in the New York and national press, and even helped land a gem that any business would covet: three hours as the backdrop for television's *Good Morning New York.*

Future Challenges

If Arons, Gottfried, and Visser have their way, New Yorkers won't be the only people enjoying the rock 'n' roll supermarket. The company has ambitious expansion plans, hoping to open its first stores outside Manhattan shortly, probably in neighboring New Jersey. Because its reputation and product line lend themselves to the Internet, the company plans to eventually take its concept nationwide and even worldwide via the Web. The founders recognize the myriad challenges that come with such a move, particularly ensuring that the Gourmet Garage experience translates well to other markets. Many retailers have found it difficult or even impossible to maintain a particular experience on a larger scale.

Gottfried acknowledges that understanding the different consumer bases in new markets, learning what they want, and developing the appropriate logistics infrastructure to serve those shoppers will be difficult. But he also believes that the challenges are surmountable. The most difficult challenge, and one key to the success of the company's expansion, will be finding the types of buildings that fit the Gourmet Garage philosophy and turning those spaces—an old train station, a former courthouse, or an abandoned police barracks, for example—into successful stores. It will require equal parts hard work, location, and magic, Gottfried pointed out.

"There is something about entering any physical space that makes it either sympathetic to people or not, and it cannot be totally planned," said Gottfried. "My father used to say that people enter a store and try to find a reason *not* to buy. If you can build a space that creates a positive attitude in people, sort of, 'Hey, what can I find in here?', then you've done it right. The problem is, it's not reducible to a formula. There's only one way to do it, and that's roll the dice."

SELF-DIAGNOSTIC: EXPERIENCE

- Are your employees trained to demonstrate respect in all their interactions with customers, and do your human-resource measures and metrics reinforce that training?
- How do you show your customers that you actually care about them?
- Do you have the kind of knowledge you need to be meaningfully intimate—as opposed to being intrusive or feigning intimacy—with your customers?
- Do you offer your customers something they simply can't get from anyone else?
- Do you have a sense of your customers' broader needs and concerns, or is your knowledge of their lives confined to their purchasing behavior?

CHAPTER 8

Making Consumer
Relevancy Work

As we've demonstrated, Consumer Relevancy is a process that aligns business operations and offerings to new or targeted markets and moves them forward over time. So how do you do it? What does it take to develop the Relevancy strategy and build the infrastructure that facilitates it? Every Relevancy application is unique, but the operational process remains the same across a wide range of industries and enterprises. It begins when a company—using the Relevancy framework—assesses how its offerings are defined by its customers, the mass market of potential consumers, its management, employees, and, in some cases, supply-chain partners.

If you think your company might need a little Relevancy, try this experiment: Ask your senior managers to take out a blank sheet of paper and write down which of the five attributes (access, experience, price, product, service) you dominate in. Now ask them to write down a second attribute they believe you're differentiated on. Finally, ask them to list any of the three remaining attributes on which they believe you're failing to at least meet your direct competitors. If you have perfect alignment in the responses and nobody has suggested that you're below market par in your performance on any of the attributes, conduct the same test with some of your front-line employees. Now try your spouse, your family, and your neighbors. If everyone agrees, congratulations, you're probably doing a great job. If they don't agree, you are a candidate for Relevancy.

Assuming you're prepared to concede that Relevancy *might* be for you, it's time for the next step. Start by conducting a survey of enough customers to ensure a broad base of respondents to find out how existing customers view your company and competitors, and where they would place all of the companies on a Relevancy matrix. We had one client who discovered that his customers had a much broader sense of the competitive set than he did. While he was worried about three direct competitors, our initial research discovered that his "loyal" customers regularly shopped at more than a dozen firms, nine of which he refused to even acknowledge as viable competition.

The next step is to move beyond your existing customers, taking a similar survey instrument out to consumers (who may or may not be your customers), again with enough range to ensure statistical validity. If you operate across multiple consumer bases, we advise augmenting the survey with several geographically and demographically dispersed focus groups, which will provide additional filters for understanding the survey results. As in the case of the customer survey, the objective is to plot a matrix of how consumers see you and your competitors.

The next step is to conduct a similar internal survey asking your key managers to identify your company's, and your competition's, primary and secondary Relevancy attributes. Once again, this exercise should be followed up with interviews to help round out management's perspective. Similar surveys and interviews should be conducted with a wide cross-section of employees, from the corporate office to field locations. In some cases, it may also help to conduct the exercise with vendors and other trading partners.

Once you've gathered all these perspectives, the combined results should be mapped on a Relevancy matrix. This provides a quick visual representation of your key stakeholders' alignment—or lack thereof.

There is tremendous power in this exercise, which large businesses can perform in six weeks, smaller businesses in two. This power comes from identifying gaps between various constituents. A business that does not have alignment experiences value leakage, which occurs anytime a business system under-delivers against a corporate value proposition.

Invariably, our client work surfaces these misalignments, even among members of the key executive team. We've actually refereed some near-fistfights in executive boardrooms—these discussions can be very emotional as the functional heads of a business champion the dominance and importance of their area of responsibility.

This isn't to say that you don't want your HR director to be world-class in his or her recruitment practices or your CFO to exercise world-class financial modeling, but it is to say that you don't want them to think that labor-cost control is the most critical element in a company attempting to dominate on service.

Letting departmental responsibility get confused with market offering is the first step on the slippery path to the myth of excellence. The effective leader of new product development may be doing an excellent job running his or her department while being at industry par in product. The same holds true for the store-operations executive who keeps labor costs way below industry average while remaining at par in service. All executives need to understand that a disproportionate amount of corporate resources should be devoted to the functional areas that reinforce the company's dominant or differentiating attributes in the consumers' minds. This requires the entire executive team to be on the same page, which is rarely the case. As individuals, most good executives strive to be world-class in their functional area, often confusing functionality with market positioning, and will fight tooth and nail for resources and capital. Many executive "teams" operate this way, with the predictable outcome being that the company ends up world-class at nothing—poorly differentiated and therefore not thought of by consumers at the moment of need. These teams have been seduced by the myth of excellence, and their lack of alignment sends mixed signals to employees and customers.

The results of this misalignment are never pretty. "I'd say our real strength is pricing," one CEO told us. "We used to have a price-impression problem years ago, but we've fixed all that." The next day, the company's

HR director told us, "I think pricing is still an issue. I make great money, and I'm loyal, but I still shop the competition for some of the items we carry. Money or no money, loyalty or no loyalty, I just can't bring myself to pay these kinds of prices." We secured that job, and when our work was finished, it was clear the target market sided more with the head of HR than with the CEO.

Once an executive team comes to alignment on its primary and secondary attributes, it can compare how various stakeholders perceive it versus how it would like to be perceived. If executives have one perspective and store management and/or store employees another, the firm may have both a communications and a reward-and-measurement problem. If there is misalignment between management and potential customers, advertising and marketing problems exist. Store operations and advertising are suspects if there isn't agreement between current customers and potential customers. We are reminded of a very successful client that had a wonderful market position as a product/experience company. Butchers in the meat department, fresh sushi made in the store, a wonderful wine selection complete with a sommelier, a humidor stocked with expensive cigars, and gourmet cooking classes. Yet every week, the front cover of the store's advertising circular screamed:

Coca-Cola twelve-packs
$1.89
Limit three
or
Tropicana Pure Premium 64 oz.
$2.49
Limit two

Clearly, a disconnect existed between the company's perceived value proposition and its customer communications. Disconnects between executives and store employees are indicative of training and education problems, while gaps between management and supplier assessments always mean there is value being lost in the supply chain.

Suppliers have the ability to adjust their offer—whether in terms of pricing, promotion, advertising, replenishment, or physical distribution—to align with channel partners' consumer-value propositions. Dollar General understands this. It approached Procter & Gamble to see if P&G could find a way to offer Dawn dishwashing liquid at a price point consistent with the retailer's "extreme value" proposition. That inquiry resulted in P&G (which has a strict policy of offering transparent and equivalent pricing to all its customers) creating a special smaller package of its non-concentrated formula that could be sold at a price point consistent with Dollar General's market position. The bottom line: With the exception of Wal-Mart, Dollar General is the world's largest Dawn retailer.

Asking suppliers to hit precise price points, even when it requires modifications in standard package sizes or formulation, allows Dollar General to remain true to its business model. At the same time, its partnership and alignment with manufacturers adds real consumer value while increasing sales for all trading partners.

Substantial differences between self-perception and market perception foster individual executive rationalization, which in turn leads to collective corporate denial. Brand degradation and loss of market share inevitably follow. It's a pattern of corporate behavior practiced by American automakers in the 1970s, organized labor in the 1980s, and regional mass merchandisers in the 1990s.

Recently, we worked with a company whose market share had been in steady decline for five straight years. Puzzled by the steady loss of customers and sales, we performed a Consumer Relevancy assessment and found significant misalignments around the price and product attributes between management on one side and employees, customers, and consumers on the other. Given the company's historical market position, we weren't too surprised by the misalignment on the pricing attribute, but the product finding surprised all of us. After all, this company had just expanded its in-store inventory by more than 100 percent and offered what was objectively the highest quality and greatest product variety and selection available. Further assessment revealed several critical problems. First, many customers were overwhelmed and confused by the increased variety. Second, the new products were drowning out the local products customers knew and loved. And finally, while the new products were of high quality, in many cases they simply weren't appropriate or relevant to the existing customer base. The result: Customers told us they no longer felt comfortable in the stores. Our client has taken steps to address both the price and product perception issues, and is regaining customers.

The alignment assessment also gives companies a chance to measure their progress with respect to any attribute as often as they like with any or all constituents. Consumer Relevancy is modular. It should be used holistically to set strategy, but it can also be exercised in pieces when attempting to measure tactical progress.

Conducting an alignment assessment inevitably forces companies to face a series of critical decisions, beginning with the reinforcement or reselection of primary and secondary market attributes, decisions with far-reaching impacts on the business. You may find you're well positioned—competing on attributes that your customers and consumers in general value. If that's the case, the prospects for future success are solid, and you should focus your attention on prioritizing and implementing operational improvements that support your current position. However, if instead you're watching customers defect to competitors, direct or indirect, and your prospects for future success are questionable, it's time to consider competing on different primary or secondary attributes.

A word of caution here: The decision to change a primary attribute is risky and should only be undertaken with great caution. Over time, brands such as Kmart, Holiday Inn, Buick, Sears, TWA, JCPenney, and dozens of others have struggled because consumers didn't adjust to their changing value propositions. It is easier, and less risky, to change your differentiating attribute, especially when your dominant attribute remains constant. A product-dominant retailer can change its differentiating emphasis from price to experience, as Best Buy did, or a product-dominant company can move its differentiation point from price to service, as Home Depot did.

Switching your dominant attribute is hard, for several reasons. First, today's consumers are extremely skeptical and cautious, requiring constant communication, relentless policy execution, and patience. Second, the operational implications of switching are hard on employees, who, like the population at large, are generally change-averse. Third, such a move almost always involves a short-term decline in financial performance, as both the market and the organization adjust. For all public companies and most others, this is increasingly hard to do.

Still, there are times when shifting your dominance attribute is exactly the right thing to do. Gordon Bethune changed the fortunes of Continental by reorienting the company to focus on service. Evian became one of the dominant brands in the bottled-water category when it focused on making its product more accessible. RadioShack has successfully migrated from a price-dominant to a product-dominant retailer, probably—given the strong growth in Internet electronics retailing—just in the nick of time.

The hard work begins once these kinds of macro-decisions have been made. Consumer Relevancy is not a magic bullet. It involves making the strategic choices we've outlined and then moving into highly customized implementations. That said, there are a couple of general rules that apply.

First, when making priority tradeoffs, emphasize those activities that bring all your attribute activities at least to par. Every day that you are not meeting customers' minimum criteria on all five attributes, your brand is being damaged. Second, you have to know both what you're not and what you are. Consumer Relevancy is all about making choices. No organization can be great at everything; all executives must be aligned; and resource decisions must be made in a manner that ensures that the majority of resources, time, and effort go to those areas that will strengthen an agreed-upon value proposition.

Dollar General doesn't have a frequent-shopper program, nor does it advertise—these are expensive activities inconsistent with its price/access position. Wal-Mart doesn't attempt to create an industry-leading experience for its customers; instead, it invests in supply-chain systems and infrastructure that allow it to relentlessly drive down net landed cost. Orvis isn't trying to gain mass distribution, and if it did, it would dilute its products' cachet among fly fishermen. And we doubt you'll see VF Corp.'s Wrangler brand on the high-fashion runways of Paris anytime soon.

That's the top-line look at Consumer Relevancy, but every senior-level executive knows that process maps and theory rarely translate directly into results. In fact, we've added more qualitative elements to most of the Relevancy applications, our own participant anthropology—everything from shopping with customers to actually "becoming" customers by anonymously using an offering. We've discussed businesses over drinks and dinner and spent untold numbers of hours just walking around. We've struck up conversations on airplanes and at ball games, and the results have verified what the research told us. Alignment is the critical first step in moving from offering transactions to establishing relationships, from value addition to the addition of values.

The Human Side of Relevancy

As we stated earlier, there isn't a standard approach to Consumer Relevancy. Like a mechanic's toolbox, Relevancy contains a set of tools and methods for tuning up a business. And the most important of those are human resources. Human resources are the secret weapon in the Relevancy war: Companies whose human-resource pools "get" the Relevancy message are companies that win. In an age characterized by regulatory human-resource constraints and employee free agentry, when loyalty often counts for little to nothing, human resources are critical to domination on any attribute. In fact, without the right people in place, it's all but impossible to effectively differentiate your business on any attribute.

For instance, a business competing on experience needs to hire people with a passion for its mission. The success of experience-oriented companies as diverse as Southwest Airlines, BMW, and the Ritz-Carlton Hotel Co. hinges in large part on positive interaction between employees and customers. Employees in an experience-dominant business are responsible for executing the company's culture, since they have a direct impact on customers' impressions and memories. In these companies, compensation and performance measures generally emphasize feedback from customers, as well as observations by management on how employees handle customer interactions—both positive and contentious.

By contrast, companies competing on product must have employees who can intelligently speak about those products: what they are, how they're used, and how they work. This characterizes firms like Williams-Sonoma, The Home Depot, and Best Buy and is most critical for businesses whose products are complex (consumer electronics), expensive (automobiles), or trendy (recorded music and fashion). Compensation should be based on work experience with related products, and should reward continuing education. Rewards and performance measures generally are based on demonstrated merchandise knowledge and customer feedback.

It's generally true that price-dominant companies from Dollar General to Red Roof Inn need to expend fewer absolute dollars per unit of sale than, say, service- or experience-dominant companies. As a result, they often focus on recruiting "diamonds in the rough," smart individuals with good people skills who can be easily trained and motivated. Often these individuals are recruited for part-time work from specific hiring pools (working mothers, housewives, teenagers, and retirees). Price-dominant players are looking for disciplined individuals comfortable with working in an environment of standardized processes and procedures.

Of course, there are exceptions to this model. We remember spending time with the head of a night-stocking crew of a major Canadian retailer. The crew boss was retiring after almost thirty years of service, and his average crew member had more than twenty years with the company. Needless to say, with that much seniority, the crew was at the top of the employer's pay scale for hourly workers. But they also were the most productive stocking crew (measured in terms of standard performance and the absence of negatives such as absenteeism and shrink) in the company, clearly providing good labor dollar value even at a fairly high price.

But such exceptions aside, as a general rule of thumb most price operators' reward-and-measurement systems should be based on a handful of relatively simple and easily understood measures, focused on compliance to a clearly communicated, repetition-based standard of performance. This emphasis on process and repetition is a hallmark of most well-run, large price-dominant companies. Employees who thrive in a price-dominant company might not feel comfortable in a product or experience culture, and vice versa. Again, we need to invoke the earlier caveat about employees like seniors and housewives who may be drawn to price-dominant companies because of flexible hours, liberal hiring policies, and frequent hiring cycles (retention often being a problem in such companies). The psychology and success model of price-dominant companies is unique, and so they must develop the ability to understand the success predictors of their model, and hire against them.

Access-dominant companies make things easy and convenient for their customers, as well as solving problems and creating solutions for them. This requires employees who are sensitive to the specific sales and service demands of their environment, with the interest and ability to resolve problems and suggest total solutions. Tide, Gerber, and Gatorade's call centers are staffed with people trained to easily answer consumer questions regarding product usage and suggest solutions to customers having a crisis related to fabric care, infant nutrition, or hydration. Kozmo.com and Circles' employees need a passion for making deadlines and derive satisfaction from solving their customers' problems—whether it's a late-night beer delivery, finding low-fat grocery products, or booking a hotel room in New York during Christmas week. Access-dominant companies need to find reward and recognition metrics that encourage independence, creativity, and an eye for deadlines and details.

Service-dominant companies face perhaps the most critical hiring, training, and retention challenges, because they need people with great interaction and communication skills. Working on this book, we often marveled at how service-dominant companies from Lands' End and Allstate to Citibank and Dell—which draw from exactly the same labor pool other companies do—manage to find people who apparently love what they do. Their employees communicate enthusiasm and seem to adjust their companies' offering on the fly at the point of customer interaction. Employees at service-dominant companies must be accommodating, not intrusive; capable of learning and communicating their learning; and capable of crafting real-time, customized decisions. Their reward-and-measurement systems should be grounded in continuing education on product or service, as well as direct customer feedback and satisfaction measures. Great employees at service-dominant companies are often higher-paid than their peers at price- or access-dominant companies. But like workers at product- and experience-dominant companies, best-of-class service workers must share a passion for their company's mission and vision and may forgo some direct compensation in favor of "psychic income."

Where Leadership Comes In

Of course, no army—no matter how skilled or well-equipped—can win without a strong general. As in all corporate change initiatives, the importance of the role of the leader simply can't be overestimated. Understanding Consumer Relevancy's importance, continuing to emphasize its importance, and being able to command the resources necessary to ensure its success aren't the same thing. If you as a leader don't deliver a clear Relevancy message, live the implications of that message, and make sure all your employees understand how they help deliver on that message, your company will never become Relevant.

Good leaders are hard to find. Consider this story about Joe Antonini, the former chairman, president, and CEO of Kmart. Several years ago, at a student-sponsored business forum at Western Michigan University, Antonini gave a presentation full of excitement about Kmart's future, punctuated at about every third sentence with a reference to Wal-Mart. During the question-and-answer portion of the presentation, a little gray-haired lady stood up in the back of the room and said, "Mr. Antonini, I thought you were the chairman of Kmart." He laughed and replied, "I am, madam. I'm the chairman, president, CEO, and COO." Looking a bit confused, the lady said, "Well, all through your speech, you talked about Wal-Mart." Antonini shot back, "Yes, that's right. I compared us to them because they're our biggest competitor." Without hesitating, the lady pressed on: "Exactly what is it that makes Wal-Mart so effective at competing against you?" The room suddenly fell into total silence. No one seemed to breathe as Antonini took two full minutes—an eternity on a stage—to respond. "I'd say that Wal-Mart's greatest asset is the fact that we're their biggest competitor."

Clearly, Joe didn't get what the little old lady intuitively understood. Wal-Mart was doing something different, starting with Sam Walton's true genius—getting ordinary people to do extraordinary things. Under Antonini, Kmart believed it was doing the right things and refused to change, while Walton always said, "This is okay. This is great for what we're doing this year. But we need to do it differently next year." Indeed, to Joe Antonini's detriment, Sam Walton succeeded in getting his company to refine its execution against its basic strategy, year after year.

Walton did everything possible to push the company in the right direction. He believed in consistency, so everyone knew what Wal-Mart was supposed to deliver to its customers, and everyone delivered. He believed in accountability, so everyone was on the spot to deliver on Wal-Mart's promises, and he checked up on them. He believed in communication, so (before the rise of the Internet) a satellite system brought the news to the organization in real time, and everyone knew what the management team knew. He believed in profit sharing, so all employees had an opportunity to share in the company's success.

Wal-Mart's management know it is not enough to dictate goals—you have to teach every single employee how his job and responsibility align with the company's goals. This requires an obsession with, and command of, the details of the operation and an ability to deliver a clear, consistent message and philosophy to the entire company over and over again.

Above all, it's vital that corporate leaders understand that Consumer Relevancy can be sustained and transferred from one leader to another and from one part of the company to another. Wal-Mart has successfully exported its philosophy to Mexico and other places around the globe.

Making Better Pancakes

One last point about putting Consumer Relevancy into practice. We were in Amsterdam working with a group of senior executives. It was our first real work session utilizing Consumer Relevancy, and we were struggling to articulate the principles and get complete, mutual understanding. It had been a hard day and with jet lag, language barrier challenges, the heat in the room, and the difficulty of achieving alignment, everyone was tired and a little frustrated.

At around 6 P.M., a senior executive sat back in his chair and said, "I now understand Consumer Relevancy. I get the difference between product value and human values, between content and context. My problem is that I agree with everything you say, because all of this stuff has been around since the dawn of commerce. If I get you right, the ingredients haven't changed, it's the recipe. We're still using the same stuff, but we need to emphasize some things more and some things less. It's like making pancakes. Sometimes you use a little more egg to make them rise; sometimes you use a little more milk to make them thin. You always use the same stuff, but the mixture changes depending on what you're trying to achieve. Do I get it?"

He did.

CHAPTER 9

Supply-Chain Realities

SOMETIMES MYTHS COLLIDE, and when they do, gods who have been worshiped for generations are often unceremoniously dumped from their heavenly perches. It happened when the Greek gods clashed and fell to the gods of the Romans, and it happens every day to less divine presences in the marketplace when the myths of excellence of suppliers come face to face with those of the distributors.

The difficulties that manufacturers or resellers experience trying to align against real consumer values are compounded when their offering is directly influenced by trading partners' business practices. More often than not, the values of either side of a transaction are overshadowed by some quality of the other side's market positioning. Resellers of high-end goods—from luxury-car dealerships to specialty electronics retailers—would have inherent difficulty trying to dominate their market spaces on price-oriented values. By the same token, the temptation to at least attempt to differentiate their businesses around product-oriented value claims might prove all but impossible to resist. On the other hand, manufacturers of fast-moving consumer packaged-goods from paper towels to canned vegetables often find their products positioned on the basis of price and/or access value propositions, regardless of product quality or efficacy.

The final outcomes of the subtle and delicate relationship between a product, brand, or service and its resellers or channels of distribution are critical to forming consumers' value and Relevancy perceptions. This relationship is brokered every day in the streets, with manufacturers pressing product efficacy and marketing information on one side and retailers and other resellers leveraging their direct interface with the consumer and shelf space on the other. While manufacturers remain the primary authors of the content aspect of a transaction, it is the retailer who, more often than not, exerts dominant influence over its context.

This isn't particularly good news for manufacturers targeting mass distribution markets. By virtue of their control of the point-of-sale interface, reselling channels hold more and more sway with consumers. Therefore, it becomes increasingly more important for manufacturers to find ways to build effective relationships directly with consumers. This is easier said than done, since resellers want to retain exclusive ownership of the consumer relationship and the data associated with that relationship. Still, some manufacturers such as Krispy Kreme, Patagonia, and Gateway are having success as hybrids, acting in effect as both supplier and retailer. But more branded giants are struggling with slow real growth, market-share declines, and capital flight to more attractive sectors.

We know consumers value simplicity, clarity, speed, and ease of transaction over disorienting efficacy claims, warring marketing slogans, and exploding line extensions. These consumer values are inherently difficult for manufacturers to build directly into a piece of furniture, a diaper, or an engine. It is much easier for resellers to build and express these values into the context in which products are sold.

This helps explain the rise of private-label products in the consumer packaged-goods industry. Today, store brands are a $50 billion business in the food, drug, and mass-merchandising channels, up from $30 billion in 1996, according to the Private Label Manufacturers Association and Information Resources Inc. Their market share has also grown. Store brands accounted for more than 20 percent of unit sales and almost 16 percent of dollar volume in supermarkets in 1999, compared with 18.6 percent of units and about 14 percent of dollars in 1995.

This isn't to say that brands aren't still a big business across the planet. Even in China, which operates under controlled market rules, the Haier Group's Haier brand of household appliances increased in value by $1.58 billion from 1994 to 1999, paralleling similar growth among other Chinese brands. Lianxiang Group's Legend brand of computers increased in value by $1.55 billion during the period; TCL Group's TCL brand of televisions increased $1.31 billion; Sichuan Changhong Electronic Group's Changhong (electronics goods) brand increased $98 million; and Konka Group's Konka brand of televisions appreciated $75 million over the five years.

The competitive advantages of controlling both sides of a transaction help explain the success of retailer-controlled brands such as the Gap's denim lines, and Gateway going direct to consumers, and exclusive marketing agreements between a manufacturer and reseller such as Kmart and Martha Stewart. Branded manufacturers that ignore the power of vertical integration do so at great peril.

Conventional supply-chain wisdom relies on tools that simply fail to address the realities of the modern market—especially the reality of who the new consumers are and what they want and demand from business. For example, longitudinal demographic and sales data have historically formed the basis of many companies' short- and long-range marketing, merchandising, and advertising plans. But Consumer Relevancy demands more. It requires another layer of information, one that provides context in addition to traditional content and that allows us to look at end users not in the traditional demographic terms we've always used to measure them, but in new ways—grouped by values and their affinity toward one of the five Relevancy attributes.

The lessons learned from Consumer Relevancy ought to force all supply-chain partners to look beyond transactions to motivation and behavior. For example, one project we worked on ultimately grouped seniors and teenagers as a cohort for a reseller of multimedia entertainment products and other durable goods. Both age groups were looking for the same set of characteristics (not being rushed, a comfortable place to meet friends, coffee and snacks, easy-to-find information on artists), yet they obviously wanted very different products and a very different environmental look and feel. And somewhat ironically, both cohorts wanted something installed in that environment the retailer hadn't thought of—couches! We assume teenagers and senior citizens use couches in different ways, but both cohorts felt couches would have improved their total experience with the retailer. Ultimately, this work impacted the layout and design of the store, with a central snacking area that served both ends of the store, one of which was configured for Generation Y, the other for the sixtysomething set. Sadly, to date at least, there still aren't any couches in the stores. In this case, we discovered not just what products consumers wanted but the kind of environment in which they wanted to make their purchases. This approach has profound implications for issues as diverse as trading-partner selection and allocation of marketing and promotional dollars, advertising, and consumer services. Our families, forced to endure more than two years of nonstop badgering about what they and their friends think about this advertisement or that service, now actually laugh out loud at the stream of product feature and function advertising. "What about service?" they ask. "Why is it that if I call the 800 number before 9 A.M. or after 4 P.M. I get a recording?" "I called to ask about a product of theirs and where to buy it, and their only response was to tell me to ask the manager at the store where I shop to order it." From our perspective, most companies spend way too much on advertising and way too little on consumer services.

In 1999 advertisers in the United States spent $215 billion trying to influence consumer opinion through messages placed everywhere from the Yellow Pages to public restrooms, a 6.8 percent increase over 1998 spending levels, according to Robert J. Coen, senior vice president and director of forecasting for Interpublic's Universal McCann. And as this book was going to press, it was estimated that advertising spending might increase an additional 8.3 percent by the end of the year 2000, reaching the $233 billion level. Yet by any objective measure, that spending is increasingly less and less effective. Why? Because the core message of most advertising is focused on price and product features and functions, rather than the development of a balanced message of content and context. Too much advertising is concerned with creating transactions rather than building relationships and emphasizes value over values. In short, it mirrors all of the mistakes being made by most businesses.

This mistake is multiplied by every step a business is removed from the ultimate consumer. As a result, almost all manufacturers and suppliers run the risk of becoming less and less relevant to consumers over time. Consumer Relevancy ought to drive manufacturers to do two things: first, to adjust the message of their advertising to reflect a better balance between content and context; and second, to focus more resources and effort on building consumer-defined values-based relationships with target customers.

This is clearly seen in the area of new-product development. Endless added features, new and improved formulations, concentrates and blends, functions added just because they can be, and the other tricks of covering a lack of real innovation with the veneer of newness aren't appreciated by consumers and often contribute to their confusion. Companies are well advised to confine their new-product development to concepts that offer true—consumer-defined—innovation, address real consumer needs, or offer perceptible consumer benefits. For Dell, RadioShack, Compaq, or Acer, this might mean offering consumer training courses.

Some manufacturers intuitively recognize this principle. BMW clearly understands the power of marrying content and context. The company offers its best customers the opportunity to put their high-end cars—and equivalent models from other manufacturers—through a series of high-performance tests. These tests serve two purposes. First, from a content point of view, they establish BMW as world-class, high-performance vehicles. And second, from the standpoint of context, pre-qualified car enthusiasts get to spend a day doing controlled spinouts, bending the cars through obstacle courses, going into full lock-ups at 70 miles per hour, and testing the limits of their skills, clearly adding to the "BMW experience."

For food companies like Kraft, Kellogg's, Kroger, Ahold, and Del Monte, this might mean offering nutritional counseling or sponsoring mobile cooking schools. Many companies attempt to use the Internet as a vehicle for blending content and context. Kraft's website (www.

kraftfoods.com) attempts to establish a form of online community for harried mothers and other people interested in simple, quick meal preparation. Procter & Gamble's Tide website (www.tide.com) helps consumers find the closest Tide retailer to their homes as well as solve individual fabric-care problems. As of this writing, neither site offers the opportunity to join a chat room, but we think both could be improved—from a context point of view—by creating an opportunity for consumer interaction.

Consumer Relevancy can also be used to help organizations move past new-product development into areas as diverse as brand strategic positioning to enterprise-level brand portfolio management.

The same questions haunt all companies, whether in Asia, Europe, or the Americas. For manufacturers, these questions include "Should the spending on either a high-end or low-end brand be discontinued, allowing for the development of value-added services for the brands that are relevant for a larger market?" and "Is a given high-potential brand deserving of more resources than a so-called corporate heritage brand long associated with the company but failing for several years?" In other words, should Procter & Gamble have supported Pringles during decades of underwhelming sales, or should Kraft have retained ownership of its Kraft Caramel brand? The answers aren't always obvious.

In our first example, Pringles has finally become a robust and profitable brand, largely because consumers' attitudes toward snacking have changed—in no small part thanks to the existence of brands like Pringles. In the Kraft example, as much as consumers loved those little caramels, they loved them only at certain times of the year, making it difficult for Kraft to justify keeping them in its brand portfolio. In a parallel example, should a global company like DaimlerChrysler keep the majority of its R&D funding tied up developing new fuel-efficient minicars for the developing world rather than designing expensive high-performance sports cars for luxury buyers?

Retailers face questions such as "Should I trade promotional allowances for more effective, consumer-friendly, in-store assortment?" and "How do I match the brands I offer to the consumers I serve?" So should Wal-Mart, for example, promote its own laundry detergent and make better gross margins, or should it promote Tide? Should Williams-Sonoma stock Calphalon cookware only, or should it also stock Revere Ware?

Consumer Relevancy also has broad impact in the area of trading-partner selection, especially at a time when the environment in which a product is offered is at least as important as the product itself. As we noted in Chapter 1, Gitano jeans were once moderately high-fashion wear prior to being introduced into Kmart. Maybe channel selection wasn't the only cause of Gitano's fall from fashion grace, but June 12, 2000, when VF Corp. paid a bankrupt Fruit of the Loom $18 million for Gitano's trademarks and inventory, had to be a sad day for brand watchers with long memories.

When you look at categories as diverse as carbonated beverages and moderately priced pens and pencils, ubiquitous distribution, or at least near-ubiquitous distribution, is clearly important. But for manufacturers, not all channels are equal. Some are inherently more profitable. Others drive volume, but only at the expense of short-term profitability and long-term brand degradation. Given this, do Sony's high-end phones belong in RadioShack? If the answer to this question is "yes," then how much support should Sony give RadioShack versus a high-end electronics retailer? Should Sony segment its brands, or manufacture lower-end private-label items for RadioShack? Is the relationship best maintained at a rigid, standardized level, or should Sony engage in joint product development in order to offer products unique to RadioShack that are more closely aligned to its customers' needs? How much should Sony invest in training RadioShack employees about its products? Ideally, every manufacturer would like to enjoy both the benefits of widespread distribution and the advantages of customizing against specific consumer target groups. Trading partners can maximize their profitability over time by aligning with companies whose Relevancy attributes are consistent with their own.

Consumer Relevancy forces a redefinition of competition to include companies that aren't—at first blush—directly competitive. If Barnes & Noble had defined competition in terms of broadening consumer access— and defined access as something other than the number of physical locations—it might have anticipated an Amazon. The pattern holds true in any industry where traditional companies suddenly face the threat of a new competitor. Sam Walton redefined competitive pricing to mean not just low prices but fair and honest pricing and ultimately ended up globally dominating in a category (food and beverage products) in which he initially didn't even compete. The mass marketing of consumer fax machines by Sharp, Panasonic, Brother, and other manufacturers almost instantly redefined part of the competitive environment for delivery companies like Federal Express and UPS, reshaping how customers thought of access and service.

Sometimes the threat is more oblique. The surveying companies that helped lay out what became the interstate highway system probably weren't conscious of the fact that they were delivering a body blow to the power of the railroads, but they were. Similarly, Dell's and Gateway's offers of computer customization and functional next-day delivery were initially hard for traditionally retail-dependent computer companies to counter.

Consumer Relevancy is even more critical in the business-to-consumer Internet space, where the context-dominance lines still aren't firmly established. It is clear that the Internet represents a great opportunity for manufacturers to directly interact with consumers and build and strengthen relationships. But direct fulfillment costs aside, as with so much related to Consumer Relevancy, a manufacturer's Internet positioning—from site design and content to navigational mechanisms, to the opportunity to build and define community, to actual goods and services offered, ought to be shaped by what consumers—not the companies themselves—think is important.

Consumer Relevancy also impacts a manufacturer's alliance and acquisition strategy. Generally, we advocate manufacturers getting more involved in channels that directly interact with consumers, whether this means setting up consumer-direct operations, vertically integrating, or creating other strategic alliances. The closer a manufacturer can get to doing business directly with consumers, the more Relevant they should become, assuming they know how to pay attention. However, we recognize that commerce doesn't occur in a vacuum and that traditional channel partners—particularly large-scale retail distributors—aren't likely to applaud any move by their suppliers to get closer to the end user. The Home Depot, for example, will not allow any suppliers to use their websites to directly sell any of the products the chain carries. At the same time, the alliances between Amazon and a variety of publishers, including the publisher of this book, haven't seemed to damage the relationship of those publishers with Borders and Barnes & Noble. Procter & Gamble, which birthed Reflect.com, a customized beauty website, spun off that business and now enjoys a new relationship with some of its fiercest physical-world competitors—a relationship that benefits Reflect users, P&G, and its "competitors." Ahold USA, the American arm of the Netherlands-based international retailer, purchased Peapod and significant assets of Streamline (before its final collapse) as a way of getting closer to consumers.

At the end of the day, most manufacturers are dependent upon their distribution channels for determining consumer perceptions of access, experience, service, and price, a fact that can sometimes place them at odds with their customers. David Nichol launched the President's Choice line of consumer packaged goods at Canada's Loblaw supermarket chain around the value proposition that consumers shouldn't pay a "brand tax" when private-label brands are "as good or better" than national brands. Chips Ahoy found itself used (in a negative light) to promote the efficacy of President's Choice Decadent Chocolate Chip cookies. The choice facing the Chips Ahoy brand manager was simple—let his brand get attacked by a customer or lose distribution in Canada's largest supermarket chain, not exactly a "Lady and the Tiger" choice since there was a hungry tiger behind both doors.

Think of a foodservice company providing a superior-quality product, say, Kobe beef, to a dirty restaurant with rude service and high prices. The danger is that Kobe beef can become associated with those negatives in the consumer's mind. In today's society, the old adage of "Build a better mousetrap, and the world will beat a path to your door" is generally untrue. Access is dependent largely on the channel, whether that channel is owned by the manufacturer or a third party. Even the Internet, with its promise of ubiquitous distribution, is suspiciously dependent on such decidedly old-economy concepts as supply chains and reverse logistics.

Frito-Lay and Coca-Cola both acknowledge that their distribution infrastructures are key to their competitive domination of their categories. Yet for some brands, domination on the access attribute can, ironically, cause damage. For generations of college students east of the Mississippi, Coors was once considered the Holy Grail of hops-based beverages, commanding a premium bootleg price and high social-status points. Coors' popularity continued despite the fact the beer wasn't pasteurized, and as a result the taste of many of those brews so carefully transported across the country by Volkswagen vans was, to put it charitably, sub-optimized. It didn't matter. But once Coors expanded its distribution and began to compete nationally, it became just another beer, and its price point and cachet suffered accordingly. There are dozens of other examples.

Indie bands that sign deals with major labels—gaining significantly improved distribution—are often attacked by their most rabid fans for "selling out." Vernor's ginger ale, once the pride of Detroit, lost its sense of uniqueness—even in the Motor City—once it went into broader distribution. And a growing number of people have discovered that they don't really need to go to Orlando to experience Disney World or Universal Studios when they can buy souvenirs at the local mall.

Service also is often reliant on the channel. Custom-mixing paint, tailoring suits, and automotive detailing are all examples of real channel-dependent customization. Differentiation can be achieved in several ways: by directly reaching out to consumers after a purchase; by analyzing purchases made by individuals or households; through customized product communication; affinity marketing; and even new-product development. The Internet can play an important role in helping manufacturers dominate on experience or service, while simultaneously reducing their reliance on the channel. If a manufacturer's website provides interesting and helpful information, allows for order-status checking, in-stock availability, meaningful interaction, and community development, it has the potential to raise its grades on these two attributes.

This is a lesson profitably learned by brands and companies like Tide, Pampers, General Mills' Quisp, and CNN, which have managed to improve their grade on service or experience by creating positive direct interactions with consumers on the Web. It will become increasingly more and more important for manufacturers to focus on this as the next generation of consumers comes of age, unless they're prepared to cede context in cyberspace to their trading partners in the same way they have in the physical world.

SELF-DIAGNOSTIC: SUPPLY CHAIN

- Do your trading partners mirror your primary and secondary value propositions, or do their offerings stress attributes that conflict with those on which you go to market?
- If you're a manufacturer, are you concerned with losing control of the context in which consumers see your products, and, if so, what are you doing about it?
- If you're a retailer, what position do you take when your trading partners go direct to consumer, i.e., do you see their efforts as brand building or an attempt to pirate sales?
- If you're a reseller, have you thought through your Relevancy positioning and, if so, how have you communicated it to your trading partners?
- If you're a manufacturer, have you established clear and coherent strategies for developing effective context that addresses the values of the current—and upcoming (wired)—generations of consumers?

CHAPTER 10

Consumer Relevancy
and the Future

As WILLIAM A. SHERDEN pointed out in *The Fortune Sellers: The Big Business of Buying and Selling Predictions,* prediction is the world's second-oldest profession, in spite of the fact that it lacks the moral integrity, intellectual acceptability, and general social respectability of the first. So why bother talking about the future at all? There are several reasons. First, because whatever else we believe about the future, most of us would agree in principle that it will be different from what we know today, and that difference may be accompanied by either opportunity, or threat, or both. Second, because with any luck, the future is inevitable. And finally, because in the rapidly changing world and business climate in which we find ourselves, none of the old rules that most of us learned during the course of our careers seem to work quite as well as they used to, assuming they work at all.

As Jasper Kunde, cofounder of Denmark's Kunde & Co., one of Scandinavia's largest integrated advertising agencies, noted in his book *Corporate Religion: Building a Strong Company Through Personality and Corporate Soul,* "The problem for all international companies is that budgetary controls based on forecast sales are technical, dead mechanisms.

Most management tools have their roots in the past, when the only interesting thing is the future. I've heard people say, quite seriously, that there is no point in trying to predict the future. But if you don't have ideas about it, or really want to be part of it, you have already lost."

Exercise

Here are two examples designed to demonstrate both the opportunity offered by thinking about the future and the dangers inherent in that opportunity. Imagine for a minute that you are in charge of strategic planning for your company. You're charged with creating a ten-year plan to help your company leapfrog its competition, dominate its market, and even expand into totally new offerings. Fair enough? All right, now let's add an increased level of difficulty. Close your eyes for a moment and imagine that it's 1957. Ozzie and Harriet are the symbols for the perfect lifestyle, the happily married suburban couple with two impish but obedient children. Everyone on the block drives the same kind of car; everyone on the block eats together and serves their families Campbell's soup; all the houses look alike; everyone (who's anyone) shops at the same stores for the same products; everyone watches the same three television stations.

Now, fast-forward ten years to the Summer of Love. Those impish kids are openly taking drugs, scoffing at all authority figures, having sex in public, and questioning the same corporations their parents identified with so strongly. Think for a minute. Was the "future" of 1967 visible from 1957? The right answer is "yes and no." Certain elements of what became the future were already in place—elements such as television and all those baby-boomer hormones just waiting for the opportunity to manifest themselves. The civil rights movement was tracing the template of mass protest in the South. And around the world, in a place most Americans couldn't find on a map, a Southeast Asian freedom fighter named Ho Chi Minh was battling to free his nation from the French. So connections could have been drawn, inferences could have been made, and maybe somebody could have crafted a story anticipating "the sixties," but it's still doubtful anyone could have sold the potential of marketing a social revolution to a corporate audience.

Let's take an example that might be more familiar to a contemporary audience: the Internet and the revolution that has followed in its wake. Close your eyes again, and imagine that it's now 1989. The smartest corporate minds are gathered together in a remote location, thinking about the decade to come and attempting to map out successful future business strategies. The ARPANET (Advanced Research Projects Agency Network), a sophisticated system of linked computers, had been created in 1969 as a way of protecting the U.S. Department of Defense's computer system against nuclear attack. The French had demonstrated the commercial viability of a mini-Internet (Minitel, launched in 1981), and writers such as theologian Pierre Teilhard de Chardin (*The Phenomenon of Man,* 1955) had, with considerable amounts of poetic license, imagined a global communications network uniting the planet, later described by novelist William Gibson (*Neuromancer,* 1993) as "cyberspace."

But the truth is that when the digital market hit (as had happened in France with Minitel), the pornography industry was the only commercial enterprise that really seemed to have figured out how to make money through online commerce. Perhaps no surprise, then, that most of the attendees at our hypothetical 1989 meeting would have failed to include the Internet, the World Wide Web, cyberspace, e-commerce, or any similar idea in their ten-year plan. And yet what did the Internet change? Why, just about everything, of course. Yet, from the point of view of 1989, the future—in this case a future already partially developed and at most only four years away—was inconceivable except to a handful of computer whizzes. But if you were around then, you shouldn't feel too bad. After all, even Bill Gates, the whizzes' whiz, managed to miss the call.

In all fairness, it isn't that easy to draw linear connections even in retrospect. One can see how the intersection of, say, all those boomer hormones and the invention of the birth-control pill helped bring passion to the Summer of Love, but keep in mind that the existence of guns and trigger fingers at the same time didn't result in a Summer of Slaughter. You could fill volumes with people's foolish predictions about the future, so why should we think about the future at all? Perhaps that's a question best addressed to the railroad industry, network television, etc.

The Case for the Future and the Future of Relevancy

At the beginning of this book, we suggested that while the attribute elements (price, service, access, product, and experience) of Consumer Relevancy have remained unchanged since the days of commercial prehistory, their specific definitions have changed radically at any given period. Now, if we believe the future is—at least in any significantly meaningful sense—unpredictable, or difficult to predict at best, how can we be so sure the attributes will continue to be present in whatever digital or physical markets may emerge, or have any sense of what their meaning might be? The simplest, but perhaps least satisfying, answer relies on a historical approach. We believe it is impossible to find an example of free, or at least quasi-free, market conditions in which the Relevancy attributes aren't present. Of course, this alone isn't enough to guarantee that the Relevancy model will hold true in the future.

While this isn't a social-anthropology textbook, we'd like to go out on a limb and suggest that the attributes are somehow inherently integral to the way people go about commerce. We're not positing some form of commercial "law" here but, rather, suggesting that the attributes emerge as almost preconditions to commercial relationships. In all relationships, there is some form of buyer, some form of seller, some object or service being bartered for, and some medium of exchange, all of which intersect at some point in time and space. Whether the exchange occurs in the digital boundaries of cyberspace or at the corner deli, we can expect to find the same ingredients present. The cornerstones of the Relevancy theory are quarried out of our sense of self-awareness, our awareness of the ability of others to positively and negatively influence us, and the necessity for a common set of values on which to base exchanges. We can't conceive of a world in which something of a perceived value isn't exchanged for something else with its own perceived value. And if such a world is possible, you won't need business books to prosper in it.

What We Can (Tentatively) Know for Sure About the Future

In Chapter 1 we cited Jonas Ridderstråle and Kjell Nordström, the shaved-headed bad boys of the Stockholm School of Economics, who end their *Funky Business: Talent Makes Capital Dance* by noting, "People expect good stuff. They have become used to great value for money. And they can get that from almost all companies around the world. So, being great is no longer enough. . . . By focusing only on the hardcore aspects of business we risk becoming irrelevant. And, trust us, irrelevancy is a much greater problem than inefficiency." We couldn't agree more, but for significantly different reasons. Ridderstråle and Nordström believe that "[t]he only way to create real profit is to attract the emotional rather than the rational consumer and colleague by appealing to their feelings and fantasy." While we agree that Relevancy is the key to building a strong business today, and will be mandatory to even being in business in the future, we strongly believe it is the customer rather than the enterprise who increasingly defines Relevancy. And while we also agree that emotions are important across all of the attributes, we're not prepared to throw out the rational aspects of transactions quite so quickly. So, let's take a look at why it's Consumer Relevancy rather than, say, Corporate Relevancy.

We think the supremacy of the enterprise, the once near-sovereign right of a business to arbitrarily define its commercial terms of engagement with the consumer, is a casualty of the transition from the Industrial Age to the Information and Post-information eras. Consumer Relevancy isn't something businesses can unilaterally offer—it is something they must research, understand, and incorporate into their goods and/or services. Consumers alone know how they define the attributes. One way to think about how Relevancy might work in the future is to think about why we have found it so easy to divide the past into ages, eras, epochs, or other linguistic pigeonholes. Put another way, an easy way to think about the future is to consider how we think about the past. Some methods of dividing up history rely on dominant socioeconomic activities—Hunter/Gatherer, Agrarian, Industrial, Information ages. Others look at the dominant technology or invention of the time—Iron Age, Bronze Age, etc. Still others look at history along military or governance lines—the Age of Charlemagne, the Roman Empire, the Cold War Era, and so on. There are, of course, those who attempt to divide history by activity—the Renaissance, the Age of Exploration, the Atomic Age.

We have looked at all these classification systems and decided they essentially come down to a matter of resonance—what seemed to make sense to the people of the period (or at least what we can impose as making sense to the people of the period). We believe that the rate of social change has accelerated to the point that we no longer have the luxury of having a generation to absorb the convergence of social forces, discontinuities, and technological innovations that typically characterize an age. In fact, we believe that we have already moved out of the Information Age, even though most of you may still feel a bit frustrated as you try to cope with its impact. Rather than worry about what to call this Post-information Age, we've opted for describing how to recognize it. Every "age" generates its own language, symbols, and metaphors, which in turn are incorporated into the language of commerce. We've looked at the most recent three ages and what we see as the dominant metaphors and how those metaphors have been translated into business, advertising claims, and commercial opportunities (see Table 10.1).

Clearly, in order to be Relevant to the consumers living through an "age," business must learn how to effectively translate its language, goods, and services into offerings that resonate with the contemporary consumers. For example, one could argue that part of the problem Monsanto encountered in marketing genetically modified food in Europe was that it couched the offering in essentially Industrial Age language. The concentration on issues of crop yield, pest reduction, etc., would have resonated well in the Industrial Age, when consumers were in awe of chemistry-based claims. But they were perceived as threatening to the Post-information Age audience, with its concerns about corporate pollution and environmental toxicity. A more appropriate campaign might have started with advertising

TABLE **10.1**

The Science of Commerce

SOCIOHISTORICAL "AGE"	DOMINANT SCIENTIFIC METAPHOR	DOMINANT BUSINESS CLAIM	TYPICAL ADVERTISING CLAIM	DOMINANT BUSINESS OPPORTUNITY
Industrial	Chemistry	Product efficacy	"Better living through chemistry" (DuPont)	Improve measurable product functionalities
Information	Physics	Fusion of product and services	"Unleashing the power of connectivity" (Intersil)	Extend value through network of providers
Post-information	Biology	Coevolution of business and consumer ecosystems	"Growing to meet your changing needs"	Appreciation and reverence for life

focusing on the problems of world hunger, especially in terms of its impact on children and the opportunity to prevent needless death and disease. The product would have been identical in both scenarios, but the reception might have been a bit different.

Industrial Age claims still abound ("Wonderclean makes your clothes 75 percent whiter, brighter, or whatever"), but they lose their Relevance to contemporary audiences. Are we supposed to rush out, for example, and buy a car because it isn't like the one our fathers drove? What kind of Relevancy is that? In a world where many products seem to perform with the same level of efficacy (outside a laboratory), what good are claims that can be verified only by a chemist? These are more than just academic questions.

To be successful in the future (and, we'd argue, the present), corporations need to learn how to address consumers on their own terms. Product efficacy is great, but it may not be Relevant to an environmentally aware consumer if it comes at the cost of air, land, and/or water pollution. Right-hand-turn access into a parking lot is important, but not as important to a working single mother who has just picked up her children from day care as the ability to find what she needs and get out of a store with a minimum of chaos. Price is clearly important, but to the upscale couple with no children, a high price tag might be more attractive than a low one. Service and experience are almost entirely subjective even by rigid Industrial Age measures. So what's a company to do?

Well, let's begin with the notion of being open to new possibilities, new language, and new ideas. One literally has to learn how to speak the language of the consumer. Recently we flew back from New York with a woman who worked for an advertising agency specializing in "ethnic marketing." Her company had just been bought by a New York–based company that wanted the Detroit-based firm's knowledge but was wrestling to understand why. "They just don't get it," she complained. "They want to do more business in the African-American community, but when they look at a product they don't see the same thing we see. For example, when they look at a Jeep, their mental image is a guy in climbing boots standing on the top of a mountain staring at a sunset. When an African-American urban consumer looks at that same vehicle, they see an upscale luxury vehicle. And when we try to explain this to New York, they just don't seem to understand how urban consumers relate to their vehicles."

The problem was obvious. We had encountered the same issue years ago when we had suggested to a car company that it market fully "tricked out" sport utility vehicles complete with interiors by FUBU and Phat Farm and sound systems whose bass ranges could create potholes. We were told these kinds of cars would be "appropriate" only in urban areas. How, then, we asked, do you account for the fact that hip-hop sells so well in the suburbs of Minneapolis and Des Moines and that for one fateful week in 2000 two very Caucasian Detroit "home boys"—Eminem and Kid Rock—had the number one and two best-selling albums in the country with their respective versions of a sound "only African-American audiences can understand"?

The point here is that different things have different meanings to different people at different times. We know it's a little tough to think about, so we prepared Table 10.2, which shows alternative imaging across the three most recent historical ages:

TABLE 10.2

The Transformation of Symbols, Meanings, and Conventional Practices—from the Industrial to Post-information Ages

AREAS/OBJECT	INDUSTRIAL	INFORMATION	POST-INFORMATION
Computation	Slide rule	Computer	DNA computation
Medicine	Scalpel	Laser surgery	Genomic manipulation
Communication	FedEx	E-mail	Sentient software
Business presentation	Overheads	PowerPoint	Virtual reality
Ideal employment model	"For life"	"For now"	"Free agent"
Sources of insights on the consumer	Traditional longitudinal demographic models; focus groups	Scan data; Internet cookies	Only what the consumer lets you see
Products	Built to last	Inherently obsolete	Evolve with user
Organizational model	Hierarchical	Team	Ad hoc
Automobile	Transportation	Status	Mobile environment
Educational model	Learning	Continuing education	Unlearning, relearning
Community	Physical	Virtual	Physical/Virtual
Retail	House products	Sell products	Educate consumers
B2B trading models	Linear supply chains	Non-linear value chains; networks	Economic webs
Air travel	Luxury	Necessity	Selective necessity
Dominant financial expert	Bank	Broker	Individual
Social goal	To belong	To excel	To be fully realized
Consumer attitude toward business	Implicit faith and evolving skepticism	Cynicism	Selective faith based on information
Medicine	To cure disease	To prevent disease	To extend both quality and duration of life
Dominant learning tool	Print	Screen	Streaming multimedia
Marketing tools	Mass marketing	Mass customization	User demand
Enterprise goal	Growth and profit	Survival	Evolution and learning
Artifact	The factory	The chip	The idea

Into the Ether: Consumer Relevancy Online

Some might argue that in the commercial world of the future, the world of e-commerce, whether business-to-business or business-to-consumer or both, some of the Consumer Relevancy attributes begin to lose their luster. Of course, that's not our position. We believe the attributes will endure, taking on different specific meanings appropriate to the times. Table 10.3 suggests what this change of definition might look like:

TABLE 10.3

The Future Face of Commerce

ATTRIBUTE	COMMERCE TODAY	FUTURE COMMERCE
Access	Location and ability to navigate through a location	Link to portals
Experience	My response to your environment	Your ability to customize an environment for me
Price	Unit cost	Total costs
Product	Inherent features	Upgrades
Service	You recognize me	You represent me

Of course, this is only one set of possibilities. We don't suggest that we can actually predict the future, but we do think it's important for every business to find ways to think about how its future may be different from its present and the implications of that change on its offerings. One way to get at this is through one of the oldest communication devices known to human beings: the story. We're big believers in the power of the story and what we see as an increasing future role for corporate storytellers. The case for storytelling has been documented in any number of books, from Rolf Jensen's *The Dream Society: How the Coming Shift from Information to Imagination Will Transform Your Business* to Jim Taylor's and Watts Wacker's *The 500-Year Delta: What Happens After What Comes Next* and *The Visionary's Handbook: Nine Paradoxes That Will Shape the Future of Your Business*.

But as we think about the future of Consumer Relevancy, we're intrigued by the use of a very special kind of story, the scenario. Scenario planning is a mainstay in the toolboxes of most futurists, and appropriately so. Every scenario planner has a unique methodology he or she claims to be "the" way to do scenario planning. We're not interested in weighing in on whose method is best. In fact, we're about to offer an exercise that combines some of the best features of all the methodologies—bottom-line scenario planning for the Consumer Relevancy set.

Basically, the idea is this: Since the future is unknowable, is there a method that can help you anticipate what might happen, help you think about what might happen in a different way, or test your readiness to cope with several alternative futures? The answer for scenario planners is a decided "yes." The construction of scenarios involves a fairly comprehensive process of identifying trends and uncertainties that might impact a business, an industry, or even a government. But again, we're not as interested in the methodology as the output—the scenario itself is really nothing more than a story about what life might look like in a future or several futures. We've saved you the methodological heavy lifting and cut to the bottom line. So here are the results, five stories about the future that examine whether or not our five attributes—price, service, access, product, and experience—will survive in the increasingly complex world of the third millennium. Here we go:

Price: The Price Was Right . . . and Wrong

Luke's finger paused millimeters above the garage-door digipad. In his mind he knew what sat behind the door: his Global Motors' Rocketbike, the XTRM16 model, sitting on its stand, a gleaming black-and-chrome vision of speed and power and a perpetual reminder of how much he still had to learn about the world. His parents had warned him that any deal that seemed too good to be true probably was, or some such Information Age cliché, but what did they know? They had grown up before people even had personal bots programmed to find them goods and services that they weren't even aware they wanted, all at price points that were—at least marginally—affordable.

His bot had found the bike on Lama Line, the Sino-Tibetan cyber-exchange. It was a classic, built in 2025. Luke was so excited that he made the mistake of telling his father about the bike, only to hear a thousand paternal reasons he shouldn't get it, ranging from "It isn't safe" to some story about losing credits on Lama Line years ago. His parents' "bots" were programmed not to shop on bootleg exchanges, but all the kids knew cybershops like Lama Line were where the really "evo" stuff could be found. Besides, he had been making his own money on his website since he was nine, and his bot wouldn't have suggested it if he couldn't afford it.

So Luke had ordered the bike, which came exactly as advertised. Even his parents had to know that misrepresentation of products on any exchange could result in permanent unplugging, thanks to the Universal Consumer Protection Act of 2015, which regulated commerce on what Luke called the Exchange but what his parents, with their terminally retro flair, still insisted on calling the Web. Even Luke had to admit the sale price seemed too good to be true, but that's why you jacked into places like Lama Line in the first place. It seemed like a bargain, such a deal, that he had never bothered to check the service agreement, which—he quickly learned—compelled him to ship the bike back to Lhasa every 10,000 miles for service at the only authorized dealer on the planet. And while the bike itself was a steal, the shipping and service fees were plain old-fashioned robbery. Without service the bike couldn't be certified road safe, and without certification it couldn't be insured. No insurance, no plates; and no plates, no riding.

The deal of a lifetime proved too expensive, and so the bike sat on its stand, a silent reminder of how he had been cheated. Luke had been so mad he had deleted his bot's central memory, in a programming maneuver known as a LoBOTomy, turning it into a cybersquash. But it didn't help—his credits were still irretrievably gone. What's worse, he had to admit Dad was right—a higher honest price was better than a lower-priced "deal."

Service: Don't Worry About a Thing, Sir, I'll Take Care of It

Adam flew through his bills with an enviable economy of keystrokes, until he came to his monthly Walworldmarket invoice. Pausing, he stopped to consider how much easier the company made his life. When his firm had transferred him to Scandinavia, Adam had felt more than a little apprehensive. There were all the language and logistics issues, but working in another country didn't mean you really *belonged* there.

Feeling a little sadder and less confident than he would have wanted to admit, Adam had walked to his "neighborhood" Walworldmarket on his second day in Stockholm. Swiping his "Guest" card on his way in the door, he shuffled down the first aisle. "Good afternoon, Adam," he heard a voice boom behind him. Startled, Adam turned to see whom the voice belonged to. "Oh, I'm so sorry," a smiling giant of a man said. "Perhaps I startled you, or perhaps your profile needs updating. Is it still permitted to call you by your first name? Oh, I'm being so stupid! My name is Jonas, and I have the very great privilege of managing this store. Tell me, er, Adam, what brings you to Stockholm, and how can I assist you?"

Almost despite himself, Adam began to relax. He had, it seemed, unwittingly caused the only person he had really "met" in his adopted city to feel off balance, which was exactly how he felt. "No, no, Adam's fine, and you didn't startle me—it's just that I wasn't planning on anyone recognizing me. Actually, I moved here yesterday. My company transferred me to oversee the Digicom business, but, well, how did you know I was me?" Relaxing a bit, Jonas said, "I didn't, until your card swipe triggered a radio-frequency signal to be sent to my pager containing a brief profile—where you're from, what you preferred to be called, and so on. Please, may I offer you a coffee or tea?" Adam liked Jonas's openness and honesty. "That'd be fine," he said, "but I don't quite remember this kind of treatment back home."

Smiling, the Swede pointed Adam toward the dining room. "That's because at Walworldmarket, we pride ourselves on not just identifying our customers but, in effect, acting as their full-service representatives. Your profile indicates that when you're at home—well, your old home, that is—

you preferred to use our automated ordering service, our digital shopping list, and other fairly passive services," said Jonas. "Naturally, we respect your preferences and concentrate on making sure those systems get you what you really want. We screen out advertising messages and new product offerings we know you wouldn't like, for example. However, it's been our experience that when one of our guests is so far from home, they often need slightly different service. So when I knew you were in the store, I appeared, frightened you, and then generally made a fool of myself, all in the name of good service."

For the first time since he had found out he was being transferred, Adam laughed out loud. "Jonas, you're great. I was beginning to think I'd never meet anybody besides the people I work with. I'm glad you recognized me for what I am—a stranger very far away from home and grateful for a friendly face." Now it was the Swede's turn to smile. "Well, to tell you the truth, the store really speaks for itself. The aisle scanners offer automatic translation of package graphics and convert the price into any of the world's twelve currencies. Outside of a few items, you'll find much of the inventory remarkably like what you would see in the States. And I'll assign a shopping assistant to help you program your shopping profile to reflect the difference in selection and introduce you to some of our fine domestic products. We're happy to have you as 'our' customer now." Adam thought for a moment. "Jonas, if it's all right with you, could you walk me through that profile, and do you know of any good restaurants in the neighborhood? I'm not really much of a cook, even with a quantum oven." "It would be my pleasure to help you with the profile, Adam," Jonas said. "But I'll only recommend a restaurant if you allow me the pleasure of taking you out to dinner this evening—if, of course, it would be convenient, er, I mean . . ." "It would be more than convenient," Adam said. "You know, I'm really pretty hungry. I'm starting to feel like my old self again. I must have just had a touch of jet lag."

Access: Flying the Friendly Ties

Gabriel sank back in the seat of the Virgin Transglobal 878 and gathered his thoughts. He logged on to the screen that had, just seconds before, been concealed under his left armrest, choosing from a keypad menu ranging from "Somatic Options" to "Entertainment," "Shopping," and the rather innocently labeled "Commerce." Reluctantly, Gabriel pressed "Commerce," noting that it seemed the most-used key on the pad. He entered his secure user code and watched as the screen before him hiccuped into life. Using the screen's visual monitor to guide the mouse, he selected the "Expenses" icon. Using the built-in scanner, Gabriel entered his last two hotel bills and his airplane-ticket receipts. The data were immediately integrated into his corporate expense portfolio. Gabriel sipped his mineral water, waiting for the polite but firm digital red flag he knew the airline ticket would trigger. A few seconds later, it appeared—a small blinking message that read, "The firm thanks you for your prompt expense download and wishes to remind you that coach class on planes in the 867 series or below is recommended for all trips of less than 2.5 hours between continents."

Huffing to himself, Gabriel reached for the digital keyboard. "Integrate this expense entry against the secured reason for this trip," he typed. And, he thought to himself, when you do you'll notice that traveling on Virgin's 878 series allows me to access the company's Executive Class service portal, which connects me to its Advanced Translation desk, which comes in handy when one is preparing a presentation for a company in Ulan Bator and doesn't speak any Mongolian dialect! There were other benefits as well. Virgin's alliance partner in central Asia ran the only decent hotels south of Lake Baikal, east of Turkey, and west of central China. No ticket on Virgin, no access to the hotel. In addition, the hotel chain was linked to the only reliable transit company in the region, and staying there also gave you access to a translator-guide, although Gabriel didn't need that service this trip. And, if that weren't enough, his medical provider had a Medlink agreement with the hotel's Wellness Network, which guaranteed that should a runaway pony run over his foot, Gabriel could receive adequate medical care until he could get home.

These not-so-subtle benefits were probably lost on the firm's accountants who, rumor had it, were really sentient software programs that had overpowered the people who had been chained to them years ago and were now exacting revenge on any carbon-based life form they could coerce. "The integration you requested has been completed, and your

incremental travel expenditure has been approved. You're reminded, however, that under normal conditions coach class on planes in the 867 series
or below is recommended for all trips of less than 2.5 hours between continents." Smiling to himself in spite of his impatience with policy, Gabriel
hit the "Shopping" icon on the keypad and scrolled through a list of
Virgin's exclusive trading partners' newest offerings. "Yeah," he thought,
"and if I wasn't on an 878, it might be just a tad more difficult to have
this beluga caviar airlifted to my hotel room. Oh, well, anything for
the firm."

Product: Mirror, Mirror in My Hand

Sierra stared in amazement at the pocket-size Life Minder sitting in the box
before her. She was nearly 45, and some form of the Life Minder had been
with her since her father bought her first unit when she had graduated from
college. That model had come with a Retro graphics hologram case that,
whenever it was in use, downloaded antique digital footage of classic oldies
singers like the Backstreet Boys, Boyzone, and Ricky Martin from one of
the 460 MTVSONY Media Stations orbiting the earth.

Most Life Minders offered the same basic functions. Essentially digital
diaries, the machines allowed users to record their impressions of life, sample music and video, and capture digipics or holographic representations
of important life events. The text, music, or video images could be recalled
any number of ways, from a straight chronological report (what was I
thinking when I was twenty-seven?) to events (birthdays, etc.), general sub-
jects (jobs, school, and so on) to more intimate issues (from loves to fears).
Advanced models like Sierra's would even trace the development of a user's
thoughts on specific issues from global trade to political philosophy, allowing the owner to retrace the development of what Sierra grudgingly had to
admit were young adult (thirty-five to fifty-five) biases. And given the competitive nature of the global personal-communications industry, almost
every company producing Life Minders offered the same service agreement: twenty-five years parts and labor, covering everything except for
direct user abuse (this happened a lot when people referenced former

spouses and employers); free upgrade downloads for the lifetime of the original owner (policed by retinal scans); and free translation services for the lifetime of the machine if the original owner willed it to a direct descendant living in a different Language Zone.

But Sierra's father had paid a little extra for a feature she hadn't appreciated at the time. Her version of the Life Minder actually "learned" from her entries and ordered new cases when it deemed appropriate. At first, Sierra was a bit disconcerted whenever the Life Minder ordered itself a new cover. "I haven't changed," she'd whisper to herself. "I'm not getting older." Acceptance came in waves. It was easy, for example, to get rid of the Backstreet Boys but a little harder when the high-resolution mirror case was replaced by what the manufacturer called the "Soft Focus" case. Eventually, though, Sierra understood that her Life Minder was like all great products—it morphed into something better whenever something better was really useful. She smiled at the new case that would house the memories of her lifetime, until, of course, a better model came along.

Experience: Color My World

Zack had been looking forward to going to the gym all day. His muscles ached from the tension of simultaneously trying to coordinate procurement bids from 186 corporate nation-states. The actual tracking of the bidding was all done digitally, of course, but even in 2045 no machine could detect the subtle differences between a microsecond market fluctuation, which could be caused by anything from viral progressions through any given workforce on any given day, to the increasingly frequent transmission errors and what Zack liked to call "the Blink" in an obscure homage to an old Information Age business phrase his mother had explained to him when he was younger. Zack had amassed a fortune in credits by sensing the difference, hedging the market, and buying or selling accordingly. "Yes," he thought to himself, "you blink, and I buy or sell, and you sit and wonder how I knew you were sweating through the climate control when I'm two thousand or three thousand miles away from you."

Any number of increasingly sophisticated infinite-regression complexity programs had been developed that attempted to do what Zack seemed to intuit, but in the long run, they weren't any more successful than the early chaos analyzers that people had tried to use to predict fluctuation patterns in the old stock exchanges. In fact, Zack didn't know how he did what he did—he just knew that it worked and it was profitable.

With all his success, Zack could have joined any health club in the city. A number of them had actually solicited his business, offering to waive his fees in exchange for having the city's most successful and sought-out financial adviser as a member. But Zack liked the Jungle Club, insisting, in fact, on paying a full membership. It wasn't that the Jungle Club offered anything that different from a product or service standpoint, as most of the major clubs offered the same equipment, from pools to personalized digital trainers who tracked every calorie burned and, unfortunately for some, apparently every one ingested. Almost every club analyzed a variety of factors, from age to weight to performance profiles, and then ordered specifically designed menus for the following week. And most of the better clubs sent abbreviated weekly or monthly reports to a designated health-care provider.

In most respects, the Jungle Club was like all other comparable clubs, but it was significantly different in one critical—at least for Zack—respect. The club's Mood Rooms were actually modified to reflect a customer's daily mood. Entering the club, Zack was greeted (by name, of course) by his health concierge. "Good evening, sir," the concierge said. "Would you care for the Custom Environment as usual?" "Yes," Zack said. "Very well," the concierge said. "Let's just step up on the machine for a moment." "The machine" was really a sophisticated health meter that sampled a variety of things, from pulse rate to skin temperature to retinal reaction to a series of varied images, and calibrated a subject's mood. That information was then fed into the club's central memory unit, which compared it with past data, searched through an active and passively constructed (user) data bank, and modeled the appropriate environment.

No matter how many times Zack went to the club, he never experienced quite the same environment. The music was by the same group but from a different year; the visuals might be similar, but the perspective was subtly different; and programmed environmental elements (smells, humidity, wind) differed ever so slightly, even between days when Zack would have sworn he felt exactly as he had the day before. The concierge had told him that some people's environments never changed. "But yours, sir, always has to change," he said. "After all, you're always trying to feel that difference in things, aren't you? Give you exactly what you are comfortable with, and you'll be vaguely uncomfortable. You're happy only when you're looking for that little difference." And that, Zack had to agree, was exactly why he kept coming back to this place, even with so many new places bidding for his business. At the Jungle Club, they recognized a hunter when they saw one.

We hope these stories help you see both how the attributes might survive and how their definitions might change. As we said earlier, we can't predict what the future will really look like, but we do know one thing: From the time the first person traded a shiny stone for some brightly colored feathers, all commercial transactions have had certain things in common, and those things are our five attributes. Markets are changing daily. Industries are consolidating. E-commerce is fighting for its rightful place in the commercial tableau. Consumers have climbed out of the convenient demographic boxes we've forced them into and burned those boxes behind them. The complexity of the speed, breadth, and depth of change we face today will pale into insignificance in the face of the change we believe will come. Technology will extend ubiquitously into every corner of our lives. Our search for values will become ever more complex and, in all probability, more difficult. But in this sea of change, we believe there are four beacons whose convergence will define what our future will become:

1. As long as there are people, they will collectively engage in some form of commerce and individually seek out some form of personal-value reinforcement.

2. As long as there are transactions, the five attributes will be present.

3. As long as those attributes are present, they will be measurable.

4. And as long as they are measurable, it will be possible to craft successful, competitive, and profitable market offerings around them, provided those offerings incorporate the contemporary values of the times.

Around the industrialized world, consumers have learned to recognize the power of their own voice, and that voice will not—and cannot—be silenced. It's not difficult to hear that voice, but the real business advantage will fall to those companies that not only hear it but also listen to it and shape their offerings accordingly. And based on what we've found in our work on Consumer Relevancy, that's something much easier said than done.

Notes

1: Field Notes from the Commercial Wilderness

1 Kalle Lasn, *Culture Jam: The Uncooling of America*™ (New York: William Morrow, 1999), p. 40.

2 Based on Robert D. Putnam's analysis of poll data archived at the University of North Carolina and quoted in *Bowling Alone: The Collapse and Revival of American Community* (New York: Simon & Schuster, 2000), p. 47.

3 George Bishop, "What Americans Really Believe: And Why Faith Isn't as Universal as They Think," *Free Inquiry*, July 1, 1999, p. 41.

4 Ronan McGreevy, "Church Invites Whole Nation in for Supper," *The Evening Standard*, March 2, 2000, p. 5.

5 Huston Smith, *Cleansing the Doors of Perception: The Religious Significance of Entheogenic Plants and Chemicals* (New York: Jeremy P. Tarcher/Putnam, 2000), p. 146.

6 "America's Education Choice," *The Economist*, April 1, 2000, p. 17.

7 "1 in 3 of Poor Aren't Covered," snapshot, U.S. Census Bureau data, *USA Today*, July 7, 2000, p. 1a.

8 Steven Greenhouse, "Running on Empty: So Much Work, So Little Time," *The Journal Record*, Dolan Media, November 10, 1999.

9 Cherry Norton, "Stressed Managers Complain of E-mail Overload," *The Independent*, February 24, 2000, p. 9.

10 Results of 1999 symposium, sponsored by the WHO, "Culture, Society, and Depression"; results reported on the World Health Organization website, www.who.org.

11 "Rise in Antidepressant Use at UW–Madison," as reported by the Associated Press, AP Newswire, October 4, 1997.

12 *Foreign Policy*, p. 70, April 1, 2000.

13 "Zenith Media Publication's Advertising Expenditure Forecast, 1990–2000," Zenith Media, 2000.

14 Zenith Media.

15 Kalle Lasn, p. 23.

16 *Ibid.,* p. 24.

2: The New Model for Consumer Relevancy

1 Calmetta Coleman, "Lands' End Warns on Sales, Sinking Stock," *The Wall Street Journal,* November 12, 1999, p. B8.

2 Valerie Seckler, "Target's Successful Formula: Upscale Trends with Discounts," *Women's Wear Daily,* November 11, 1998, p. 2.

3: Would I Lie to You?: The Overrated Importance of *Lowest* Price

1 Debbie Howell, "The Right Reverend of EDLP," *Discount Store News,* May 24, 1999, p. 46.

2 Laura Heller, "Leigh Stelmach, Dollar General: A Singular Sense of Mission," *Discount Store News,* December 8, 1997, p. 49.

3 Jennifer Negley, "Dollar General Is Poised to Grow," *Discount Store News,* November 3, 1997, p. 13.

4: I Can't Get No Satisfaction: Service *with a Smile?*

1 Sheila M. Puffer, "Continental Airlines's CEO Gordon Bethune on Teams and New Product Development," *Academy of Management Executive,* August 1999, pp. 28–35.

2 *Ibid.*

3 *Ibid.*

4 *Ibid.*

5 *Ibid.*

5: I Still Haven't Found What I'm Looking For: Access, *Physical and Psychological*

1 Todd Lapin, "Get Rich . . . Quixtar!", *Business 2.0,* August 1, 1999, pp. 135–44.

2 Lisa Singhania, "Selling-Giant Amway Makes Leap Online," *Cincinnati Enquirer,* September 24, 1999.

3 Priscilla Donegan, "Wired for Sales," *Grocery Headquarters,* April 2000, p. 44.

4 Winn-Dixie Stores Inc., 1999 Annual Report, p. 8.

5 Angela Hardin, "Tops Sizes Up Smaller Store Format," *Crain's Cleveland Business,* November 15–21, 1999, p. 1.

6 "Wal-Mart Announces Expansion Plans," company news release, October 5, 1999.

7 "Saddle Brook Named Third Villager's Hardware Site in the Garden State," company news release, December 8, 1999.

8 *Ibid.,* p. 4.

6: Why "Good" Is Good Enough: Choice and the Issue of Product *Bandwidth*

1 Priscilla Donegan, p. 44.

7: Do You Really Get Me?: The Experience *Factor*

1 Howard Schultz, as quoted in "Interview with Howard Schultz: Sharing Success," *Executive Excellence,* November 1999, p. 16.

Index

About the Authors

FRED CRAWFORD is an executive vice president with Cap Gemini Ernst & Young (CGEY), the major international management consulting and systems integration firm. He is an internationally recognized strategist who has worked with a wide variety of global companies.

In his current role as managing director of the consumer products, retail, and distribution practice at CGEY, he works with some of the firm's largest and most important clients. He is a sought-after speaker for industry events and a frequent contributor to business and trade publications.

RYAN MATHEWS is a futurist with FirstMatter, a Westport, Connecticut–based futuring consultancy recognized for providing creative and innovative business solutions. A popular international speaker and consultant, he is recognized for his expertise and understanding of consumer goods, demographics and lifestyle analysis, and work in the areas of e-commerce and the information economy. He has provided consulting services and advice to a variety of international companies, including Coca-Cola, Unilever, General Motors, and Procter & Gamble.